How to Care for Your Parents' Money While Caring for Your Parents

How to Care for Your Parents' Money While Caring for Your Parents

The Complete Guide to Managing Your Parents' Finances

Sharon Burns, Ph.D., C.P.A.

Raymond Forgue, Ph.D.

McGraw-Hill

New York   Chicago   San Francisco   Lisbon   London
Madrid   Mexico City   Milan   New Delhi
San Juan   Seoul   Singapore
Sydney   Toronto

The *McGraw·Hill* Companies

1 2 3 4 5 6 7 8 9 0   DOC/DOC   0 9 8 7 6 5 4 3

ISBN 0-07-140866-5

This publication is designed to provide accurate and authoritative information in regard to the subject matter covered. It is sold with the understanding that neither the author nor the publisher is engaged in rendering legal, accounting, or other professional service. If legal advice or other expert assistance is required, the services of a competent professional person should be sought.

> —*From a Declaration of Principles jointly adopted
> by a Committee of the American Bar
> Association and a Committee of Publishers*

McGraw-Hill books are available at special quantity discounts to use as premiums and sales promotions, or for use in corporate training programs. For more information, please write to the Director of Special Sales, Professional Publishing, McGraw-Hill, Two Penn Plaza, New York, NY 10121-2298. Or contact your local bookstore.

Library of Congress Cataloging-in-Publication Data

Burns, Sharon.
    How to care for your parents' money while caring for your parents :
the complete guide to managing your parents' finances / by Sharon Burns
and Raymond Forgue.
        p.   cm.
    ISBN 0-07-140866-5 (alk. paper)
    1. Aging parents—Finance, Personal.   2. Retirement income.
3. Investments.   4. Adult children of aging parents—Handbooks, manuals,
etc.   I. Forgue, Raymond E.   II. Title.
    HG179 .B86 2003
    332.024'0565—dc21
                                                    2002154747

Contents

Preface

The twentieth century brought phenomenal life expectancies to which we have now become accustomed. The senior citizen population grew faster than any other age cohort between 1990 and 2000. This growth rate will only accelerate over the next two decades as more and more of the 76 million baby boomers simultaneously enter retirement and attempt to provide care for their aging parents.

An increasing number of senior citizens will lead to an increasing demand for caregivers. Americans will not shirk their responsibilities to their parents. About 90 percent of the respondents in a national poll said, "Grown people have a moral responsibility to take care of their parents." According to an American Association of Retired Persons (AARP) study, the privilege of parental caregiving falls on one in four American households. All told, over 22 million households in America provide care to an aging parent, sibling, or other relative. And this number doesn't include those who arrange to have others provide such services as house cleaning, lawn mowing, and financial management—many from a distance.

By some estimates, 83 percent of such caregivers are female. Historically, women have had more limited experience in managing financial affairs. Most women report that even if they are experienced, they do not feel comfortable about their financial know-how or do not feel confident in making significant financial decisions. And men are affected too.

Assuming a caretaker role is commendable and honorable, to say the least, but the emotional and financial stresses placed on children who serve as their parents' caregivers are often hard to bear. Caregivers' work lives are affected significantly through lost time on the job, lost wages, delayed promotions, and other work stressors. Caregivers' personal lives are also affected, as they must take time away from their own family, relate to siblings in new and unprecedented ways, and make decisions with their parents' very lives at stake. Caregivers need adequate resources to enable them to cope with the task at hand. Parents' financial resources are often limited, making it even more important that the caregiver be armed with the financial information and knowledge that they need.

This book was written to provide such resources. It provides a basic primer in personal financial management that focuses specifically on the needs of those who are, or will become, involved in their parents' financial lives. The authors have extensive experience as financial management educators. They have been active and successful in their careers. Both are also providing financial guidance and assistance for their own parents.

Acknowledgments

The authors wish to thank all those who provided support and encouragement throughout this book project. Each offered suggestions, guidance, research, or editorial remarks as this book developed: Jill and Larry Birchfield, Bill Bussing, Sheila Clark, Zachary Eickhoff, Lauren Smith, and Carol Hite. Barry Neville provided excellent editorial skills, and Jessica Faust served as an able and efficient agent. Special thanks are due Ruth Mannino for her editorial guidance. Many thanks to John Wolff for his loving support of this project and for serving meals that energized and enthused us as we traveled this journey.

Sharon Burns   Ray Forgue
April 2003   April 2003

1

Introduction

Jim and Frances Taylor have been married for 54 years. Jim has been retired for almost 10 years. He was the breadwinner, and Frances was a full-time homemaker. The couple raised four children on their modest income. Jim is healthy, but Frances was diagnosed with Alzheimer's disease about 5 years ago and is starting to decline significantly. She is no longer able to handle household tasks. Jim has tried to take up the slack, but it has been difficult for him. He has been caring for Frances lovingly, but he is increasingly finding himself unable to meet her needs.

Two of the Taylors' children live within 10 miles of their parents. Sue Crawford, the eldest, is 52. She is a nurse and works full-time at a local hospital. Her husband is a police captain. Their children are grown, and they have three grandchildren. Jim and Frances's youngest child, Mason, age 44, has never married and is the banquet chef at the best hotel in town. He visits his parents about once a month. The two other children live quite a distance from their parents and siblings. Betty, age 46, is a single mother with two children still at home. She lives in Oregon and works as a librarian. Brent, age 45, is a colonel in the U.S. Army, stationed in Germany. His family lives in Georgia. Brent has been pushing his siblings to address the rapidly approaching need to step into their parents' lives. Sue fears that the bulk of the responsibility will fall upon her.

YOUR INTEREST in this book indicates that you are facing, or are about to face, a critical turning point in your life, not unlike the one that Sue and her siblings are facing. It is one that people commonly encounter during late middle age or early in their retirement years. The change does not relate to your retirement. It relates to your involvement in your parents' lives. And it probably means getting directly involved in their financial affairs. Most people recognize that their parents may eventually come to depend on them for day-to-day personal care and for assistance in health-related care. But few imagine that they will have to help manage or even fully manage their parents' finances.

Yet that is exactly what is happening. The fastest-growing segment of the U.S. population consists of those over age 70. This is in some ways a positive development, reflecting improvements in the health status of the elderly. But there is often a downside as well. As they approach age 70 and beyond, many people's financial position becomes more tenuous. For some, this is because their income and financial assets decline to the point where they cannot cover the basic needs of day-to-day living. For others, their ability to manage their finances declines as their mental and physical abilities deteriorate. Some older people, perhaps your parents, simply need someone to help them pay their bills, balance their checkbook, and perform other routine tasks. But others reach a point where they are simply unable to handle their financial affairs at all.

The Two-Edged Sword: Emotions and Knowledge

Perhaps you purchased this book because you are nervous about getting involved in your parents' financial life. Perhaps you wonder if you can handle the emotional aspects of the task. Or perhaps you feel that you don't know enough to tackle the specific financial issues that people face late in life.

Emotional Aspects of Managing Your Parents' Money

It is understandable that you would have emotional concerns over the prospect of managing your parents' money. Getting involved in our parents' finances intrudes upon three key aspects of our relationship with our parents. One, both parents and children value their ability to handle their own affairs. Two, they guard their privacy. Three, they try to avoid conflict. Let's examine each of these three issues and how they affect your thoughts about managing your parents' money.

Independence is one of our most strongly held cultural values. Many of our ancestors left their families and traveled long distances to make it on their own. We revere that pioneer spirit of hard work and self-sufficiency. As children, we strove to become independent of our parents. Our first savings account, our first credit card, our first car, and our first home were major milestones by which we measured our independence. But independence works both ways. You became an independent adult, and your parents became independent of you. That independence is prized, nurtured, and protected. Children who for years told their parents "I can take care of myself" begin to hear the same thing in return. Parents guard their independence by resisting help. And when someone resists your help, it is natural to back off.

We also value our privacy. "None of your business" is a common response to questions about our finances. Even if we don't actually say it, we think it. Perhaps you have asked your parents about their finances. What did you hear back? A common response is, "Just fine, honey," which is designed to change the subject. More forceful responses can include "I don't want to talk about it, and don't ask again." Rarely do parents offer information, and when they finally do, the situation has often become critical. Some parents fail to recognize that they need financial assistance. Parents may be embarrassed, feeling that they did not manage their money well. And their children will feel uncomfortable pushing their parents to talk about a topic that they do not want to talk about.

Finally, we don't like conflict. Why does "money talk" lead to conflict? Money is one of our most emotionally laden resources. It involves numbers, arithmetic, and "cold" facts. It also involves feelings that are very deeply and personally held. These feelings are highly individualized. When children and parents begin talking about money, their individual differences come out into the open. Perhaps you and your parents do not agree on how to spend or invest money. Perhaps your parents do not agree. Siblings further complicate the situation. It is understandable that you would not want to open yourself up to this conflict.

Americans are taught not to discuss money with others. Parents rarely discuss finances with their children while they are growing up. And when they do, the focus is on the child's finances, not theirs. Talking to Mom and Dad about their money is not high on people's list of fun things to do. But it is often necessary.

Knowing What to Do

Even without these emotional concerns, you may feel that you do not know what to do. You may feel that you lack the skills and knowledge necessary to help your parents. You may feel that you have not managed your own financial affairs well enough. You may feel that you lack sufficient knowledge to tackle money issues that you have not experienced. And even if you have been successful, you may not be sure you can translate that success to benefit your parents.

Fortunately, the nuts and bolts of handling your parents' money are similar to those of handling your own. Money comes in, and it is spent. Assets are accumulated and can be used to provide income. Debts must be paid. Homes, vehicles, health, and lives must be insured. Taxes must be calculated, minimized where possible, and paid. Investments must be managed. The distribution of estates must be planned.

It is the details that are somewhat different when you are dealing with someone else's money, especially that of your elderly parents. You are the one who suffers the consequences when you make a mistake with your own money. Your parents will suffer the consequences if you make a mistake with theirs. You do not want to let them down.

This book addresses both the emotions involved and the knowledge needed to handle your parents' money. Each chapter addresses a specific topic and focuses on issues that are directly relevant to your new role in your parents' life. The approach is simple: Knowledge brings competence. Competence breeds confidence. And confidence reduces the emotional tensions involved. We discuss all of the basic financial topics that you will need to understand in order to manage your parents' money well. We provide the necessary information and offer worksheets, illustrations, and checklists that show you what to do and how to do it. As a result, you can become confident in your new role.

When Is It Time to Get Involved?

Perhaps you are wondering whether you should get involved at all. What signals will tell you that it is time to act? Educators have long recognized the concept of the "teachable moment." This is when students are open to and want to learn because of something inside themselves, not something external. This allows students to internalize what they are learning and have it become part of their bag of tricks, so to speak.

Are you at a teachable moment? We'll assume you are. You are reading this book. But what about your parents? To answer, we can borrow a distinction from the health-care field. Health-care providers distinguish between critical and chronic concerns. A critical concern is usually tied to a specific event, such as a heart attack, an accident, or a stroke. Action must be taken quickly. Chronic concerns are those that build over time but are not immediately life-threatening. High blood pressure, diabetes, and dementia are examples of chronic concerns. Actions must be taken, but they can be introduced gradually and become more complex should the situation worsen.

Critical and chronic concerns can exist in finances, as well. Perhaps one of your parents has had a critical medical emergency and physically cannot deal with finances. The situation may be permanent or temporary. Or, as with the Taylors, it may be that one of your parents is chronically ill and financial affairs are becoming more and more difficult. Maybe your parents are healthy, but their income has dropped because their retirement funds have run out. Perhaps medical expenses have rendered a modest income insufficient. Or perhaps your parents have fallen victim to one of the many frauds that are perpetrated on the elderly. Table 1.1

Table 1.1 Signals That You May Need to Get Involved with Your Parents' Money

Signal	Suggested Responses
Late fees, prior balances, and second notices on routine household bills; utility cutoffs	Offer assistance, set up a bill-paying calendar, ask to see bills, sort your parents' mail, have utilities put in your name
Frequent complaints about not having enough money, restricted activity because of lack of funds, seemingly unwarranted scrimping	Keep track of day-to-day income and expenses, set up a budget, monitor large and unexpected expenditures
Checking account problems: overdrawn accounts, bounced checks, excessive fees, unrecorded ATM activity	Offer to reconcile checking accounts, have your name put on accounts so that you can monitor transactions and balances, take control of the checkbook and/or debit cards
Credit card problems: going over the limit on credit cards, missed payments, late payment charges, rapidly increasing credit card balances, charges from unknown sellers	Consolidate debt through balance transfers, close unneeded credit card and charge accounts, monitor account statements, put credit cards on bill-paying calendar, set a payoff date and make the payments necessary to pay off by that date, cut up credit cards, challenge suspicious charges
Large, unplanned and/or automatic withdrawals or transfers from savings and investment accounts, especially those for sweepstakes entry; gifts to unknown charities or persons	Obtain account transaction histories to determine how long these practices have been going on, stop automatic payment agreements, get business reputation reports from the Better Business Bureau, contact local or state consumer protection agencies
New friends who appear to overstep normal boundaries, gain access to parents' accounts or credit cards, turn parents against family and other friends, or otherwise exercise undue influence	Discuss appropriate boundaries with the friend and with your parent, obtain physical control of checkbook and charge cards, write "photo ID required" on the back of charge cards, contact law enforcement authorities if necessary
Severe illness that includes memory loss or cognitive impairment or lengthy incapacitation	Gather bill payment records, check registers, and account statements; consult current financial advisers and insurance agents; develop basic financial statements (balance sheet and cash flow statement); review sources of income and retirement accounts; inquire about and, if necessary, supervise development of a will and living will, health-care surrogate, and durable power of attorney documents
Death of first parent	Confer with the surviving parent as to his or her understanding of the financial situation and ability/willingness to handle things alone; notify financial advisers and insurance carriers and update policies and contracts; update the survivor's will, living will, health-care surrogate, and durable power of attorney documents

highlights some signals that can alert you to the need to become involved in your parents' finances.

Who Should Manage Your Parents' Money?

You may be the only person in the family who is available to assist your parent. But more likely there are several people who could help. You may have brothers or sisters who might assist. Your parent may have siblings who could help, too.

What should you take into account when deciding who should step in to provide assistance? There are three factors that should be considered. One is proximity. How close to your parent does the person live, and how often does the person interact with your parent? Someone who lives nearby but who works 60 hours per week may not be a good candidate. Ideally, the helper should be someone who can have direct face-to-face contact with your parent several times per week.

The second factor is expertise. The person providing assistance should be someone who understands personal financial matters, either through formal education or from experience. This book is designed to help you upgrade your knowledge.

A third factor is willingness. Who will accept the responsibility? Handling your parents' finances and dealing with the paperwork and interpersonal aspects of the job can be difficult and time-consuming. Someone who understands the pressures involved and can accept those pressures will make the best caretaker. Sentimentality should not play a role in this decision. Just because someone is the oldest child, is close to the parents emotionally, or feels the most responsibility does not mean that he or she is the best person for the job. In many cases there really is only one person available. But when there are several people who could take on the role, the choice should be based on objective factors and should be acceptable to the parents, the person who will provide the assistance, other children, and, as appropriate, members of the extended family. The basic requirement is trust. Will the caregiver have the trust of everyone involved, especially the parents?

Family Dynamics

A primary key to your success as your parents' money manager will be your ability to understand and deal with each member of your family. In the example that opened this chapter, from one family (Jim and Frances) there evolved five families (Jim and Frances, and four children with their individual families). Changing one part of this system changes all parts, some reluctantly. Several factors will influence how you handle your new responsibilities and how your parents and siblings react to the situation. These include the concepts of boundaries, consistent patterns of behavior, and a desire for continuity. In addition, each person has her or his own values and attitudes regarding money. This process involves an immense amount of understanding: of where your parents were and are, of where each of your siblings is in the system, and of your own place in this evolution. The greater the involvement of a family with one another and with the process of caretaking, the greater the impact each will experience.

Boundaries

Each of us, your parents included, has a strong desire for privacy, independence, and control. But the caretaking situation that you now find yourself in is the exact opposite. If you are to manage your parents' money successfully, they must share details of their financial life with you. And they may be voluntarily or involuntarily facing the reality that they can no longer manage their own affairs. In addition, your brothers and sisters may have thoughts and feelings about the situation that are significantly different from yours. Brent is concerned that his parents need assistance. While Sue is also aware that they need assistance, she has additional concerns. Because she is physically close to her parents, it is likely she will bear the greatest responsibility for their care. And she is also concerned about the impact on her family life. She knows she will be stepping over boundaries. Her approach will be benefited by recognizing when that is about to happen, by communicating the recognition and need to do so, by getting her parents and siblings to accept the changes, and by being clear about the new boundaries that will form.

Consistent Patterns of Behavior

Each of us could face the exact same task, such as bill paying, and address it in an entirely different manner. We develop patterns of behavior that work for our own family. As Sue left her parents, married, and established a family of her own, she formed new behavior patterns. It is likely that her financial management patterns are different from those of her parents. And, this might cause conflict. For example, suppose that Jim and Frances paid bills as soon as they arrived. Therefore, they were always writing checks and mailing payments. Because Sue works outside the home and there thus are other claims on her time, she and her husband put all their bills in a basket and pay them on the 25th of the month.

Sue wants to handle paying her parents' bills in the same way. However, her parents are concerned that they will "get a bad reputation" for late payment, and just seeing the bills on their desk worries them. To top it all off, Brent is hearing about all of this from his parents and is emailing his sister to please take care of their parents' business affairs.

Desire for Continuity

Many people strive for continuity in their lives. They want things to continue as they are. However, as Jim and Frances age, it becomes less likely that their patterns and environments will remain the same. And, because external factors (health, income, expenses) are changing, the Taylors, their children, and their physical environment will need to adapt. Instead of Jim and Frances being the parents, the children will find themselves parenting their parents at times. Parenting your parents means that your lives have come (or are coming) full circle. The continuum in life is not a straight line, but a circle. Each of the five families will have to find its place and attempt to feel comfortable in this new family system.

Values

Conduct a simple survey. Ask each member of your family about his or her first real memory of money and the emotions that come to mind. Then ask how those feelings reverberate in their financial lives today. You will find that each has a different answer. We all value the financial aspects of our lives in different ways. Your own values will affect the manner in which you want to handle your parents' money. But their values will come into play, as well. Your parents may feel that it's very important to maintain their home's physical appearance. Yet, they tell you that they are not hiring extra personal assistance because they "can't afford it." But if they didn't have the professional landscaping done each year, they could afford to hire an aide to help bathe your mother three times a week. So whose values are more important? As money manager, you will need to work with your parents to understand their values and, as far as possible, adhere to their priorities, not yours. However, if your parents' health or safety is at stake, you may need to intercede and do what you think is best for them.

Attitudes

In addition to values, we all have different attitudes about money. Our attitudes were formed as we grew, from our environment and from events in our lives. It is likely that your attitudes about money differs from that of your parents. For example, Sue may see no problem with hiring household help. While her parents know that they can afford it, they still resist spending money for such a luxury. Frances thinks that she's letting Jim down by not keeping "a good house." Jim knows that she can't maintain the house, and that he can't either. While he can adapt his thinking to allow for hiring help, Frances continues to resist.

Change

Your parents' situation will force changes in their lives, your life, and your siblings' lives. As you take on new responsibilities, the relationship between you and your parents will change. Because they wish to maintain the boundaries that have been established, they may resist relinquishing control. Or, they may rely on you to just do it. This adds stress to your life and is likely to reduce the time you have for your family and your work activities.

In addition, your siblings will view you differently. Some will be relieved that someone is handling the caretaking, and as long as it's not them, fine. Others will want to be the authority or manager but do none of the actual work. Still others may be jealous and be afraid that they are "missing something" or that you're getting special treatment. Ideally, the family will meet as a group, develop a clear understanding of the reality of the situation facing your parents, and explore options for change. Tasks might be assigned depending on proximity to your parents, the special skills or knowledge each of you has, or the time each of you has available to dedicate to caretaking. Regardless of which of these "families" you belong to, good communication will ease the transition and, hopefully, increase the competence and confidence with which all family members handle this new phase of life.

Will the process go smoothly? No one knows. Can the process go smoothly? It certainly can. But it will do so only if all concerned have a clear understanding of what needs to change and what options for change are available, and if they also openly explore the impacts of those options before one of them is selected. In short, change can be managed competently and confidently, with open communication.

Being a Good Communicator

Money provides the economic goods and services that we all need and want. But money also is connected with complex motivations, including freedom, trust, self-esteem, guilt, indifference, envy, security, comfort, power, and control. When talking about financial matters with your parents, it is important for you to recognize how they value money emotionally. Your parents will want to hold on to their fiscal autonomy as long as possible, and they may be embarrassed to reveal details about their earnings, spending, and debt. You can overcome these obstacles by discussing money with sensitivity and compassion. Here are some tips for discussing your parents' money with them.

Get to Know Your Own and Your Parents' Approach to Money

The first step in learning to talk with others about financial matters is to understand your own approach to money. Perhaps you could make a list of the things that money means to you. Consider the emotions described in the previous paragraph to help get you started. Make a list of your financial fears, or "what would happen if . . ." After your parents separately make such lists, you will have much to discuss together. It will be constructive to discuss any differences between how you view your finances and how your parents view theirs.

Learn to Manage Financial Discussions

Give your parents time to express their views when discussing financial matters. If talking proves too difficult, have them write things down. Don't start talking about something out of the blue. Schedule the time and place for financial talks, decide on agenda items, and leave other topics for other times. When necessary, agree to disagree or to postpone difficult decisions until a later time—not to procrastinate, but to wait until the timing is better.

Avoid "You" Statements

"You" statements are usually seen as critical or blaming statements. "You" statements begin with something like "You always . . . ," "You never . . . ," "You should . . . ," or "If you don't, I will . . ." These statements have a high probability of being resisted. They shut off discussion and bring out defensiveness. Instead, tell your parents that their needs and wants are important.

Avoid Telling Your Parents What to Do

Beware of statements that begin with "I need you to . . ." or "You should . . ." These statements are seen as attempts to exert power. Such phrases as "I think" and "I feel" are helpful when discussing money. Even better are such statements as "How would you like us to handle . . . ?" "What can I do to help?" and "What would make things easier for you?"

Focus on Commonalities

Successful communication about money requires that the effort be aimed toward agreeing on common goals and reaching a consensus of opinion. Consensus goes beyond compromise. It results in each party internally and truly accepting the decision or course of action.

Follow Through on Your Discussions

Achieving consensus requires that family members talk about finances regularly, particularly when money decisions are not pressing. Decisions that are made should be acted upon. People who are just learning to discuss money matters often focus their attention on current financial activities and short-term issues to the exclusion of long-term financial planning. Try to use these discussions to establish long-term strategies for dealing with your parents' money. Good planning prevents crises.

The Journey Begins

The remainder of this book is divided into four parts. Part I focuses on basic money management. Chapter 2 begins by discussing the personal cash flow statement. This statement is a tool for determining where your parents' money has been coming from and where it has been going. Chapter 3 then discusses the personal balance sheet and how it can be used to assess your parents' current financial status. The balance sheet focuses on their assets and debts and, ultimately, their net worth. In Chapter 4 we provide tools to help you develop your parents' budget. The budget is a road map for your parents' future. Chapter 5 looks at issues related to the use of credit among the elderly. Its major focus is on solving debt problems. Chapter 6 focuses on personal income taxation issues that are especially relevant for retirees.

Part II covers issues related to protecting your parents' assets through insurance and appropriate investment strategies. Chapter 7 provides a basic understanding of insurance with a focus on automobile and homeowner's insurance. This chapter also addresses appropriate policy limits and how to make sure that your parents will be reimbursed as fully as possible after a loss. Chapter 8 provides a comprehensive overview of investment fundamentals. It includes a discussion of asset allocation strategies that are appropriate for retirees. Chapter 9 explores your parents' life insurance plan. Chapter 10 covers the important topic of Medicare. Chapter 11 describes the Medicaid program and its relationship to decisions about nursing home care.

Part III covers two primary areas of your parents' consumption of goods and services. Chapter 12 explores housing options and decisions. Factors involved in the deciding among the single-family house, apartment, assisted living, and nursing home options are emphasized in this chapter. Chapter 13 discusses common frauds perpetrated on the elderly, how they can be recognized, ways to avoid them, and how to address the situation if one of your parents has been defrauded.

Part IV focuses on the plans and procedures for transferring your parents' estate. Chapter 14 covers estate planning and what can be done prior to death to protect the estate and ensure that it transfers according to your parents' wishes. Chapter 15 discusses the probate process that occurs after a parent's death. It provides information that is useful to the executor of the estate. Part IV concludes with Chapter 16, which provides guidance on what you can do to plan your own finances based on what you have learned from working with your parents'.

Part I

Basic Money Management

2

Income and Expenses

Frances Taylor has always handled all the money matters for her family. As Frances's health declined, Jim took on that role. But now that Frances needs more care, Jim has not been able to keep up. Their daughter Sue Crawford has offered to step in, but Jim is unable to help her very much. For the past few months, Sue has ensured that the bills were paid. It has become clear to her that more money is going out than is coming in. When she expressed her concerns, Jim said that whenever he needed a little extra money he would take it out of their savings account. He likes to take Frances out to dinner because she can no longer cook and it brightens her spirits. Occasionally, they go to a movie, and Jim plays golf a couple of times each month.

GETTING INVOLVED in your parents' finances must be approached with hardheaded logic and emotional kid gloves. You want to be sensitive to the concerns and feelings of family members, but you need to apply sound financial management techniques, too. The two approaches are not mutually exclusive. "Crunching the numbers" can be done with sensitivity, but where do you get the numbers to "crunch"?

Usually, children become involved in their parents' lives when a crisis is looming or has already occurred. A common first thought is, "What is going on? Where is the money coming from? Where has it been going?" These questions were on the top of Sue's mind.

The Personal Cash Flow Statement

Fortunately, these questions can be answered in a businesslike way by applying one of the basic tools of business analysis, the cash flow statement. Just like a corporation, a family or individual has income (money coming in) and expenses (money going out). These two concepts form the bases for your parents' "personal" cash flow statement.

Personal cash flow statement: A document summarizing income and expenditures for a past period of time.

Your parents' cash flow statement (also called income and expense statement) will show whether their income is sufficient to meet their needs. Because most of their income is received on a monthly basis, you will probably want to complete a cash flow statement for your parents monthly. You can then compile the monthly statements into an annual statement. The cash flow statement consists of three sections: total income received, total expenditures made, and net gain (or deficit, if negative), which is the difference between total income and total expenses.

Income

When you prepare a cash flow statement, include income from all sources, including wages, salaries, government benefits, gifts, commissions, interest, dividends, and inheritances. To be counted as income, the funds should have come from outside rather than inside the household. For example, stock dividends, which are received from a company, are income. The sale of shares of stock, which is simply converting shares that are already owned to cash, is not income.[1] Some sources of income are received on an irregular basis, perhaps quarterly or annually. They should not be overlooked (see Table 2.1), but they should be counted only in the month in which they are actually received.

Expenditures

All expenditures made during the period covered by the cash flow statement should be included. Most people separate the expenses by whether they are fixed or variable. Fixed expenses tend not to vary over time and are outside of one's immediate control. Examples are rent payments and automobile installment loans. Variable expenses are expenditures over which an individual has control, including such items as food, utilities, entertainment, and clothing. There is no definitive set of categories for the expense section, but all expenditures need to be classified in a way that is consistent from month to month. Some expenditures occur on an irregular basis, perhaps quarterly or annually. They should not be over-

---

[1]Note that profit on the sale is a form of taxable income called capital gains. This must be reported to the IRS. See Chapter 6.

Table 2.1 *Common Sources of Income and Types of Expenditures for Retirees*

Sources of Income	Types of Expenditures
• Wages, salaries, and tips	*Fixed Expenses*
• Social security retirement benefits	• Savings and investments (regular, fixed
• Military pensions	deposits)
• Public assistance	• Retirement plan contributions (employer's
• Pension income from one or more prior	plan, IRA)
employers	• Housing (rent, mortgage loan payment)
• Distributions from IRA or 401(k)	• Automobile (installment payment, lease)
retirement savings plans	• Insurance (life, health, renter's/homeowner's,
• Interest and dividends received (from	automobile)
savings accounts, investment, bonds,	• Installment loan payments (vehicles,
or loans to others)	appliances, furniture)
• Support from family members	• Taxes (federal income, state income, local
• Other income (gifts, tax refunds, rent,	income, real estate, social security, and
royalties)	personal property)
• Supplemental Security Income (SSI) benefits	*Variable Expenses*
• Annuity income received	• Meals at home
• Rent received from rental property owned	• Meals away from home
• Stock dividends (received quarterly)	• Utilities (electricity, water, gas, telephone)
• Bond interest (received semiannually)	• Transportation (gasoline and maintenance,
• Mutual fund dividends (wtihout sale of	licenses, registration, public transportation)
actual shares)	• Medical expenses
	• Medicines (prescription and over-the-counter)
	• Clothing and accessories
	• Gifts
	• Domestic help
	• Household furnishings (furniture, appliances,
	curtains)
	• Cable television
	• Personal care (beauty shop, barbershop,
	cosmetics, dry cleaner)
	• Entertainment and recreation (hobbies,
	socializing, videotape rentals, movies)
	• Contributions (church, the poor, other
	charities)
	• Vacations and travel
	• Credit card payments
	• Personal allowance
	• Savings and investments
	• Miscellaneous (postage, books, magazines,
	newspapers, membership fees)

looked (see Table 2.1), but they should be counted as expenditures only in the month in which they are actually paid.

Net Gain

Net gain (deficit) shows the amount remaining after expenditures are subtracted from income. It is important that you be honest with yourself and your parents. If your parents don't have the income they need to meet their expenses and are selling shares of stock in order to do so, that needs to be seen clearly. Even if a deficit is covered by a stock sale or a savings account withdrawal, it is still a deficit.

A parent who has consistent deficits in cash flow has to be getting the money to meet expenses from somewhere. Some use credit cards to make ends meet. Most retirees make savings account withdrawals or sell assets to meet expenses. This is acceptable during retirement, but it should be acknowledged. Eventually the assets may run out.

The Iron Laws of Personal Finances

Net gains or deficits are the basis for two fundamental tenets of personal financial planning. First, people get ahead only when their income exceeds their expenditures. This means that their overall net worth (discussed more fully in Chapter 3) will grow only if they have money left over at the end of the month. Second, people fall behind when their expenditures exceed their income. In other words, their net worth will decline if they spend more than they receive. Typically, income exceeds expenditures until the retiree reaches about age 70. Thus, most seniors continue to build wealth even after their retirement. But by the time a child becomes involved in his or her parents' finances, the opposite is generally true. And in many cases, by the time a child becomes involved, there is no wealth remaining.

How to Obtain Information for the Cash Flow Statement

Preparing your parents' first cash flow statement may seem like so much guesswork. You probably have not been personally involved in their finances. They may not have kept good records, and their memory may have deteriorated. Some parents hide spending or a reduction in income from their children because they don't want them to know about these things.

Figure 2.1 Illustrated Spending Notebook Page

Spending Category: Food Away From Home	$ Amount
January 4 —Dinner	$ 20
January 8 —Lunch after golf	$ 8
January 10—Lunch, Jim and Frances	$ 13
January 15—Dinner with friends	$ 22
January 18—Dinner with Sam (Sue's son)	$ 34
January 21—Dinner, Jim and Frances	$ 16
January 22—Lunch after golf	$ 7
January 24—Dinner, Jim and Frances	$ 19
January 31—Dinner, Jim and Frances	$ 21
Total	**$160**

They may even be ashamed because they feel that they haven't been handling things well. However, most of the information is readily available.

Every check written, purchase receipt, bank account statement, and investment account report can serve as a source of information for the income and expense statement. Of course, if your parents keep poor records and save few documents, preparing a sufficiently detailed income and expense statement will be difficult. If this is the case, you may want to keep detailed records for a month before preparing your first statement.

Purchase a small spiral notepad to keep track of things on a day-to-day basis. Your parents may be able to do this for themselves, or they may need your help. You can use categories such as those in Table 2.1 as headings for the pages in the notebook. Figure 2.1 provides an example of such a page. Each time your parents make an expenditure, it is recorded on the appropriate page for its category. At the end of the month, the total for each page will be the total for that category. As we'll see in Chapter 4, these records can also be the basis for developing a budget.

Sue asked her dad if she could take a more active role in their day-to-day finances. She suggested that she could be of more help if she could get a handle on where their money was coming from and where it was going. Jim agreed to keep a log of what was being spent if Sue would set up a notebook for him to use and call him every day to help him enter the data. The notebook page for "food away from home" is given in Figure 2.1 as an example. The resulting cash flow statement is presented as Worksheet 2.1.

Worksheet 2.1 Cash Flow Statement for the Taylors

January 1, 2003–January 31, 2003

Income	Dollars	Percent
Jim's social security	$1,063	37.87
Frances's social security	657	23.41
Interest and dividends	123	4.38
Annuity	334	11.90
Jim's pension	550	19.59
Gifts	80	2.85
Total Income	**$2,807**	**100**
Expenses		
Fixed Expenses		
Rent	$706	25.15
Homeowner's insurance (monthly)	38	1.35
Automobile insurance and registration (monthly)	68	2.42
Life insurance	56	2.00
Savings at credit union	60	2.14
Federal income taxes (monthly average)	150	5.34
State income taxes (monthly average)	58	2.07
Medicare supplement insurance	155	5.52
Cable TV	45	1.60
Personal property taxes	60	2.14
Pledged church donation	100	3.56
Total fixed expenses	**$1,496**	**53.29**
Variable Expenses		
Food (at home)	$215	7.66
Utilities	230	8.19
Household operations	40	1.43
Gasoline, oil, maintenance	210	7.48
Medical expenses	165	5.88
Medicines	120	4.28
Clothing and upkeep	30	1.07
Food (away from home)	160	5.70
Entertainment	40	1.43
Gifts	135	4.81
Personal allowances	100	3.56
Personal care	70	2.49
Charitable contributions	90	3.21
Miscellaneous	100	3.56
Total variable expenses	**$1,705**	**60.75**
Total Expenses	**$3,201**	**114.04**
Surplus (deficit)	**($394)**	**(14.04)**

The first thing that Sue noticed was that her parents had overspent their income for the month by $394. This would amount to over $4,700 for one year. She worried about how long this pattern could continue. She noticed that $60 was going into another savings account that Jim said was intended specifically for holiday gifts for their children and grandchildren. Jim felt that all the spending was necessary or very important to the couple.

Final Thoughts

In spite of the seemingly bad news, Sue and Jim's effort to develop a cash flow statement has accomplished their goal. They now have a good picture of Jim's income and expenses. There is no substitute for taking this step. The job is easier if you can reconstruct the past few months from existing documents and records. If necessary, keeping track of every dollar spent for a month or two will pay off in the long run. It is not unusual for retirees to spend more than their income. Sue's next step is to determine whether Jim's investments and savings are sufficient to provide the additional funds he needs to cover his expenses over time. Chapter 3 provides the information needed to take that next step.

3

The Balance Sheet

Sue Crawford's concern over how her parents' bills were going to be paid deepened when she discovered that they were spending almost $400 per month in excess of their income. Her dad was taking the money out of their savings account. How much was in the account? What would happen if the money ran out? Where else could he get funds? To whom did her parents owe money? Now that her mom was very ill, how could her dad afford the increased medical care expenses? All of these questions were running through her mind.

ONCE YOU HAVE an understanding of your parents' income and outflow, you might think that the logical next step is to work out a budget to get the two into balance. That is probably what you would do for your own finances: You would focus on cutting your spending to match your income or increasing your income to match your spending. We will wait until the next chapter to discuss budgeting, however. For the elderly, there is an interim step.

This interim step is needed because of two realities your parents are probably facing. First, many of their expenditures either are fixed or, although theoretically variable, can't easily be reduced. Thus, they can have a tough time reducing expenditures. For example, spending on health care can be wildly variable, but there isn't a whole lot that can be done about it. Second, because they live on a relatively fixed income, they may have an equally tough time increasing their income.

How, then, do the elderly make ends meet? In the language of family economists, they practice dissaving. But for the elderly, dissaving is usually intentional. Their goal is to dissave slowly enough so that they don't run out of money. In fact, it is typical for the elderly to want to have a little (or a lot) left over to pass on to heirs.

The key is not necessarily to spend less than is coming in. The key is to make sure that the savings will last. But what savings? Basically, we are talking about the assets that your parents have accumulated over their lifetime. These assets may be in the form of savings accounts, retirement savings plans, stocks, bonds, mutual funds, real estate . . . any number of things that could be tapped, sold, or cashed in to generate funds. Therefore, it is vitally important to know your parents' assets and liabilities.

The Personal Balance Sheet

In Chapter 2 we borrowed a tool used by businesses, the cash flow statement, to look at the flow of money into and out of your parents' financial accounts. We are going to borrow another business tool in this chapter to analyze your parents' assets. That tool is the balance sheet (also called a net worth statement). The balance sheet lists assets (what your parents own) and liabilities (what your parents owe). The difference between their assets and their liabilities is their net worth. Their net worth can be tapped to provide the extra funds needed to balance income and expenses.

> **Balance Sheet:** A document summarizing one's financial condition at a specific point in time.

Assets

Assets include all goods, property, and financial assets that your parents own. They are measured at their fair market value, or their value as of today. They are not measured at the amount that was originally paid for them or what it would cost to replace them.

> **Fair Market Value:** The price that a willing buyer would pay a willing seller.

It is useful to classify your parents' assets into three categories: monetary assets, use assets, and investment assets. These three types of assets are used in different ways to meet financial needs. Monetary assets are cash, bank accounts, and other near-cash assets that can be readily converted to cash. They are primarily used for living expenses, emergencies, and savings. Use assets are physical items whose primary purpose is to provide maintenance of a lifestyle. They are "used up" or consumed over time to provide transportation, housing, and other aspects of day-to-day living. Investment assets are tangible and intangible items acquired primarily for generating income or with the expectation that they will go up in value. For retirees, investment assets provide flows of income to replace or supplement employment income. Table 3.1 provides a listing of commonly owned assets.

Liabilities

The liabilities section of the balance sheet includes all debts that your parents owe to others. Liabilities are measured at their payoff amounts, including the principal and any accrued interest. This equals the amount it would cost to pay off the loan today.

For example, the outstanding balance on a credit card would be listed as a debt on the balance sheet. This amount varies during the month. A simple phone call to the customer service number for the card (located on the monthly statement) will give you the balance at any time. The same is true for vehicle, home, and other installment loans. Future interest is not included, and it is not accurate to use the sum of the remaining payments on a loan. Liabilities are usually separated into short-term (a debt

Table 3.1 Common Assets and Liabilities of Retirees

Assets	Liabilities
Monetary Assets	*Short-Term Liabilities*
Cash on hand, checking accounts, savings accounts	Personal loans (owed to other persons)
Savings bonds, certificates of deposit	Credit card charge accounts, travel and entertainment credit cards
Money market accounts	Professional services unpaid
Money owed to a parent by others	(doctors, dentists, chiropractors, lawyers)
	Taxes owed but unpaid
Use Assets	
Automobiles, motor homes	*Long-Term Liabilities*
House, mobile home, condominium, vacation property	Automobile and other installment loan balances
Household furnishings and appliances	Home mortgage balance
Personal property (jewelry, furs, tools, clothing)	Home equity loan (second mortgage) balance
Other "big ticket" items	Loans from cash-value life insurance policies
	Personal loan balances
Investment Assets	
Stocks, bonds, mutual funds	
Retirement accounts, IRAs	
Life insurance and annuities (cash values only)	
Real estate investments	

to be paid off within 1 year) and long-term (a debt to be repaid more than 1 year in the future).

Net Worth

Your parents' net worth is the dollar value that remains when liabilities are subtracted from assets. Net worth is determined mathematically by subtracting liabilities from assets:

Worksheet 3.1 Balance Sheet for a Retired Couple—Jim and Frances Taylor

January 31, 2003		
	Dollars	Percent
ASSETS		
Monetary Assets		
Cash on hand	$260	0.25
Savings account #1—credit union	1,500	1.44
Savings account #2	40,147	38.56
Total monetary assets	**$41,907**	**40.25**
Use Assets		
Personal property	9,000	8.64
Automobile	11,500	11.05
Total use assets	**$20,500**	**19.69**
Investment Assets		
Life insurance cash value	5,400	5.19
Annuity cash value	36,300	34.87
Total investment assets	**$ 41,700**	**40.06**
Total Assets	**$104,107**	**100.00**
LIABILITIES		
Short-Term Liabilities		
Dentist bill	$120	0.12
Credit card debt	1,545	1.48
Total short-term liabilities	**$1,665**	**1.60**
Long-Term Liabilities		
Total long-term liabilities	**0**	**0.00**
Total Liabilities	**$1,665**	**1.60**
Net Worth	**$102,442**	**98.40**
Total Liabilities and Net Worth	**$104,107**	**100.00**

$$\text{Net worth} = \text{assets} - \text{liabilities}$$

or

$$\text{Net worth} = \text{the value of what is owned} - \text{the value of what is owed}$$

The Taylors' balance sheet is shown in Worksheet 3.1.

Any number of financial activities can alter your parents' net worth. Changes in the fair market value of an asset will affect both the asset and net worth sections of a balance sheet. For example, if a vehicle valued at $12,520 last year depreciates (as most use assets do) to $11,000, net worth will decrease by $1,520 if all other assets and liabilities remain the same. Second, liabilities can increase as more debt is acquired or decrease as loan payments (principal portion only) are made.

Three Financial Ratios

The information provided in a balance sheet is very useful. It is even more useful when it is looked at in tandem with the information in the cash flow statement. By comparing specific pieces of information from the two statements, you can get a feel for your parents' financial situation. We'll use the example of Jim and Frances Taylor to illustrate three financial ratios that will help you to better understand your parents' financial condition.

Assets-to-Debt Ratio

The assets-to-debt ratio shows whether the Taylors are technically solvent. This ratio is calculated by dividing total assets by total debts. For the Taylors, the assets-to-debt ratio is 62.5 ($104,107/$1,665). This is an excellent result and reflects their low level of debt. An assets-to-debt ratio greater than 1.0 reflects solvency and a positive net worth. Retirees should have ratios of 25 or more because they should carry little debt.

Debt-to-Income Ratio

A second ratio is the debt-to-income ratio, which is calculated by dividing debt repayments (excluding mortgage payments) by gross monthly income. A figure of 20 percent or less is recommended for people during their working years. But for retirees a ratio below 10 percent is recommended. The Taylors have built up a credit card debt that needs to be paid off. They plan to pay $140 on the debt in order to get it paid off in one year. Thus, for the Taylors, the debt-to-income ratio is 4.99 percent

($140/$2,807). While this is apparently low, it reflects a relatively low payment on their credit card debt.

Investment Assets–to–Net Worth Ratio

The third ratio is the investment assets–to–net worth ratio. This figure is calculated by dividing investment assets by net worth. For the Taylors, this ratio is 40.7 percent ($41,700/$102,442). This reflects the facts that they have a large asset—a savings account, which is a monetary rather than an investment asset—and that they do not own a home. As one approaches retirement, this ratio should increase and should approach 70 to 90 percent (lower for homeowners). In later retirement years the ratio declines, since investments have been used to meet living expenses.

Obtaining Information for the Balance Sheet

Preparing your parents' balance sheet may seem like a difficult task. But the information can be found with a little effort. Start with the most recent monthly statements from your parents' various bank, investment, and credit accounts. Then make a list of their household furnishings and other items of personal property. You do not have to include all use assets, especially if they would never be sold to raise money. However, the balance sheet can be used again in estate planning, so you want to include all items that have market value. You may have to estimate approximate dollar values for some use items, and other items, such as jewelry and collectibles, may need to be appraised. Remember to value such items at their fair market value. The dollar values of homes and vehicles can be based on what similar items are currently selling for. Sometimes the best you can do is estimate what items could bring at a garage sale. Sentimental value should not come into the picture. Just be reasonable. Remember, you are trying to be businesslike.

How Long Will the Money Last?

Part of your parents' retirement income probably comes from savings and investments built up over the years. The key question is, how long will the money last? The answer depends upon three factors: (1) the amount of money in the nest egg, (2) the rate of return earned on an investment or savings account, and (3) the amount of money that is withdrawn from the account each month. By spending at a rate that will not deplete the funds too rapidly, you can ensure that the funds will last the desired number of years. Table 3.2 provides factors that can be multiplied by the amount in a retirement account, investment fund, or savings account to determine the amount available for spending each month.

Consider the case of Jim and Frances Taylor. They have been tapping a savings account to make ends meet. In a recent month they withdrew $394. Jim wants his $40,147 nest egg to last 15 years, assuming that it will earn a 4 percent annual return in the future. The value in the table in the "15 years" column and the "4 percent" row is 0.0074. Multiplying 0.0074 times $40,147 reveals that Jim could withdraw $297 every month for 15 years before the fund was depleted. Since he has been withdrawing about $100 per month more than that, Jim should be concerned that he will run out of money earlier than he would like. In fact, Jim will run out of money in about 10 years if he continues to withdraw $400 per month ($400/$40,147 = 0.01, which is close to the 10-year figure in the 4 percent row of Table 3.2).

As you can see, this calculation is crucial for the Taylors (and for any retirees and their children). In this case, there are several options available. One is to move the money out of the savings account and into an alternative investment earning a higher rate of return. Perhaps a money market mutual fund or a bond mutual fund would be appropriate. But these bring additional risk (especially the bond fund). Or, Jim could plan on the money lasting only 10 years. The rationale might be that he would prefer to spend the money now and live more frugally later. Jim is being conservative because his life expectancy is closer to 90 than 85. But will he really need as much income when he is in his late 80s? Thinking

Table 3.2 Estimating Withdrawal Rates from Savings or Investment Accounts*

Rate of Return	5	10	Years 15	20	25
3%	0.01797	0.00966	0.00691	0.00555	0.00474
4%	0.01842	0.01012	0.00740	0.00606	0.00527
5%	0.01887	0.01061	0.00791	0.00660	0.00585
6%	0.01933	0.01110	0.00844	0.00716	0,00644
7%	0.01980	0.01161	0.00899	0.00775	0.00707
8%	0.02028	0.01213	0.00956	0.00836	0.00772

*For a given interest rate, multiply the dollar amount of the asset by the factor for the number of years you wish the asset to last. The result is the dollar amount that can be taken each month without exhausting the asset during the planned time period.

through these questions is difficult for both parents and the children who are attempting to help them. Both must confront the economic realities and at the same time confront the parents' mortality.

Final Thoughts

The balance sheet provides a snapshot of your parents' financial situation at a given time. But it is an ever-changing picture. You will want to prepare a balance sheet each year. Net worth will naturally decrease if assets are being tapped or loans are taken out to meet expenses. But it is entirely possible that assets could grow in value and debts decline, so that net worth increases. You will want to make an honest appraisal of how long any savings or other income-producing assets will last. If necessary, you will want to adjust your parents' budget. Chapter 4 covers budgeting.

4

Budgeting

Sue Crawford now understands her parents' financial situation much better. She knows that her father is withdrawing almost $400 per month from savings, and that at that rate he will run out of money in 10 years. Her father wants the money to last 15 years, and this means that he should be withdrawing about $100 per month less than he has been doing. But Sue is still worried. Interest rates have been pretty low in the last couple of years, and even if he cuts his withdrawals by $100 per month, Jim will need to earn 4 percent after taxes to have his money last 15 years. If interest rates remain low, he will run out of money even sooner. Maybe he should withdraw even less. But how will he make ends meet at this lower withdrawal rate?

SUE CRAWFORD has helped her dad with some bill paying. And she has helped him better understand his situation by preparing a balance sheet and a cash flow statement. But she hasn't really become directly involved in her parents' finances. No hard decisions have been made, decisions that are necessary given her parents' situation.

Sue must help her father translate what they now know into action. They need to bring Jim's spending under control. He needs a budget. And budgeting is about making choices and carrying out a spending plan. This chapter provides tools that you can use to help you develop a budget for your parents. We start by putting the budgeting process into perspective by discussing the nature of budgets. Then we talk about the steps involved in budgeting.

> **Budget:** A plan for income and spending focused on meeting financial goals.

The Nature of Budgets

The word *budget* carries lots of meanings. To some people, it means discipline. To others, it means a straitjacket. Some people love to keep track of their money and assess their success. Others avoid budgeting like the plague. But a budget is really just a tool for reaching financial goals.

Financial goals evolve over a person's life cycle. Young adults are most concerned with acquiring a home, vehicles, furniture, and other consumer goods. Middle-aged adults may focus on their children's education and their own retirement. During retirement, the goal is to maintain the desired standard of living in the face of reduced income. Often, retirees are concerned about outliving their wealth and becoming dependent on others. Those are Jim Taylor's big concerns.

This focus on goals puts budgeting into perspective. Budgeting starts by considering the end result. Budgeting is a means to an end, not an end in itself. Helping your parents live within their budget demands that you take a realistic look at their future income and expenses in light of what they want.

How do you know what they want? You can ask. Sue knows that her father likes to take Frances out to dinner once in a while. He wants to get out with his friends for golf and socializing. He wants to make ends meet on a regular basis. And he wants to be able to pay his own way given his retirement benefits and savings.

There is another way to know what your parents want: You can look at how they live. That is, you can examine their actual spending pattern. That pattern is summarized in the cash flow statement discussed in Chapter 2. The cash flow statement tells what has been going on. The balance sheet tells your parents' current status. And the budget lays out a plan for future income and spending given available resources.

Budgeting is also personal. No two families will or should have the same budget. However, it does sometimes help to see a typical spending pattern. Table 4.1 provides the average amount spent in various categories by the typical older household. These figures can be guidelines, but that is all they should be. Each family must look at its own values, goals, resources, and behaviors and come up with its own plan. There is no right or wrong way to budget your money. What's right is what works. This is true both for where the money comes from and goes and for the budget mechanisms used. Some people use detailed charts and computer programs for budgeting. Others use notebooks and calculators. The methods do not matter as long as the goals are reached.

Table 4.1 Typical Spending Patterns for Older Households

Item	Age 65–74	Age 75 and Over
Income		
Wage and salary income	$9,174	$2,147
Self-employment income	860	757
Investment income	1,810	1,991
Social security income	17,011	15,529
Other income	494	409
Total Income	**$29,349**	**$20,563**
(After-Tax Income)	**$27,833**	**$19,759**
Expenditures		
Food at home	$2,760	$2,106
Food away from home	1,418	971
Shelter	5,114	4,034
Utilities	2,438	1,937
Household operations	498	839
Housekeeping supplies	511	322
Household furnishings and equipment	1,110	634
Apparel and related services	1,130	701
Transportation	5,797	2,875
Health care	3,163	3,338
Entertainment, reading, and education	1,718	898
Personal care products and services	479	368
Alcohol and tobacco	484	254
Cash contributions	2,022	1,618
Personal insurance and pensions	1,379	460
Federal income taxes	1,338	574
State and local income taxes	200	83
Other taxes	257	147
Miscellaneous	761	553
Total Expenditures Including Taxes	**$32,577**	**$22,712**

Source: U.S. Department of Labor, Bureau of Labor Statistics, Consumer Expenditure Survey, 2000.

Steps in the Budgeting Process

Budgeting can be broken down into five distinct steps: setting goals, establishing a budget ledger format, deciding on the monetary targets for income and expenditures, putting the budget to work, and, finally, evaluating success and revising the budget as necessary once the budgeting period is over. Then the process begins anew. Figure 4.1 outlines the steps in the budgeting process.

Figure 4.1 Steps in the Budgeting Process

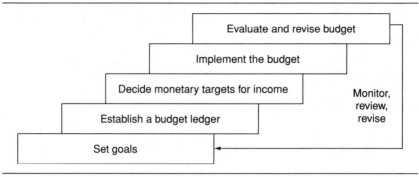

Setting Financial Goals

Financial goals should be as specific as possible. They should include specific dollar amounts and target dates as appropriate. Jim Taylor wants to maintain his spending for dinners out with Frances and his own social life. These goals are general in nature, but his cash flow statement provides the dollar amounts that he has been spending for these purposes and, thus, the target for future spending. He also wants to make sure that he does not overspend his income by so much that he withdraws money from savings too fast. His general goals translate into these financial goals:

1. Continue to spend $160 per month on meals away from home.
2. Continue to spend $40 per month on recreation.
3. Cut spending by approximately $200 per month to slow the withdrawal rate from his savings account.

Note that Jim has no goals that involve savings. This is not unusual for retirees, as they often are withdrawing from savings to meet day-to-day living expenses. Savings goals are a little more complicated than Jim's goals. Let's assume that Jim wants to purchase a new vehicle in 3 years and put 40 percent down. The make and model he wants to purchase sells for $20,000 today, so he would need $8,000 down. Dividing by 36 months indicates that he would need to save $222 per month. This simple calculation would get him close to his goal. But three factors are missing. The first is the effect that inflation will have on the price of the vehicle in 3 years. He might have to save a bit more to counteract inflation and still meet his 40 percent down payment goal. The second factor he must consider is the interest he will earn on his savings. Whatever interest he earns will help him reach his goal by letting him save somewhat less than $222 per month. Third, he must also account for the taxes that he must pay on the interest earned on the savings. You can usually ignore inflation, interest rates, and taxes for goals to be achieved within 1 or 2 years. For longer-term goals, you will need to include these factors in order to calculate a realistic monthly savings goal. Fortunately, there are a number of Web sites that provide calculators to assist you. These sites include www.bankrate.com, www.money.com, and www.Kiplinger.com.

Many people become discouraged when they try to set goals because they quickly perceive that some goals must be delayed. They wonder which goals they should attack first. One rule of thumb is to pay off high-interest credit cards first. Then move on to deciding among the various other goals. You will need to help your parents sort out their priorities. It is important to keep in mind that every action carries not only the cost of the action taken, but also the opportunity cost of not achieving the alternatives that were forgone.

Establishing a Budget Ledger Format

Developing a budget requires that you decide on a budget format. This requires setting up a ledger as a way to record income and expenditures during the month. Within the ledger, you will establish classifications for income and expenditures. The ledger will be almost identical to the cash flow statement in this regard. Only the dollar amounts will differ. You can create your own ledger or purchase forms at an office supply store.

> **Ledger:** A form, booklet, or computer file for maintaining income and expenditure records.

Many people use computerized ledgers because they are especially suited to making adjustments, corrections, and updates. Quicken and Microsoft Money are two popular versions of these software programs. Or you can develop your own using a spreadsheet program such as Microsoft Excel or Corel Quattro Pro.

Most people budget on a monthly basis. This works well for retirees because they generally receive social security, pension, and annuity checks on a monthly basis. Using a monthly time period also enables them to identify and control financial activities that occur monthly, such as rent, utilities, and other bills. A monthly budget can be compiled into an annual budget and the results of implementing the budget summarized into the two main financial statements (balance sheet and cash flow statement).

Deciding on Budget Targets

The next phase of budgeting focuses on making decisions about the sources of funds as well as how they will be spent. You should begin by estimating your parents' total gross income from all sources. Then make estimates for their various spending categories. Your estimates must be realistic, and you will have to resolve conflicting needs and wants by revising your estimates (usually downward) as necessary to meet their goals. Bear in mind that a budget is a working tool, and that it should remain flexible.

People usually find that their initial expense estimates far exceed their income. Sue is facing this problem, as her dad has been outspending his income by almost $400 per month. To make ends meet, Jim can (1) increase income, (2) reduce expenses, (3) withdraw money from savings, or (4) borrow money. Jim and Sue have already decided against choice 1 because to increase his income, Jim would have to either go back to work or invest in riskier investments. And Jim does not want to take on additional debt (choice 4). By default, Jim has been withdrawing from savings even though he hasn't been budgeting. He wants to slow his withdrawals, and in order to do so he must focus on reducing his expenses.

Retirement Plan Distributions

Most of your parents' income probably comes from two sources: social security and a retirement pension that pays a monthly benefit. As we discussed earlier in this chapter, if your parents' income is not enough to meet their living expenses, they will have to withdraw funds from their savings or other retirement assets. A significant amount of their assets may be held in individual retirement accounts or in 401(k) or 403(b) plans. They may choose to withdraw funds from these accounts in order to supplement their monthly income.

The IRS allowed your parents to save funds for retirement in IRAs and 401(k) and 403(b) plans on a tax-deferred basis. Because the IRS has never taxed the assets in these "qualified" retirement plans, it requires your parents to begin withdrawals at age 70½ regardless of their need for income. The withdrawals are taxable in the year of withdrawal. Generally speaking, the IRS taxes each withdrawal. Withdrawals from Roth IRAs are not taxable. Funds contributed to employer-based plans on an after-tax basis will not be taxed upon withdrawal either.

Each year after they reach age 70½, your parents will have to make a "required minimum distribution (RMD)." The required minimum distribution is based on the balance of the account on December 31 of the previous calendar year and the plan owner's age during the year of withdrawal. The IRS publishes a required minimum distribution table, shown here as Table 4.2. To determine the amount of the required distribution, you need to divide the account balance at the end of the previous calendar year by the divisor shown next to your parent's current age in Table 4.2. For example, if Jim, who is 75, had a balance of $30,000 in his IRA at the previous year's-end, his required minimum distribution would be $1,310.04 (30,000/22.9). (He can, of course, take more.) The withdrawal needs to be made by December 31 of each year or the IRS will assess a sizable penalty for late withdrawal.

Table 4.2 Required Minimum Distribution Factors

Age	Applicable Divisor	Age	Applicable Divisor
70	27.4	93	9.6
71	26.5	94	9.1
72	25.6	95	8.6
73	24.7	96	8.1
74	23.8	97	7.6
75	22.9	98	7.1
76	22.0	99	6.7
77	21.2	100	6.3
78	20.3	101	5.9
79	19.5	102	5.5
80	18.7	103	5.2
81	17.9	104	4.9
82	17.1	105	4.5
83	16.3	106	4.2
84	15.5	107	3.9
85	14.8	108	3.7
86	14.1	109	3.4
87	13.4	110	3.1
88	12.7	111	2.9
89	12.0	112	2.6
90	11.4	113	2.4
91	10.8	114	2.1
92	10.2	115 and older	1.9

Retirement Plan Distributions *(continued)*

The IRS requires that you calculate a required minimum distribution for each tax-deferred account. However, you are not required to withdraw the funds from each account; you can choose to withdraw the total required minimum distribution from any one of your tax-deferred accounts.

Although IRA, 401(k), 403(b), or other tax-deferred retirement account withdrawals must begin by age 70½, it is not that simple. A taxpayer must make his first required minimum distribution before April 1 of the calendar year *following* the year in which he turns 70½. For example, if your father turns 70 on September 15, 2003, he will turn 70½ on March 15, 2004, and not have to make his first withdrawal until April 1, 2005! However, if he turns 70 on May 15, 2003, he will turn 70½ on November 15, 2003, and have to make his first required minimum distribution by April 1, 2004.

It is possible that a taxpayer would have to take two required minimum distributions in one calendar year. Take our example above where your father turns 70 on September 15, 2003. He must make his first withdrawal by April 1, 2005. The amount of that RMD would equal his account balance on December 31, 2003, divided by 26.5. He would then have to make his age 72 withdrawal by December 31, 2005. The amount of his age 72 RMD would be the account balance on December 31, 2004 less his April 1, 2005 withdrawal divided by 25.6 (the age 72 divisor).

From Worksheet 2.1, Sue determined that Jim had been spending approximately $3,200 per month. Her discussions with Jim helped them decide to cut savings withdrawals in half and to reduce expenditures to about $3,000 in order to make ends meet and pay off the credit card debt. Therefore, their immediate task is to decide where to make cuts in Jim's expenses until they have reached their targets. To some extent this is a trial-and-error process. They used the figures from Jim's cash flow statement and made adjustments until his projected expenses were $3,000. As indicated in Worksheet 4.1, they ended up reducing planned expenditures in the following areas: gifts, food at home, food away from home, personal allowances, charitable contributions, gasoline, clothing, personal care, and miscellaneous. While it is sometimes uncomfortable, the process of reconciling needs and wants is a healthy exercise because it identifies what is important in your parents' life. You might find it worthwhile to

Worksheet 4.1 Budget for the Taylors

February 1, 2003–February 28, 2003

Income	Dollars	Percent
Jim's social security	$1,063	37.87
Frances's social security	657	23.41
Interest and dividends	123	4.38
Annuity	334	11.90
Jim's pension	550	19.59
Gifts	80	2.85
Total Income	**$2,807**	**100**

Expenses	Dollars	Percent
Fixed Expenses		
Rent	$706	25.15
Homeowner's insurance (monthly)	38	1.35
Automobile insurance and registration (monthly)	68	2.42
Life insurance	56	2.00
Savings at credit union	60	2.14
Federal income taxes (monthly average)	150	5.34
State income taxes (monthly average)	58	2.07
Medicare supplement insurance	155	5.52
Cable TV	45	1.60
Personal property taxes	60	2.14
Pledged church donation	100	3.56
Total fixed expenses	**$1,496**	**53.29**
Variable Expenses		
Food (at home)	$184	6.59
Utilities	230	8.19
Household operations	40	1.43
Gasoline, oil, maintenance	155	5.52
Medical expenses	165	5.88
Medicines	120	4.28
Clothing and upkeep	25	0.89
Food (away from home)	140	4.99
Entertainment	40	1.43
Gifts	60	2.14
Personal allowances	50	1.78
Personal care	50	1.78
Credit card repayment	140	4.99
Charitable contributions	60	2.14
Miscellaneous	45	1.60
Total variable expenses	**$1,504**	**53.63**
Total Expenses	**$3,000**	**106.92**
Surplus (deficit)	($193)	(6.92)

go over Jim's cash flow statement and see what cuts you might have made to reduce spending by $201 to hit the $3,000 target and pay off the credit card.

Putting the Budget to Work

Once priorities have been set and decisions have been made, it is time to put the budget into action. Sue and Jim will need to record Jim's income and expenditures during the first month and deal with any problems that arise. It is important that they keep an accurate and up-to-date record of expenditures. Many people keep a notepad in their pocket or purse for that purpose. Jim did just that as he kept track of expenses prior to completing his cash flow statement. He will need to do so again, but this time he will keep a running tally of spending against what was budgeted in each category.

Keeping track of the money is relatively easy. Controlling it is another matter; especially when the budget calls for reduced spending. There are several budget controls that you might find useful.

- *Use a checkbook.* Checks are easier to keep track of than cash. A checkbook can be used to record the business or person with whom you did business and the purpose of the expenditure. It helps to deposit 100 percent of all checks received into the checking account. Then pay most expenses with a check. Where cash is necessary, write a check for cash, indicating in the checkbook register the purpose of the cash. Periodically during the month the checkbook can be used to assess progress. Automatic teller machine and debit card transactions should be recorded in the check register immediately, along with the purpose of the expenditure. ATM and debit card receipts should be retained in a wallet or handbag and filed away safely upon returning home.

- *Keep a notebook.* Recall from Chapter 2 that a notebook can be used to record expenditures on a day-to-day basis when developing a cash flow statement. The same notebook method can be used for budgeting. One dimension is added: At the top of each notebook page, write in the amount budgeted for that category, then calculate a declining balance throughout the month. Figure 4.2 provides Jim Taylor's notebook page for gas, oil, and maintenance during the month of February. Note the declining balance from the budgeted amount of $155. If your parents reach $0 in a category during the month, they have two choices: They

Figure 4.2 llustrated Budget Notebook Page for Jim and Frances Taylor

Spending Category: Gas, oil, and maintenance
Amount budgeted: $155
Amount carried from previous month: $0

Item	Amount Spent	Remaining Balance Available to Spend
Total Amount Budgeted	**$155**	
2/1—Gas	$ 17	$138
2/8—Oil change	$ 20	$118
2/9—Gas	$ 19	$ 99
2/15—Air filter	$ 9	$ 90
2/16—Gas	$ 18	$ 72
2/23—Gas	$ 15	$ 57
2/28—Gas	$ 10	$ 47
Total	$108	

can stop spending on that category, or they can transfer a balance from another category and reduce spending in that other category.

- *Periodically monitor unexpended balances and justify exceptions.* The best method for controlling overspending is to monitor the balance in each budget classification each week. This is very easy to do if you use the notebook method. The purpose is to catch patterns that will result in overspending before the end of the month. Overspending may be justified, but a conscious effort should be made to understand the reason for the overspending. It may be necessary to reallocate spending or to offset over-expenditures with extra earnings received or with a reduction of spending elsewhere.

- *Use the envelope method.* The envelope method is especially appropriate for expenditures that are made primarily with cash. At the beginning of the month, the exact amount of money to be spent on each of these categories is placed into a separate envelope. Write the classification name and the budget amount on the outside of each envelope. As expenditures are made in a category, they can be written on the appropriate envelope and the proper amounts of cash removed from that envelope. When an envelope is empty, funds for that category are exhausted. This technique works well in controlling expenditures for variable expenses such as entertainment, personal allowances, and food.

- *Use subordinate budgets.* A subordinate budget is a budget of planned expenditures within a single budgeting category. For example, one might budget $650 for a weekend trip during a given month. The trip spending could be controlled by a subordinate budget that allocates $250 for lodging, $150 for meals, $150 for entertainment, and $100 for transportation.

The Evaluation

At the end of the month, you should evaluate the budgeting process. This step provides the feedback for examining your progress toward achieving your goals. Specifically, the purpose of evaluation is to determine whether the earlier steps in the budgeting process have worked.

Evaluation compares actual with budgeted amounts. In some expenditure classifications, the budget estimates will rarely agree with the actual expenditures. Some classifications may still have a positive balance at the end of the month. For example, Jim Taylor spent only $108 on vehicle expenses (gas, oil, and maintenance) rather than the $155 budgeted for this purpose. What should he do with the $47 balance? Some people deposit these surpluses in a savings account. Others treat them like "mad money" and spend them. Still others leave the funds in a checking account and carry the surpluses forward, thereby providing larger budget estimates for the following month. The budgeting form in Figure 4.2 allows for carrying forward balances to the next period. Jim wants to carry the balance forward in anticipation of car repairs that are likely to be needed in future months. By doing that, he will be prepared for an expenditure that might otherwise "ruin" the budget in a future month.

Because estimates of variable expenses are usually averages, it is best not to change the estimate based on a variation that occurs during just 1 or 2 months. If estimates are too high or too low for a longer period, however, you will want to make adjustments. Some fixed expenditures, such as life and auto insurance or property taxes, may not be paid monthly. In such cases, balances must be carried forward to ensure that the funds will be available when they are needed. It is a good idea to open a separate savings account—a revolving savings fund—to safeguard these funds from appearing to be unneeded surpluses. At the end of each month, you can put the surpluses in these categories into this account, so that when the bills comes due, they can be paid with the saved funds.

Whatever your goals, it should be encouraging to know that some or all of them have been achieved or that progress has been made toward achieving them. If some objectives are not met, the evaluation process helps you to determine why and to adjust the budget and objectives accordingly. Suppose Jim finds that he could not cut spending by as much as he desired. He shouldn't give up. Cutting a budget is not always successful the first month. But over time, the new pattern can take hold. Next month's budget can have amounts similar to those used in February. Jim should adjust the estimates only if they seem unachievable or unnecessary after several months.

Related Issues

Budgeting for your parents can be difficult even when their income is adequate. This is especially true when they have not been going through a formal budgeting process in the past. Two other situations warrant special consideration when working with elderly parents.

When Parents Cannot Manage Their Own Money

Unfortunately, many parents reach a point where they can no longer handle their day-to-day finances by themselves. Several techniques are useful in such cases. Develop a monthly bill-paying calendar that lists all regular payment due dates during a month. This will help you remind your parents to pay the bills, or remind yourself if you have taken over that task. You can also set up utility, insurance, rent, and other regular payments as automatic payments out of your parents' checking account. This method is particularly helpful if you must assist your parents from a distance. Another technique is to set up a credit card account specifically for making purchases at the grocery, the drugstore, and other regularly visited retail stores. The monthly statement can be mailed to the person who is assisting the parents in managing their spending. Finally, you could hire a bookkeeping service or personal financial assistant that would charge on an hourly basis. You would want to ensure that such an assistant is bonded and get references from other clients.

When Your Parents' Income Is Grossly Inadequate

Often, by the time a child gets involved, the parents' income from all sources has declined to the point where it simply cannot cover their living costs. At this point, some tough decisions need to be made. It may be necessary to begin selling some of the parents' assets, such as unneeded furniture, clothing, appliances, jewelry, and even their home. Reverse mortgages may also be used to tap the equity in a paid-for home (see Chapter 12, "Housing"). Various food assistance programs such as Meals on Wheels and programs at senior citizens' centers may be helpful in adequately meeting your parents' nutritional needs. Parents whose only source of income is a small social security check might qualify for the federal Supplemental Security Income program (www.ssa.gov or www.benefitscheckup.org). They can apply at their local social security office. They may also qualify for food stamps. Faith-based and other social service organizations can also be of assistance. The key is to make contacts in your local community and find what senior citizens' assistance offices and centers may exist.

Final Thoughts

Budgeting flows naturally from the information in the cash flow statement and the balance sheet. In fact, you should not start to set up a budget for your parents without having first developed these statements. You should also discuss your parents' assessment of their past patterns of income and spending and their current net worth with them. Explore their goals and fears, and use the budget to reach those goals and allay those fears. Your parents' budget should be unique to their situation and should not be judged by what others seem to be doing. Attention to detail is important. Maybe after a few months of successful budgeting, they can relax their day-to-day record keeping. But they should still evaluate how they did at the end of each month.

5

Credit

Carl Johnson's mother, Martha, has been bedridden for almost a month. Several days ago, she handed him her checkbook and a big packet of mail and said, "Will you pay these bills for me?" When he went through the stack, he found five different credit card bills and one installment loan statement. He had thought she only had one card: an account that they had opened jointly several years ago. Two of her credit card bills were already past due. She had not made a payment on their joint account the previous month. Martha has been carrying balances from month to month on all five cards. There were charges on the cards from places he had never heard of and many cash advances. He asked her about the loan. She said it was a home-equity debt consolidation loan with her house as collateral that she used to pay off two of her cards about 6 months ago. She told him where he could find past credit card statements, and when he went through those, he found a similar pattern. She owes a total of $14,190 and has an income of $1,250 per month. How can Carl make sense of this situation and clean up the mess?

OUR PARENTS grew up in different times with different values. This is especially true when it comes to the use of credit. Before 1960, credit was used only for major purchases, such as a home or a car. Credit cards were generally unavailable. And being in debt, even manageable debt, was a cause for concern at best and a moral failing at worst.

Today, almost everyone uses credit and lenders constantly barrage prospective borrowers with offers. Loan default rates and consumer bankruptcies are at near-epidemic levels, and the elderly are not immune to the plague. According to the Federal Reserve Board, the percentage of income used to pay debts increased for all age groups over age 50 between 1989 and 1998. This percentage is highest among the lowest-income groups. It is very easy to use credit cards to cover the costs of day-to-day living when income drops. And when health-care expenses overwhelm income, using credit cards becomes very tempting. Combine these factors with the tendency to view being indebted as a sign of moral failure, and you have the ingredients for big trouble for today's elderly—trouble that you may have to help your parents resolve.

Fortunately, there are many tools at your disposal. First, this chapter will provide you with basic information about how credit works today. Some of the pitfalls of credit that can befall the elderly are discussed next. Then we examine techniques for managing credit usage. Finally, we discuss what to do when high debt loads become a problem.

Credit Basics

Understanding the way credit works today requires focusing on the cost of credit, how credit is obtained, and how finance charges are calculated. Armed with this information, you can begin to address any problems your parents may have with credit.

The Cost of Credit

It's certainly no surprise that interest represents the price of credit. But interest is only one of the components of the finance charge. All mandatory charges, such as a loan application fee or credit life insurance premiums, must be included. Lenders are required to quote the finance charge as an annual percentage rate (APR) so that consumers can shop for credit. The lower the APR, the lower the true cost of credit. In recent years, the average credit card has carried an APR of around 15 percent. However, rates range from 8 percent to 27 percent.

Finance charge: the total dollar amount paid to use credit.

APR: The cost of credit on a yearly basis, expressed as a percentage rate.

Federal law (the Truth in Lending Act) has made it easy to shop for the best credit terms. Key pieces of information must be disclosed in advertising and on applications for credit. Such information includes the APR, how it is calculated if it is a variable rate, the finance charge, all fees, the length of the grace period, and the method used to calculate the account balance on credit cards (these topics are discussed later in the chapter). Web sites such as www.bankrate.com and www.cardtrack.com can also be used to shop for credit.

The fees that credit cards often charge add another dimension to the cost of credit. Some of these fees are assessed even when the borrower uses the account appropriately. For example, some bank credit cards charge annual fees ranging from $20 to $50. A transaction fee may be levied each time a card is used, especially for cash advances. Some of these fees are not included in the APR calculation for credit cards because they cannot be known in advance. An apparently low-cost card may actually be a high-cost card when all fees are considered. Other fees are charged when the borrower fails to honor the contract in some way. For example, late payment fees average over $30. Many credit cards carry an over-the-limit fee when the cardholder exceeds his or her credit limit. In addition, banks often impose higher punitive interest rates on the entire debt when a payment is late or the credit limit is exceeded. Rates can jump to 24 or even 32 percent. Carl's mother is in danger of having this happen because of her pattern of late payments.

Obtaining Credit Today

Lenders make two decisions related to granting credit. The first is whether to grant credit, and the second is what interest rate to charge. The decisions are based on information in the credit application and on a credit bureau report of the applicant's credit history. Under federal law (Equal Credit Opportunity Act), a lender may not discriminate among applicants because of gender, ethnicity, race, national origin, religion, age, or receipt of social security or public assistance. A lender may, however, decline a credit application because of a poor credit history.

The key to getting the best credit terms is having a good credit history. A bad credit history is like high blood pressure—it can sneak up on you. It is quite possible that Carl's mother has already hurt her credit history. Furthermore, the law requires that credit granted in two names must build a credit history for both parties. Carl's name is on one of his mother's accounts, so his credit might be affected, too.

Lenders commonly use a credit score when making credit decisions. Some lenders develop their own credit scores, but most now use scores developed by a credit reporting bureau. The best-known scoring system is the FICO score, developed by Fair, Isaac and Company, Inc. Even so, the lender makes the decisions as to whether to grant credit and what interest rate to charge. Lenders will tie the interest rate to the applicant's credit score. People with low credit scores can usually find some lender who will say yes, but the interest rate will be high. Carl's mother's credit usage pattern may have affected both of their credit scores and will affect their cost of credit in the future.

Credit scoring: A practice that allows lenders to categorize credit users according to their risk of nonpayment.

Many credit card companies pay credit bureaus to search their files for people who have certain characteristics. For example, a bank might ask for all the people who own their own home, already have a credit card, and are current on all their credit accounts. The company then sends these people a "preapproved" application for credit at a certain APR. However, preapproved simply means that the prospect will be granted credit. The offer makes no promises concerning either the card's credit limit or the interest rate. These will be determined only after the application and credit investigation. Martha Johnson got her additional four cards by responding to such offers. She is paying the highest interest rates on the cards she obtained most recently. This is because when she obtained these cards, her credit score had begun to decline because of her late payments and growing balances and the high total debt limit on all her cards.

Calculating Credit Card Interest

The monthly finance charge on a credit card is calculated by multiplying the balance owed by the monthly interest rate (the APR divided by 12). Therefore, how the balance owed is calculated is critical. Typically, the balance used is the average daily balance for the month. The lender simply adds up the balances owed each day and divides by the number of days in the month. The monthly rate is applied against that balance. Depending on how the balance is calculated, it is entirely possible to have a card with a low APR generate higher finance charges than one with a higher APR.

There are several ways to calculate the daily balance. How new purchases are handled is the important factor. Typically, they are excluded only if the account has a grace period. If a grace period applies, new purchases do not accrue interest until after the due date for the first bill on which they appear. The different ways by which average daily balances are calculated are summarized in the sidebar "How Average Daily Balances Are Calculated." Martha is carrying a balance on all her cards, so she receives no grace periods. Every time she uses one of her cards, she starts accruing interest on the amount immediately.

How Average Daily Balances Are Calculated

Lenders typically use one of four methods to calculate the average daily balance on a credit card bill:

1. **Average daily balance excluding new purchases.** With this method, the cardholder pays interest only on any balance left over from the previous month. New purchases are not added in when the interest is calculated. This method in not commonly used.
2. **Average daily balance including new purchases with a grace period.** Only if the balance was *not* paid in full in the previous month will the average daily balance calculation include new purchases. If it was paid in full, there is a grace period. This is a commonly used method.
3. **Average daily balance including new purchases with no grace period.** The balance from the previous month and any charges made during the billing cycle are included in the balance calculation, even if the previous month's balance was paid in full. This is also a commonly used method.
4. **Two-cycle average daily balance including new purchases.** The average daily balance is based on the daily balances from the last 2 months. This method is the least favorable for consumers as they pay down the credit card balance. This is not a commonly used method but it is prominent for cards heavily marketed to those with poor credit histories.

Credit Pitfalls and the Elderly

A listing of the pitfalls of credit use can be quite long, but some of them stand out because they are common or because they are problems to which the elderly seem especially prone. Such pitfalls include low minimum payment requirements, convenience checks, automatic charges, secured credit cards, credit card insurance, fraudulent use, subprime lending, and predatory lending.

Making Only the Minimum Payment

Credit card lenders require a minimum monthly payment that can be as low as 2 or 2½ percent of the outstanding balance. Paying only the minimum will keep the user in debt for a long time. An 18 percent APR card with a balance of $3,000 might have a minimum payment of $60 (2 percent). Of this minimum payment, $45 is interest and only $15 constitutes payment on the principal of the debt. At this rate, it would take almost 8 years to repay the debt even if the card were never used again. Just imagine if there were $60 in new charges on the card that month. The minimum payment would actually go toward those charges and the interest would in effect have been added to the balance. The card would never be paid off at that rate. To make matters worse, many card issuers today allow cardholders to skip a payment if more than the minimum was paid in the previous month. Interest still accrues for the month in which no payment was made, and thus the balance increases. Martha Johnson was taking advantage of this $0 minimum payment when she did not make a payment on their joint account last month.

Convenience Checks

Many bank credit card issuers periodically send "convenience checks" to their cardholders. Using these checks represents a cash advance on the account. Cash advances usually carry a higher interest rate, have no grace period, and generate a transaction fee. Martha Johnson has been using convenience checks to make payments on one credit card with cash advances from another. In effect, she wasn't paying on her debts at all and was actually falling further behind as a result of interest and transaction fees.

Automatic Charges

It is becoming increasingly common for sellers of merchandise, utilities, charitable organizations, and others who are paid regularly for services to ask customers to set up an automatic charge to a bank credit card to pay their bills. These automatic charges, when coupled with low minimum payments, can result in rapidly escalating credit card balances. A budget can quickly get out of hand because the individual items do not appear in the checkbook and keeping records is difficult. It becomes easy to borrow to pay bills and to use the money in a checking account in other ways. Martha Johnson has her newspaper and several charitable contributions set up this way.

Secured Credit Cards

A secured credit card is a credit card backed by a savings account opened at the financial institution that issues the card. The savings account serves as collateral for the card. Typically a steep application fee and an initial deposit are required. The deposit in the savings account equals the credit limit and cannot be withdrawn as long as the card is available for use. In a particularly insidious scam, some secured card issuers establish the savings account by taking a cash advance against the credit card and then start charging a monthly fee. Because the charge on the account is the same dollar amount as the credit limit, the borrower cannot use the card but must keep paying the monthly fee. If the borrower does not do so, he or she is also charged a fee for being over the credit limit.

Credit Card Insurance

Federal law limits a cardholder's liability for lost or stolen credit cards to $50 per card if the card is used illegally before the lender is notified of the loss. Even so, some companies sell credit card insurance that will pay the $50. This is an overpriced and, usually, unneeded protection. Most homeowner's and renter's insurance policies pay for such losses. Furthermore, most credit card companies will waive the $50 fee for unauthorized use as a gesture of goodwill when they are notified about a lost card promptly.

Credit Life and Disability Insurance

Credit life insurance pays the unpaid balance on a loan to the lender in the event of the borrower's death. People are often grossly overcharged for this insurance. Rates typically range from $5 to $7 per $1,000 of the outstanding balance—every month! Lenders may also offer credit disability insurance, which makes the minimum monthly payment while the borrower is disabled. However, disability is usually very narrowly defined, and, in any event, it does not pertain to those who have no job. Martha Johnson is paying about $65 per month for these unneeded protections. The premiums are simply charged to her accounts.

Privacy Issues and Fraudulent Use

With very little personal information, a clever thief can steal someone's credit identity and run up thousands of dollars in bills. Once a crook has someone's credit card number, he or she can use the information to purchase items by phone, by mail, and on the Web; take cash advances; and otherwise raid the account. The elderly are more susceptible because they may be less vigilant about reviewing the charges to their accounts. Fraudulent users may make charges at the same merchants used by the cardholder, who then may assume that the charge is valid and that she or he has simply forgotten about it. A valid charge for a magazine subscription service or other merchant may be followed by repeated unauthorized charges months later.

Another common technique is to employ a "negative option," where a repeat charge is initially authorized as part of a free trial period on some service such as lost credit card insurance. The charges will continue until the customer explicitly stops them. But the process for canceling the charges is difficult, and the information on how to do so is easily forgotten or misplaced. This is especially true for negative option offers on the Web. Often the site that must be used to cancel the service is not the same as the site where the order was originally placed.

Protecting Credit Card Privacy

- Do not disclose your address, telephone number, or social security number when using a credit card. If the merchant requires identification beyond the credit card (e.g., a driver's license), do not allow such information to be written down.
- Save all purchase and ATM receipts and check them against statements from creditors.
- Do not disclose your credit card number on the telephone to anyone you do not know or did not telephone directly yourself.
- Review your credit bureau report at least once each year.
- Report lost or stolen credit cards and suspicious billing information without delay.

Subprime Lending

As mentioned previously, lenders tie their interest rates to borrowers' credit scores. A market called the subprime market has developed in recent years to offer those who have poor credit scores a credit card with a high interest rate and onerous terms. This may be the only source of credit for some consumers. But many people with better credit scores are also targeted and pay much higher rates than necessary. The elderly fall prey to these approaches because they sometimes do not understand credit scoring and may not be aware that they could qualify for lower rates elsewhere. Martha Johnson has two subprime credit cards.

Subprime lending: High-cost loans and credit cards targeted to those with low credit scores or those who simply underestimate their creditworthiness.

Predatory Lending

The equity in a home is one of the major assets held by the elderly. Predatory lenders encourage people to open credit accounts at seemingly low interest rates, with the home serving as collateral on the loan. These loans are often marketed as debt consolidation loans because the interest rate, at least initially, is lower than that for other forms of credit, especially credit cards. The loans often have high initial fees that are included in the initial loan balance. They also tend to have very stringent default terms, so that a late payment will trigger default. Default results in the seizure of the home. The elderly are particularly vulnerable because of their fear of debt and their low levels of income. The offers push the idea that monthly credit payments can be slashed, even though the total finance charges will be higher over the life of the loan. Martha Johnson's debt consolidation loan is precisely this type of loan. Fortunately, she has been up-to-date and on time with her payments.

Managing Credit Usage

What should Carl Johnson do? What would *you* do if your parents had some of Martha Johnson's problems? A first, and not so easy, step is simply to find out who is owed, how much is owed, and at what interest rate and credit terms. This can be accomplished by preparing a debt inventory. Armed with this information, you can adjust your parents' debt by transferring balances, closing accounts, and setting some rules for future use of credit. It may be appropriate for you to set up your parents' credit accounts as joint accounts. And it may be necessary to challenge and correct errors in current and past credit card statements. You will also want to obtain a copy of your parents' credit bureau report to ensure that it is accurate and up-to-date.

Get Organized with a Debt Inventory

A debt inventory is simply a listing of all a person's debts, including to whom money is owed, how much is owed, at what APR, and for how long. For credit cards, you will want to set a payoff date and calculate the monthly payment needed to pay off the account balance by that date. When a card is currently being used, you will need to pay both the full amount charged that month and the payoff amount to reach the target date.

Carl Johnson prepared Figure 5.1 as a debt inventory for his mother. He set a goal of paying off all the credit cards within 3 years. The debt consolidation loan was for 7 years and had had an initial balance of $5,000, which had been paid down to $4,690. Martha owes a total of $9,500 on her five credit cards. Carl used Table 5.1 to calculate the monthly payment on each card based on the target payoff date. Assuming that Martha does not use the cards again, the total monthly payments on all her debts will be $421.93. The interest portion of the payments for the first month will total about $174. Only $248 of the payments will actually go to pay off the debts. Carl divided the total debt outstanding into the monthly interest charges and found that the average APR on a dollar owed was 14.7 percent. Martha has lower-cost credit available to her.

**Figure 5.1 Debt Inventory for Martha Johnson—
Before Adjustments/Transfers**

Account	Limit	APR	Balance	Payoff Date (in Months)	Monthly Payment	Comments
Consolidation loan	$ 5,000	9%	$ 4,690	77	$ 80.44	Low APR
Credit card 1 (joint account)	$ 5,000	12%	$ 1,100	36	$ 36.53	Low APR, available balance
Credit card 2	$ 1,500	10%	$ 1,500	36	$ 48.40	Annual fee $50
Credit card 3	$ 3,000	14%	$ 500	36	$ 17.09	Low APR, available balance
Credit card 4	$ 6,000	20%	$ 4,800	36	$178.37	High APR, high balance
Credit card 5	$ 3,000	22%	$ 1,600	36	$ 61.10	High APR, low balance
Total/average	$23,500	14.7%	$14,190		$421.93	High payments, high interest

Table 5.1 Monthly Payment per $1,000 of Credit Card Debt*

	Number of Monthly Payments						
APR	**12**	**18**	**24**	**30**	**36**	**48**	**60**
9	$87.45	$59.59	$45.68	$37.35	$31.80	$24.88	$20.76
10	87.92	60.06	46.14	37.81	32.27	25.36	21.25
11	88.38	60.52	46.61	38.28	32.74	25.85	21.74
12	88.85	60.98	47.07	38.75	33.21	26.33	22.24
13	89.32	61.45	47.54	39.22	33.69	26.83	22.75
14	89.79	61.92	48.01	39.70	34.18	27.33	23.27
15	90.26	62.38	48.49	40.18	34.67	27.83	23.79
16	90.73	62.86	48.96	40.66	35.16	28.34	24.32
18	91.68	63.81	49.92	41.64	36.15	29.37	25.39
20	92.63	64.76	50.90	42.63	37.16	30.43	26.49
22	93.59	65.73	51.88	43.63	38.19	31.51	27.62
24	94.56	66.70	52.87	44.65	39.23	32.60	28.77

*To illustrate, assume a credit card balance of $3,200 at 16 percent to be paid off in 30 months. The monthly payment is $130.11, found by multiplying $40.66 (16 percent row and 30-month column) by 3.2.

Carl went to work to see what he could do to lower the monthly payments and have a higher percentage of the payments go to paying off the debt. He also wanted to lower the average APR. Here is his plan.

1. Carl realized that he needed to transfer debt from the high-APR cards to the lowest-APR cards. To do so, however, he needed a higher debt limit on their joint card. He requested an increase from $5,000 to $7,000.
2. He then used balance transfers to fully pay off cards 2, 4, and 5. He transferred the balances to cards 1 and 3. Even though card 2 had the lowest APR, the fact that it was maxed out and had a high annual fee made it a poor choice for a balance transfer.
3. Carl closed card accounts 2 and 4.
4. Carl kept card 5 open for convenience uses, as discussed later. The card has a grace period for new purchases, so there will be no interest charges as long as the balance is paid in full each month.
5. Carl then revised Martha's debt inventory. He decided that it would be difficult to pay off the joint account card in 36 months, so he extended the projected payoff for that card to 48 months.

Figure 5.2 is Carl's revised debt inventory for his mother. He was able to reduce the monthly payments to $353.34, a savings of more than $68 per month. The interest portion of these payments was reduced to approximately $135, and the average APR per dollar owed went down to 11.4 percent. Note that payment on the principal of the debts went down to $218, about $30 less than before. If Carl chose, he could apply that $30 to card 1 and pay it off in just under 3 years.

Carl's plan called for no out-of-pocket transfers of funds. He simply rearranged the debts to get the balances owed on the lowest-APR opportunities available to his mother. Carl could have asked for an increase in the limit on the home-equity loan. If debt payments became difficult, however, default on that loan might occur. This would put Martha's home at risk.

Separate Convenience Use from Balances

Some credit cards have a low or no annual fee, and others have a low APR. Which is better? Generally speaking, you should choose a card with the lowest available APR if you are likely to carry a balance on the account. Alternatively, you should choose a card with a grace period

Figure 5.2 Debt Inventory for Martha Johnson— After Adjustments/Transfers

Account	Limit	APR	Balance	Payoff Date (in Months)	Monthly Payment	Comments
Consolidation loan	$ 5,000	9%	$ 4,690	77	$ 80.44	Low APR
Credit card 1 (joint account)	$ 7,000	12%	$ 6,600	48	$173.78	Low APR, small available balance
Credit card 2	$ 0	10%	$ 0		$ 0	Account closed
Credit card 3	$ 3,000	14%	$ 2,900	36	$ 99.12	Low APR, no available balance
Credit card 4	$ 0	20%	$ 0	36	$ 0	Account closed
Credit card 5	$ 3,000	22%	$ 0	12	$ 0	Account paid off; use but carry no balance
Total	$18,000	11.4%	$14,190		$353.34	Lower payments, lower interest

and no annual fee if you are likely to pay your balance in full each month. The grace period makes the APR irrelevant when no balance is carried. Carl kept credit card 5 open for convenience items; Martha will pay this bill in full monthly. He has convinced her to lock away cards 1 and 3 to ensure that she will not use them.

> The bank credit card business is highly competitive. Do not hesitate to contact your current card issuers to request a lower annual fee, a lower APR, or a higher credit balance, as appropriate. Make sure the issuer knows that you are shopping for the best terms, and then switch cards if necessary.

Monitoring Billing Statements

Once Carl had established his plan to realign his mother's debts, he turned his attention to the particular charges on the accounts that he felt were in error. The Fair Credit Billing Act (FCBA) allows cardholders to dispute billing errors on revolving credit accounts. Charges can be disputed for up to 60 days after the date the first bill containing the error was mailed. Once notified, the lender has 30 days to acknowledge the notification and must either correct the error permanently and return any overpayment (if requested) or provide evidence showing why it believes the bill to be correct (such as a copy of a charge slip) within 90 days. Creditors cannot assess interest on or apply penalties for nonpayment of the disputed amount while the dispute is being investigated. Back interest and penalties may be assessed if the disputed item is ultimately shown to be legitimate. Carl found several items that he wanted to dispute, and he took the following steps as outlined under the law:

1. He sent written notice of the errors to the credit card issuers. The notice must be in writing to qualify for the protections provided under the Fair Credit Billing Act. As is typical, there was a separate "Send Inquiries To" address on the billing statements.
2. Carl also notified the particular merchants involved. Again, he did so in writing. This step is not required by the FCBA, but as a practical matter it speeds up the process.

3. He provided photocopies (not originals) of the necessary documentation. He kept the originals to challenge any finding by the company that no error occurred.
4. Carl withheld payment for disputed items. For cards 2, 4, and 5 he paid the remaining amount owed via balance transfers. This helped to isolate the disputed items. As required by the FCBA, the card issuers immediately credited the accounts for the amounts in dispute. Once the investigations are complete, he can pay off any amounts owed on the accounts and close accounts 2 and 4 as planned.

Carl next turned his attention to charges that were automatically being placed on his mother's accounts. He drafted letters to the card issuers and the particular entities making the charges asking to have them stopped. His mother must sign the letters (except those for account 1) because the accounts are in her name.

Resolving Errors in Credit Bureau Files

Carl is concerned that his mother's credit problems have become part of her credit history file at the major credit bureaus. The federal Fair Credit Reporting Act (FCRA) requires that credit bureaus provide consumers with a credit report upon request. The report is free if the file was used to deny credit within the past 60 days; otherwise, a modest fee may be charged for a report (in some states one free report is allowed per year). To obtain the reports, he contacted each of the three major credit reporting bureaus.[1] Again, his mother had to make the formal request for her file, but Carl could assist her in doing so. When he receives the reports, he can take steps to get the information corrected should he find errors or omissions.

Dealing with Overindebtedness

What signs should children look for that indicate that their parents are having debt problems? What steps can then be taken? What protections do your parents have if their debts have been turned over to collection agencies? And finally, how does bankruptcy apply to the elderly?

---

[1]Equifax (https://www.econsumer.equifax.com),
TransUnion (http://www.transunion.com/Personal/OrderOnline.asp), and
Experian (http://www.experian.com/consumer/index.html).

Fair Credit Reporting Act Procedures

The FCRA outlines the following steps for resolving errors and omissions in credit bureau files:

1. The consumer notifies the bureau in writing that he or she wishes to exercise the right to a reinvestigation under the FCRA.
2. The bureau must reinvestigate the information within 30 days. If the bureau cannot complete its investigation within 30 days, it must drop the information from the consumer's credit file.
3. If the information was in error, it must be corrected. And if a report containing the error has been sent to a creditor investigating the consumer's application within the past 6 months, a corrected report must be sent to that creditor.
4. If the credit bureau refuses to make a correction (perhaps because the information was technically correct), the consumer can provide his or her version of the disputed information (in 100 words or less) by adding a consumer statement.

Key Signs of Credit Difficulty among the Elderly

The typical signs of credit trouble are similar across all age groups. Late payments, skipped payments, repossession, and harassing phone calls are clues. But there are certain red flags among the elderly that differ from those among younger credit users. Some stem from their having grown up in an era when debt was seen as a bad thing. Others relate to the difficulty of keeping track when multiple accounts are open. This was Martha Johnson's problem. If you observe any of these signs, you will need to probe more deeply while being sensitive to your parents' feelings.

1. Using credit cards for day-to-day expenses. This is a heretofore taboo use of credit that the elderly are unlikely to engage in unless they are in real trouble.
2. Borrowing from family members. Family members are a lender of last resort.
3. Paying only the minimum amount due. This leads to long-term debt obligations.
4. Home-equity borrowing. Home ownership is sacred for many elderly people.

5. Silence when asked. Many elderly people see debt problems as a sign of failure.
6. Talking about money difficulties while seemingly doing fine. The outward appearance of sufficient income may indicate that credit is being used to pay for things.
7. Seeming confused or defensive when discussing finances. This is a sign that things have gotten too complicated.

Two special cautions are important here. The first is that credit problems can quickly escalate. This is because most credit contracts contain an acceleration clause. Even if the lender does not exercise the clause right away when a default occurs, it can do so at any time. Do not ignore warning letters! The second relates to repossession. When a lender takes back collateral or repossesses property because the borrower defaults on a loan, the borrower often still owes part of the debt because of a deficiency balance—that is, because the sale of the asset at auction brings less than the remaining balance of the debt. This can occur whether the repossession is forced or voluntary. The asset is lost, and money is still owed.

> **Acceleration clause:** A contract provision that makes the entire debt due on demand if default occurs.

> **Deficiency balance:** The debt that remains after a repossessed item is sold.

Helping Your Parents Get Out of Debt

What should you do if you begin to realize that your parents are overextended?

1. Determine what your parents owe and to whom they owe it. Carl Johnson did this when he developed his mother's debt inventory. Paying off debts provides a better rate of return than savings accounts and most investments.
2. Restructure the debt, if possible. Again, this was part of Carl Johnson's response. It may be necessary to open new accounts in order to do so. This is okay as long as the old accounts are closed.

3. Contact the creditors. Creditors are more likely to work with borrowers who come to them first rather than after collection efforts begin.
4. Find good help. Creditors can be of help here. Banks and credit unions often provide advice to help debtors. Nonprofit consumer credit counseling groups can set up a debt management plan for your parents. Under such a plan, the organization negotiates with creditors to persuade them to accept reduced or partial payments and to pass the savings along to the debtor. There should be either no fee or only a low fee for setting up such a plan, and a high percentage of the money sent to the organization under the plan should go to the creditors.
5. Avoid bad help. Avoid credit repair companies and credit clinics that offer to help improve or fix one's credit history for an exorbitant fee. An accurate negative credit history can't be "fixed." Organizations that say they can do so should be avoided.

What if Debts Have Gone to Collection?

The Fair Debt Collection Practices Act (FDCPA) prohibits third-party debt collection agencies from using abusive, deceptive, and unfair practices in the legitimate effort to collect past-due debts. In spite of these protections, collection agencies can be very persistent. The FDCPA gives the debtor the right to tell the collection agency to cease making contact. The harassment must stop, but legal action may still take place. If your parent is being harassed, you should file a complaint with your state's consumer protection office. (For contact information visit www.nacaanet.org.)

Bankruptcy Is a Last Resort

Under bankruptcy, the court provides for an orderly division of the borrower's property and repayment of each creditor as fully as possible. State and federal laws govern what the debtor can keep; in general, bankrupt people are allowed to keep a small amount of equity in their homes, an inexpensive automobile, and limited personal property. Federal laws allow bankruptcy for consumers in two forms: Chapter 13 and Chapter 7. Chapter 13 is designed for individuals with regular work incomes, so your parents may not qualify. With either form, the court issues a "stay" that temporarily prevents all creditors from taking action against the debtor and prevents the debtor from disposing of assets or continuing to pay on some debts in preference to others. Chapter 7 is designed for a liquidation of assets. This option is permitted when it is highly unlikely that substantial repayment could ever be made. The assets are sold, and the proceeds are applied to the debts. The remaining debts are absolved. Bankruptcy should be used as a last resort, not as a quick fix or cure-all for overuse of credit. Bankruptcy remains on one's credit record for 10 years.

If your parents are considering bankruptcy, they should know that their retirement benefits may or may not be protected in bankruptcy court. The general rule is that traditional pension plans, so-called defined-benefit plans funded by an employer, are exempt. So are social security, civil service, and military benefits. Defined-contribution plans where the employee has funded the plan [e.g., a 401(k) plan] or has control over how the funds are invested and can withdraw funds from the plan at his or her option are generally not exempt. In terms of protecting property, debtors have a choice of using federal exemption rules or the rules of their particular state. State rules often protect homeownership at least to some degree. Legal representation, while not mandatory, is recommended for anyone considering bankruptcy. The legal costs for bankruptcy can be $700 and up.

Related Issues

There are a number of issues that often arise when addressing your parents' credit. These include the use of joint accounts, allowing others access to your parents' credit cards, and simply talking to your parents about their debt situation.

Joint Accounts

Children often consider having their names put on their elderly parents' credit accounts. This allows you to monitor the accounts and make adjustments as necessary. If one of your parents becomes incapacitated, you will be able to handle some of that parent's financial affairs using the joint account without getting the parent involved. Carl's joint ownership of a credit card made the job of rearranging his mother's debt while she was incapacitated much easier.

There are some significant risks, however. Joint accounts mean joint responsibility. Even if the parent is the primary holder of the account, the lender will pursue whichever party is more likely to pay. Any debt jointly owed with your parents will show as outstanding debt on your credit history. Similarly, slow payment, default, and other negative behaviors will reflect on your creditworthiness and potentially decrease your access to credit and increase your cost of credit. In addition, should the parent pass away the joint account holder will be responsible for the debt.

Access to Your Parents' Credit Cards

Some families choose to pay all their parents' expenses using one credit card and then pay only that one bill each month. This technique is easy to use because most stores, including grocery stores, accept credit cards. It is also possible to have utilities and other monthly service fees charged to a credit card or set up for automatic withdrawal from a checking account. In addition, more than one individual may have signature power on the account. This allows several siblings to share the grocery shopping or clothing shopping for their parents. However, you will need to have a "checks and balances" system. Your parents are liable for any charges on the account. It is prudent to have more than one individual review the credit card statements on a regular basis to avoid theft or inappropriate charges.

Using one credit card to pay all your parents' bills may have some disadvantages. To protect against theft and loss, you may not want to have more than one card floating around. Also, it may be difficult for the bill payer to collect all of the receipts in order to check the monthly statement for accuracy. However, you can store the card at your parents' home and notify your siblings where it is. Ask that each person using the card place the receipt in an envelope in the same place where the card is kept. In any event, limit the number of people who have access to the card. The card should be accessible only to those individuals who shop for your parents.

An alternative to using a credit card for purchases is to use a debit or cash card. On the surface, these cards operate in the same manner as a credit card. However, all charges are instantly withdrawn from the checking account on which the card is issued. The likelihood of overdrawing an account using a debit card is much greater, especially if several people are using the card. In addition, a user may inappropriately withdraw cash with the card.

If a nonfamily caregiver is going to shop for your parents, do not use a debit or cash card. Using a credit card in this situation will reduce the probability of misuse or theft.

Whether the credit card is used to pay monthly bills or not, life will be much simpler if only one credit card account is maintained. Maintain an account with a company whose card is accepted at most retailers, restaurants, and service providers. Cancel all other credit card accounts, especially store accounts, those that are accepted only by a particular retail store or gasoline station. Closing all but one account increases the ease of money management and record keeping and reduces the possibility of theft and your parents' liability if the cards are stolen.

To close an account, you should both call and write the company. Then cut up each card. Do not send the card back to the company. Credit card companies will not close an account that still has an outstanding balance. However, they will block future use of the card if they are requested to do so. Once the account has been paid in full, you can close the account.

Talking to Your Parents about Debt

Credit usage and debt management are more than just financial matters. They carry a lot of emotional weight as well. This is especially true if the debt is too high or if your parents simply feel bad about using credit. How do you get your parents to open up about their credit and debt situation? You can reassure them by emphasizing the following points:

- They are not alone. Credit cards and credit usage are commonplace today. Credit provides access to goods and services and helps even out the peaks and valleys of income and expenditures.
- They are not failures. Even if their debt burden is manageable, they may feel that they have been taking a shortcut by using credit. Help them recognize why they have been using credit and shift the focus from self-blame to reducing the use of credit and reducing the level of debt.
- Debt problems are resolvable. As seen in this chapter, simply rearranging a parent's debt can go a long way toward solving the problem. Further, creditors will work with people to bring debt under control. Reputable credit counseling agencies have a long history of helping people.
- Debt problems are temporary. It is sometimes hard for people to see how they will ever get back to a more manageable level of debt and pattern of credit usage. Setting up target dates for paying off debts and setting up plans for reaching those target dates can be very reassuring. Card-cutting ceremonies can signify a clear break from past patterns of behavior.

Final Thoughts

The use of credit is an increasingly important concern for retirees. You can assist your parents by having a basic understanding of how credit works today. You should focus on the cost of credit as measured by the annual percentage rate and the finance charge in dollars. Increasingly, lenders are using credit-scoring systems to evaluate applicants. Interest on credit cards can be significantly affected by the method of calculating the average daily balance on the card.

There are a number of credit pitfalls for the elderly. The use of features such as convenience checks and automatic charges can quickly add to the balances owed. Secured cards, though easily obtained, have significant hidden costs. Various credit insurance plans, such as credit life and disability insurance, can be costly and unnecessary. Privacy issues and the potential for fraud are an increasing problem related to credit. In particular, the elderly can fall victim to abuses related to subprime and predatory lending.

A key to managing your parents' credit use is the development of a debt inventory giving detailed information about all credit accounts. When balances are carried on credit cards, you will want to use a separate credit card for convenience purchases to reduce overall interest charges. You should regularly review your parents' credit card statements to ensure that they accurately reflect your parents' usage and are free from billing errors. Similarly, you should monitor your parents' credit bureau files for accuracy and have errors corrected.

Parents who are in credit difficulty may not recognize the problem early enough and may be reluctant to admit that they are having problems. There are specific signs that you should look for to determine if your parents are overly indebted. Seek help immediately if you perceive problems. Bankruptcy may be necessary in some cases but should be approached with care, as its effects are somewhat different for retirees.

It may be necessary for you to take an active role in your parents' credit usage patterns. This may entail opening joint accounts with your parents. You may want to give your parents' caregivers access to their accounts. Finally, simply talking to your parents about their credit use and difficulties will require you to be sensitive to your parents' special needs.

6

Taxes

It's April 1, and Nancy Bradshaw is frantic. She knows that her dad, Jim, has yet to file his 2002 tax return, and he is sick with the flu. He has also gone downhill in the past year and will not be able to complete his own return as he has done in the past. ("It saves money," he has always said.) In searching for her dad's 2001 tax return, it dawns on Nancy that he may not have remembered to file that year, either. This time last year he was in the hospital for heart bypass surgery. Besides, she sees copies of his 1990 through 2000 tax returns neatly stacked in his closet, but she finds no 2001 tax return. Nancy does not know much about her dad's income except that he receives social security and a monthly pension from his former employer. In addition, she thinks he has some certificates of deposit because he is always complaining about the low interest rate he is receiving. He also mentions his broker, Fred, occasionally.

THE AVERAGE TAXPAYER spends 20 hours each year preparing and filing his or her personal income tax return. The system is not easy and tries everyone's patience. You may be able to prepare your own tax return and yet need assistance in completing your parents' return. This chapter focuses on income tax issues specific to taxpayers over age 65. It provides an outline for you to follow to determine if your parents are required to file a tax return, how to file a very basic tax return, and what tax benefits you may be allowed to claim on your return if your parents qualify as your dependents.

Numerous income tax issues are beyond the scope of this chapter. Your parents will want to secure the services of a qualified tax preparer if they are subject to any special or complicated income or deduction rules. Some examples of these are outlined in the sidebar "Consider Hiring a Professional Tax Preparer."

Consider Hiring a Professional Tax Preparer

You should consider hiring a professional tax preparer for your parents if any of the following statements apply to them.

1. Their social security income is taxable (income above $25,000 if single or $32,000 if married).
2. Their income exceeds $100,000.
3. They receive income from self-employment, farming, or rental properties, or receive funds from stock sales.
4. They receive income from foreign sources or hold foreign investments.
5. They qualify for the foreign tax credit, credit for prior year minimum tax paid, or business credit.
6. They are subject to the alternative minimum tax.
7. They have given property that has increased in value to a qualified charity.
8. They are subject to estimated tax payment rules.

Completing your parents' tax return will be easier if you follow several steps, in order. You must gather information and then determine if your parents are required to file a tax return. If they are required to file a return, you will need to calculate their gross income. From there you will be able to reduce gross income to a lower taxable income by taking various subtractions, adjustments, deductions, and exemptions. Once you have calculated their taxable income, the next step is to calculate their actual tax. You then subtract any allowable credits to arrive at their tax liability. Finally, prepayments are subtracted to determine whether your parents owe additional tax or are due a refund from the IRS.

Gathering Information

It is very important that your parents file income tax returns if they are required to do so, and that both you and they take advantage of any legal adjustments, deductions, exemptions, and credits that are available. But before you can make these determinations, you will need to gather the appropriate information. Review the tax return your parents filed for the previous year thoroughly. Any documents used in the preparation of the previous year's return will also prove very helpful. A good review of their earlier tax returns and reporting documents will make the preparation of this year's return more accurate, offer consistency with previous returns filed, and reduce the likelihood of raising any red flags with the IRS. As you are examining the previously filed tax returns, you may want to look for the information and answer the questions outlined in Worksheet 6.1. Nancy will have to review her dad's tax returns for years 1999 and 2000.

Worksheet 6.1 *Important Information from Previous Tax Returns*

1. What filing status did your parents use (single, married filing separately, or married filing jointly)?
2. How many dependents did they claim? (If they did not claim themselves, did one of their children claim them?)
3. What types of income did they have?
   - Earned income
   - Interest
   - Tax-exempt interest
   - Dividends
   - Capital gains
   - Self-employment income
   - Alimony
   - IRA distributions
   - Pensions
   - Social security
4. Did they file:
   - Form 1040, U.S. Individual Tax Return
   - Form 1040A, U.S. Individual Tax Return
   - Form 1040EZ, Income Tax Return for Single and Joint Filers
   - Form 1040 ES, Estimated Payment "coupons"
   - Schedule A, Itemized Deductions
   - Schedule B, Interest and Dividends
   - Schedule D, Capital Gains and Losses
   - Schedule H, Household Help
   - Form 2120, Multiple Support Declaration (would appear in an adult child's tax return claiming the parents as dependents)
   - Form 2441, Credit for Care for the Elderly or Disabled (may appear in an adult child's tax return)
   - Schedule R, Credit for the Elderly or Disabled
5. Did they make estimated tax payments?
6. Was there an income tax refund "carryover" applied to the current year's tax liability?
7. Who prepared their return?

Reviewing previously filed tax returns is not enough. Gather all tax documents and reporting statements that your parents' banks, financial institutions, mortgage lender, and favorite charities mailed to them during January. (By law, these documents must be postmarked no later than January 31 and are mailed to the taxpayer and to the IRS simultaneously.) Interest is reported on Form 1099-INT, dividends and mutual fund capital gains on Form 1099-DIV, wages on Form W-2, and retirement income on Form 1099-R. The Social Security Administration also issues statements of your parents' benefits for the year. Reporting information that is inconsistent with the data on these statements is sure to raise a red flag and prompt a letter from the IRS. It is most efficient to have an envelope, a shoe box, or some other place into which you can toss these documents when they are received. You can then simply review all the documents before you begin the task of actually filling in the tax return. Nancy may need to contact Jim's bank, his broker, his former employer, and the Social Security office for duplicate statements.

Evaluating the Need to File a Return

Whether your parents need to file an income tax return is determined by the amount of income they received during the tax year. Their total income is compared to a filing "floor" that changes every year. Several factors, including the standard deduction amount, the personal exemption amount, your parents' filing status, and your parents' ages at the end of the tax year, are combined to determine the filing floor. Not being required to file in one year does not exempt a taxpayer from the responsibility for filing in a subsequent year. You need to evaluate whether your parents are required to file each year.

A single person who is 65 or older is required to file a return if her or his income is $8,950 or greater ($10,100 if also blind). If both of your parents are over age 65 and they file jointly, they will need to file a return if their gross income is $15,950 or more ($16,900 if one spouse is blind and $17,850 if both spouses are blind). If only one of your parents is over 65 and they file jointly, they will need to file a return if their gross income is $15,000 or more. These thresholds equal the total of the standard deduction amount and the personal exemption amount for the tax year. These thresholds change every year. Details concerning the personal exemption and standard deduction are provided later in this chapter.

Completing and Filing a Tax Return

On the surface, the income tax calculation is simple. The taxpayer simply totals her or his income and subtracts adjustments, deductions, and exemptions. The result is the taxable income. To arrive at the total tax, the taxable income is multiplied by the appropriate tax rate. Credits are subtracted from the total tax to determine the final tax liability. Any prepayments, such as withholdings from pension benefits or estimated payments made directly to the IRS, are subtracted from the final tax liability to calculate the tax liability or refund due.

The difficult part of preparing your parents' income tax return is correctly identifying your parents' various sources of income and the adjustments, deductions, exemptions, and credits to which they are entitled. If you follow the six steps given here, you should be able to complete a simple tax return. These steps are outlined in Figure 6.1.

Step 1. Determine Your Parents' Filing Status

Individuals who are single on December 31 must file as single taxpayers unless they became widowed during the tax year. In that case, they may

Figure 6.1 Steps in Filing a Tax Return

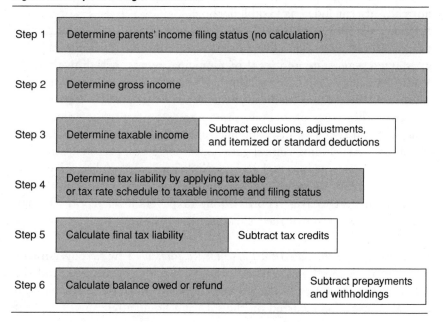

Step 1	Determine parents' income filing status (no calculation)
Step 2	Determine gross income
Step 3	Determine taxable income / Subtract exclusions, adjustments, and itemized or standard deductions
Step 4	Determine tax liability by applying tax table or tax rate schedule to taxable income and filing status
Step 5	Calculate final tax liability / Subtract tax credits
Step 6	Calculate balance owed or refund / Subtract prepayments and withholdings

choose one of the two married filing statuses. Because Jim's wife passed away 4 years ago, he will have to file as a single taxpayer.

Married taxpayers have two filing statuses to choose from. The choice they make may allow them to save on their total tax liability, depending on their level and type of income, their deductions, and other factors. These two statuses are *married filing jointly* and *married filing separately*. The taxpayers do not have to live apart to file separately. Married filing separately simply means that each spouse reports his or her income and deductions on a separately filed return. Most married couples over the age of 65 file jointly.

Step 2. Calculate Gross Income

The Internal Revenue Service's definition of income is different from the definition of income that you used in determining your parents' cash flow and budget in Chapters 2 and 4. As a general rule, all funds that your parents receive are included in the IRS's definition of gross income and are taxable. This includes interest on savings accounts, certificates of deposit, and money market accounts; dividends from stock ownership; capital gains or profits taken when investments are sold; and pension and annuity income. Withdrawals from retirement savings plans such as 401(k) and 403(b) plans and individual retirement accounts (IRAs) are normally also included as taxable income.

Some exceptions to the IRS definition of gross income are of particular interest to those over age 65 or retirees. Nontaxable income includes gifts, interest on state and local or municipal bonds, withdrawals from Roth IRAs, and benefits from long-term-care, health, and life insurance policies. Medicare and Medicaid benefits are never taxed.

Two other types of income, capital gains on the sale of a personal residence and social security income, may or may not be taxable. The threshold for excluding capital gains on the sale of a personal residence from taxable income is so high that few individuals or families will exceed it. The taxability of social security benefits depends on the amount of other income a taxpayer reports. Many taxpayers must report and pay taxes on at least some of their social security income.

Capital Gain on the Sale of a Personal Residence   Few taxpayers incur a tax on the capital gain on the sale of a personal residence, and the sale is generally not reported on a taxpayer's return. In most cases, no capital gains tax is incurred on the sale of a home after August 1997 if the homeowner meets the use and frequency tests.

The use test requires the taxpayer to have used the home as a principal residence for 2 of the 5 years before the sale. The 2 years do not have to be consecutive. In addition, the home cannot have been used for business purposes after May 6, 1997. If your parents enter a nursing facility, do not retain their home for longer than 3 years after they physically leave the home. If you do, they will not meet the 2-of-5-years use test, and any capital gains on the sale of the residence will be taxed.

The frequency test prohibits the taxpayer from using the capital gain exclusion if another principal residence was sold (and the capital gain exclusion used) in the 2 years prior to the sale of this home.

> If your parents own two homes, and they have split their time between the two, they can avoid capital gains tax on the sale of both residences with proper planning. They should sell the first home, then use the other residence as their principal home for at least 2 years. When they then sell the second home, they will not have a capital gains tax on it either.

Single persons who are selling a home are taxed only if the capital gain exceeds $250,000. Married couples filing jointly may have to pay a capital gains tax on the sale of their home if the profit is more than $500,000. The $500,000 exclusion is allowed to married couples even if only one spouse owns the home, as long as both spouses meet the use and frequency tests. If the capital gain exceeds the capital gain exclusion amount, only the amount over the capital gain exclusion amount is taxed—and at capital gains rates, which are lower than ordinary income tax rates.

> If two people intend to marry, sell one of their homes, and live in the other, the home should be sold before the marriage takes place. Otherwise, the couple would be required to maintain the other's home as their principal residence for at least 2 years in order to receive the capital gain exclusion upon its sale. If they intend to sell both homes within two years of the marriage, then both homes should be sold before the marriage, or else only one spouse may be allowed the exclusion, because the other is "tainted" by virtue of being married to the owner of the first home to sell (the frequency test).

Social Security Income   The IRS will tax some of a taxpayer's social security benefits if the taxpayer's combined income exceeds a base amount. This base amount depends on the taxpayer's filing status. If a single taxpayer's combined income is between $25,000 and $34,000, up to 50 percent of the total benefits will be taxed. If a single taxpayer's combined income is greater than $34,000, 85 percent of his or her benefits will be taxed.

> **Combined income:** Adjusted gross income [see definition of adjusted gross income (AGI) later in the chapter] plus nontaxable interest, plus 50 percent of social security benefits.

The social security taxability threshold for married couples filing jointly is $32,000. Once a couple's combined income exceeds $44,000 (married filing jointly), 85 percent of the total benefit is taxed. Worksheet 6.2 can be used to determine the taxability of social security benefits.

Worksheet 6.2 *Taxability of Social Security Benefits*

Determine the amount of taxable social security benefits by completing the following:

1. Enter the total amounts from Box 5 of Forms SSA-1099 and RRB-1099.
2. Multiply the amount on line 1 by .50 (50 percent).
3. Add the amounts on Form 1040, lines 7 (wages), 8a (taxable interest), 9 through 14, 15b, 16b, 17 through 19, and 21 (other income).
4. Enter the amount of tax-exempt income from Form 1040, line 8b (nontaxable interest).
5. Add lines 2, 3, and 4.
6. Enter the total adjustments from Form 1040, line 32, less the amount from Form 1040, line 24.
7. Subtract line 6 from line 5.
8. Enter one of the following:
   a. 32,000 if married filing jointly.
   b. 0 if married filing separately and your parents lived together at any time during the tax year.
   c. 25,000 for all other filing statuses.
9. Subtract line 8 from line 7. If zero or less, enter 0.
Note: If line 9 is zero or less, stop here. None of your parents' benefits are taxable.
10. Enter one of the following:
   a. 12,000 if married filing jointly.
   b. 0 if married filing separately and your parents lived together at any time during the tax year.
   c. 9,000 for all other filing statuses.

11. Subtract line 10 from line 9. If zero or less, enter 0.
12. Enter the smaller of line 9 or line 10.
13. Multiply line 12 by 0.50.
14. Enter the smaller of line 2 or line 13.
15. Multiply line 11 by .85. If line 11 is 0, enter 0.
16. Add lines 14 and 15.
17. Multiply line 1 by .85.
18. Enter the smaller of line 16 or 17. This amount equals your parents' taxable social security benefits.

Step 3. Calculate Your Parents' Taxable Income

The IRS allows eleven adjustments, seven deductions, and one exemption; when these amounts are subtracted from gross income, the result is your parents' taxable income. In effect, each of these items can reduce your parents' final tax liability. All have economic value equal to the amount of the adjustment, deduction, or exemption times the marginal tax rate your parents are assessed (10 percent, 15 percent, 27 percent, 30 percent, 35 percent, or 38.6 percent).

Adjustments There are eleven adjustments, and subtracting these amounts from your parents' gross income gives an income amount called the *adjusted gross income* (AGI). These adjustments include reductions for one-half the amount of the self-employment tax paid; qualified contributions to an individual retirement account; contributions to a SEP, SIMPLE, or other qualified retirement plan; alimony paid to an ex-spouse; interest paid on a student loan; qualified tuition and related education expenses; contributions to an Archer medical savings account; unreimbursed moving expenses (for employed individuals only); 70 percent of the total health insurance premiums paid by the self-employed; monies spent by educators; and penalties paid on early withdrawals of savings. In reality, few senior taxpayers benefit from any of these adjustments, and they are subject to change each year. However, the AGI is used in several other tax calculations, so you must calculate this amount before calculating further reductions in taxable income. The AGI may be found on the last line of the first page of Form 1040.

Two major reductions in the adjusted gross income are allowed in arriving at a taxable income amount. Each taxpayer may claim the higher of the standard deduction or itemized deductions and a personal exemption. Each year the IRS increases the amounts of the standard deduction and the personal exemption.

Standard or Itemized Deductions   The standard deduction is the IRS's attempt to allow a tax break for basic living expenses. It varies depending on the taxpayer's age, filing status, and whether or not he or she is blind. In 2003, single persons are allowed a standard deduction of $4,750, which is increased to $5,900 if the taxpayer is over the age of 65. A blind single person is allowed to add $1,150 to the standard deduction. Jim's standard deduction is $5,900.

For tax year 2003, the standard deduction for married couples filing jointly was $7,950. If one spouse was over age 65, the standard deduction increased to $8,900, and it increased to $9,850 if both spouses were over age 65. For each spouse who is blind, $950 is added to the standard deduction amount.

In lieu of using the standard deduction, taxpayers are allowed to reduce their adjusted gross income by the total of their itemized deductions. The taxpayer may take advantage of this rule by using the larger of either the standard deduction or the total itemized deductions. Itemized deductions are reported on Schedule A. The six types of itemized deductions are health-care costs; state and local income taxes and property taxes paid on personal residences; interest expense on mortgages and investment loans; charitable contributions; theft and casualty losses; and miscellaneous expenses, such as the cost of tax preparation services.

The rules for deducting state and local income and property taxes and interest expense are straightforward: You may deduct any of these amounts that were actually paid during the tax year. However, because of limitations, most taxpayers do not take the itemized deductions for theft and casualty losses and miscellaneous expenses. Taxpayers may claim a deduction for noninsured casualty and theft losses only if those losses exceed $100 and 10 percent of their adjusted gross income. And only the amount of miscellaneous expenses exceeding 2 percent of AGI is deductible.

Medical expenses are the single largest expense for many seniors. Almost all medical expenses are deductible for tax purposes. This includes premiums for health insurance, Medicare Part B, and most long-term-care insurance policies. In addition, the out-of-pocket costs for prescriptions and medicines, hospital and doctor visits, eyeglasses, and hearing aids are deductible. Taxpayers may deduct the cost of travel to and from medical care facilities. Travel includes mileage or other transportation costs, parking, tolls, and hotel rooms if overnight stays are required. Mileage is deductible at 12 cents per mile or the actual cost of gas and oil (not depreciation, insurance, etc.). The sidebar "Allowable Medical Deductions of Interest to Senior Citizens" provides a list of allowable medical deductions that are of interest to senior citizens.

Allowable Medical Deductions of Interest to Senior Citizens

- Acupuncture
- Air conditioner necessary for relief from allergies or other respiratory ailments
- Alcoholism inpatient treatment, meals and lodging at therapy center, transportation to AA meetings
- Artificial limbs and teeth
- Automobile: additional cost for special equipment or adaptations to hold a wheelchair—deductible in year of purchase only, not depreciable
- Braille books and reading materials for use by a visually impaired person. Deduct only the difference in cost between the regular version and the Braille version
- Contact lenses, including saline solution and enzyme cleaner
- Crutches and braces
- Decedent's medical expenses paid within 1 year of death out of decedent's estate
- Detachable home installations, such as air conditioners, heaters, humidifiers, or air cleaners, used for the benefit of a sick person
- Diet: additional cost of special food (over normal costs) if prescribed by a doctor to alleviate a specific medical condition
- Doctors' and physicians' services, including surgeons, osteopathic doctors, dentists, eye doctors, chiropractors, podiatrists, psychiatrists, psychologists, physical therapists, acupuncturists, psychoanalysts, and authorized Christian Science practitioners
- Drug addiction inpatient treatment, meals and lodging at therapy center, and transportation to therapy
- Elastic hosiery
- Exercise program if recommended by doctor to treat a specific condition (does not include programs to promote general health, even if recommended by doctor)

Allowable Medical Deductions of Interest to Senior Citizens *(continued)*

- Extra rent or utilities for a larger apartment required to provide space for a nurse/attendant
- Eye surgery, including laser eye surgery
- Eyeglasses
- Guide dog or other animal to be used by visually impaired, hearing-impaired, or other physically disabled persons
- Hearing aids and batteries
- Home improvement costs if the main purpose is to provide a medical benefit. Includes entrance or exit ramps, wider doorways or hallways, railings, support bars, modified door hardware, bathroom or kitchen modifications, detachable equipment such as a window air conditioner. (Deduction is limited to the difference between the actual cost of the improvement and the increase in the fair market value of the property.)
- Hospital care, including meals and lodging
- Household help for nursing care services only (excludes personal and household services)
- Insurance premiums, including Medicare Parts A and B (excludes loss of life, limb, or sight or guaranteed payments for days in hospital insurance)
- Laboratory fees
- Legal fees paid to authorize treatment for mental illness
- Lifetime care advance payments if part of the advance fee is allocated to medical care and the percentage is specified by the retirement home in the agreement
- Lodging expenses up to $50 per night, per person, to receive medical care in a hospital or medical facility related to a hospital
- Long-term-care insurance premiums ($2,510 if age 61–70 and $3,130 if age 71 or older)
- Mattresses and boards specifically used to alleviate an arthritic condition
- Medical conferences related to the chronic illness of a taxpayer, spouse, or dependent (excludes meals and lodging)
- Medicines and drugs (excludes over-the-counter products)
- Nursing care, including wages, employment taxes, benefits, and attendant's meals

- Nursing home if the main reason for being in the nursing home is to obtain medical care
- Oxygen and oxygen equipment
- Reclining chair bought on a doctor's advice by a person with a cardiac condition
- Stop smoking programs and prescribed drugs to alleviate nicotine withdrawal
- Swimming, if prescribed and therapeutic
- Telephone costs or repair of special equipment for the hearing-impaired
- Transplants, including surgical, hospital, laboratory, and transportation expenses, including those of a donor or possible donor
- Transportation costs, including ambulance, bus, taxi, train, plane fares, parking fees, tolls, and use of personal vehicle at 12 cents per mile or actual cost of gas and oil
- Weight loss program if recommended by doctor for a specific condition
- Whirlpool baths prescribed by doctor
- Wig for the mental health of a patient with hair loss caused by disease
- X-ray services

Only the portion of medical costs exceeding 7.5 percent of the taxpayer's adjusted gross income may be deducted.

Your parents can claim a tax deduction for cash or property donated to a charity. Up to 50 percent of adjusted gross income may be deducted in any tax year. Charitable gifts to veterans' organizations, fraternal societies, nonprofit cemeteries, and certain private nonoperating foundations are limited to 30 percent of AGI. If contributions exceed these amounts, the unused portion may be carried over for an additional 5 tax years. Any unused portion remaining at a taxpayer's death can be used for the taxpayer's final return but is not transferable to another taxpayer.

Do not give away over 50 percent of a single parent's AGI to charities in any given year. If your parent should die prematurely, the carryover deduction cannot be used.

Money or property that is donated to civic leagues, social and sports clubs, chambers of commerce, labor unions, homeowners' associations, and political groups or candidates is not deductible. Neither are the costs for bingo games, raffle and lottery tickets, or dues to lodges, country clubs, and other groups.

Your parents may be cleaning out their homes and donating used clothing, appliances, and household furniture or other items to charitable resale shops. The value of these items is deductible, but it is often hard to determine. If the total resale value of these items exceeds $500, you must file Form 8283. You can get more information about this form from IRS Publication 526. You may be able to obtain a list of items and their suggested resale value from a number of sources, such as www.taxrep.com or www.satruck.com.

You must be able to support your parents' claim for itemized deductions. You will need to keep receipts for medical care costs or cancelled checks or credit card statements for payments actually made in order to deduct medical expenses. Mortgage interest statements from the lender on Form 1098 and statements of charitable gifts from the receiving charity will provide proof of these deductions. Your checks for state and local income taxes paid should be retained. A check for payment of property taxes or a statement from the county treasurer will serve as documentation of the amount of property taxes your parents paid.

Personal Exemption   The personal exemption amount was $3,050 for each person in tax year 2003, regardless of marital status or age. Like the standard deduction, the personal exemption amount changes each year. Jim's personal exemption amount would be $3,050. Under certain conditions, children may claim their parents as dependents on their personal tax returns. This issue is addressed later in the chapter.

Step 4. Calculate the Tax Liability

Taxable income is the number you use to actually figure your parents' income tax. It is equal to the adjusted gross income less the greater of the standard deduction or itemized deductions and less the personal exemption amount. The method for calculating the tax is to use the taxable income amount to find the tax amount in the tables for your parents' filing status provided by the IRS. These tables can be found in Publication 17, in the booklet that comes with the blank tax forms, or at www.irs.gov. The tables must be used for taxable incomes up to $100,000. If taxable income exceeds the maximum income in the tables, you will need to actually calculate the tax by hand. An example is provided in Worksheet 6.3.

Worksheet 6.3 Calculating Taxes Using a Tax Schedule

Tax Schedule for 2003 for Single Filer

If Taxable Income Is Over	But Not Over	The Tax Is	Of the Amount Over
$0	$6,000	10%	$0
$6,000	$28,400	$600 + 15%	$6,000
$28,400	$68,800	$3,960 + 27%	$28,400
$68,800	$143,500	$14,868 + 30%	$68,800
$143,500	$311,950	$37,278 + 35%	$143,500
$311,950	Unlimited	$96,235.50 + 38.6%	$322,950

Assume that Jim Bradshaw's taxable income is $121,000. Using the tax rate schedule provided here, the tax is calculated as follows:

Step 1. Subtract the bottom of the tax bracket from the taxable income
($121,000 − $68,800) = $52,200
Step 2. Multiply the answer to Step 1 by the tax rate for the appropriate tax bracket
($52,200 × 0.30) = $15,660
Step 3. Add Step 2 to the tax for lower tax brackets
($15,660 + $14,868) = $30,528

Jim's tax liability equals $30,528.

Step 5. Subtract Credits to Determine the Final Tax Liability

A tax credit is the most valuable of all tax breaks. Like having a coupon at the grocery store, it provides a direct, dollar-for-dollar reduction in a taxpayer's tax liability. The two credits that apply most often to elderly taxpayers are the *credit for the elderly or disabled* and the *credit for child and dependent care*. The latter credit is discussed later in this chapter because it is typically used not by the parent, but rather by the child who must pay for care so that he or she may continue working. Once credits are identified and summed, they are subtracted to arrive at your parents' final tax liability.

Taxpayers who are over age 65 and whose income is below a certain level may qualify for the *credit for the elderly or disabled*. In addition, taxpayers who are under age 65 *and* retired on permanent and total disability also qualify for the credit. To receive the credit, the elderly or disabled taxpayer must have income below $17,500 for single taxpayers, $20,000 for couples filing jointly with one disabled or elderly spouse, and $25,000 for couples if both spouses are disabled or elderly. Schedule R is used to claim this credit. It is unlikely that Jim will be able to use this credit because he is not disabled and his income exceeds $17,500.

Caretakers who need to place a parent in an adult day-care facility or hire home day care so that they may continue working use the credit for child and dependent care. This credit is discussed more thoroughly in the section on special considerations.

Step 6. Determine if Additional Tax or Refund Is Due

To accurately calculate the amount your parents owe or the refund due them, you must identify, total, and report all prepayments. Most taxpayers make prepayments of their tax liability through withholdings from pension benefits or wages. In addition, many taxpayers are required to make estimated tax payments (see the discussion later in this chapter).

The total amount of all prepayments is subtracted from the final tax liability. This calculation may result in a positive amount, which means that your parents still owe some tax, or a negative amount, which means that they are due a refund.

Special Considerations

The discussion of income taxes in the previous section was simplified to provide an outline of the basic process of calculating income taxes owed. When you are preparing an income tax return for your parents, a number of special considerations need to be addressed. These include who can sign your parents' return, what to do with tax refunds, making estimated payments, filing and paying taxes late, the tax implications of hiring household help, and tax benefits for you as your parents' caretaker.

Signing Your Parents' Return

It is best for your parents to sign their own return. This simply avoids hassles with the IRS. However, if your parents are incompetent, you may have to sign the return. In this event, you must have a power of attorney or declaration of representative from the IRS. The power of attorney privilege for tax purposes is given to an individual by a taxpayer who completes Form 2848, Power of Attorney and Declaration of Representative. Once you have an effective power of attorney, you simply sign the return *"your name, Power of Attorney for taxpayer's name."* Form 2848 must be renewed every 3 years.

In addition to Form 2848, the IRS requires Form 8821, Tax Information Authorization, to be on file before it will release information about a return listed on the authorization form to a person other than the taxpayer.

Instead of filing Form 8821, you can check an authorization permission box at the bottom of page 2 of Form 1040.

How to Handle Tax Refunds

In some cases, your parent will be due a refund. If your parents make estimated tax payments (see the discussion in the next section) and the refund is not greater than their estimated tax for the following year, you may wish to "carry over" the refund and have it applied to the following year's tax liability. Because applying a refund to the following year's tax liability decreases the amount of estimated payments, you are less likely to forget to make an estimated payment or to incur a penalty for not making an estimated payment. In addition, it seems silly to get a refund, only to write an estimated payment check that crosses with the refund in the mail.

 Never carry over a refund amount greater than the total estimated tax liability for the following tax year.

Making Estimated Tax Payments

The Internal Revenue Service does not want to wait to receive tax payments until taxpayers file their annual returns. In addition to filing their current year's income tax return, taxpayers are required to calculate the amount of taxes that will be due on the following year's income. Because it is difficult, if not impossible, to determine tax liability before income is earned, you are allowed to base the estimated payment on the previous year's tax liability.

The IRS has determined that if a taxpayer owes less than $1,000 when he or she files a return (after accounting for tax withholding and any prior year refund carryover), the taxpayer can wait to pay until he or she files the return (as long as it's before April 15). However, if your parents expect to owe more than $1,000 when they file their return, they are required to make four quarterly payments as estimates or prepayments of their expected liability. Those who owe more than $1,000 and who did not prepay at least 90 percent of the current year's tax (which you usually don't know in advance) or 100 percent of the previous year's tax liability are assessed a penalty for late payment. Taxpayers who reported adjusted gross income over $150,000 (or $75,000 if married filing separately) in the previous tax year must prepay at least 110 percent of the previous year's tax to avoid incurring a penalty for late payment.

By the way, the quarterly basis is not really quarterly! One-fourth of the estimated taxes is due on April 15, a second payment of one-fourth is due on June 15, a third is due on September 15, and the last is not due until January 15 of the following year. Complete Form 1040 ES and send it with all payments. Make sure to write your parents' social security numbers and "1040 ES" and the tax year on the check before mailing it to the appropriate Internal Revenue Service office.

Filing Late or Paying Late

As individuals age, they often fail to keep up with the paperwork of day-to-day living. Your parents are more likely to forget to file a return if they prepared and filed their own returns without the assistance of a professional. Paid preparers normally send reminder letters or call those of their clients who fail to make an appointment in a timely fashion.

It is imperative that you prepare and file a return for a previous year as soon as you become aware that a required return was not filed. Penalties and interest for late filing and late payment are assessed only when there is a tax liability due. If a refund is due, the IRS does not require filing for a period of 3 years after the return was originally due. However, refunds are not released unless a complete return is filed.

Your parents will be assessed a late payment penalty equal to 0.5 percent of the taxes owed for each month the payment is late. In addition, interest is due on the unpaid balance at the rate in effect during the period in which the payment was due. Finally, a late filing penalty of 5 percent of the amount due per month will be charged (up to a maximum of 25 percent of the tax due).

Penalties will not be imposed if you can show that the failure was due to reasonable cause and not willful neglect. You must request a waiver of the penalty in writing. Your request should include all the facts and circumstances causing the return to be late. Reasonable cause includes the death or serious illness of the taxpayer or an immediate family member. Include the following statement in your letter: "Under penalties of perjury, I declare that I have examined this statement and accompanying information and, to the best of my knowledge and belief, they are true, correct and complete." Then sign the letter before mailing it to your IRS Service Center. Interest is typically not abated.

Taxes for Household Help

Many families employ some household assistance for their parents. The IRS requires that federal and social security taxes be withheld and paid on any compensation given to household service providers. The family is not responsible for these payments if the household help is contracted through an agency that appropriately withholds taxes. However, you are considered to be an employer if you hire the help directly.

Being an employer is no easy task. You will be required to withhold FICA (social security and Medicare) taxes from the wages of any individual to whom you pay more than $1,400 per year. The amount to withhold is 7.65 percent of the employee's gross income. You must then match this to make your contribution. In other words, you will have to pay 15.3 percent of an employee's gross income to the IRS.

And this may not be all. If the total wages for all employees in a calendar quarter exceeds $1,000, you are responsible for another 0.8 percent of wages. This 0.8 percent covers the Federal Unemployment Tax (FUTA). Only the first $7,000 of wages per employee are subject to the FUTA tax.

To report the FICA and FUTA taxes, a household employer files a Schedule H. Household employment taxes are included in the estimated tax payment calculation. In addition, you should check with your state's unemployment and workers' compensation offices to determine if you are required to pay these taxes on household employees' wages.

Each state and community will have its own rules regarding the withholding and payment of income taxes for household employees. Consult with a qualified tax preparer or your state and local income tax offices before hiring any household help.

Tax Benefits for You, the Caretaker

You may qualify for some tax benefits by virtue of your caretaking role. For example, you may be able to claim your parents as dependents on your own tax return. To qualify for this additional exemption, you are required to provide over 50 percent of the cost of your parents' support and they are not required to live with you. For purposes of this rule, *support* is defined as monies actually spent for food, lodging, clothing, medical and dental care, recreation, transportation, and other necessities. The amount to use for lodging is the fair market value of lodging, not the mortgage payment. Your parents may have any amount of income, and even be liable for income taxes, but if you provide at least 50 percent of their support costs, you can claim them as dependents. If your parents file a tax return and you claim them as dependents, they cannot claim the personal exemption on their personal return.

Many family members may need to contribute to a parent's support. When the combination of all the children's support exceeds 50 percent of the cost of a parent's support, then the children may choose which child can claim the parent as a dependent. The child claiming the parent as a dependent must pay at least 10 percent of the parent's support. However, for one child to claim a parent as a dependent when more than one person contributes to that parent's support, the other children will have to sign Form 2120, Multiple Support Declaration. The child who is claiming the parent as a dependent will attach a copy of this form to her or his return.

The *credit for child and dependent care* entitles the child to a credit against her or his tax liability if she or he incurs costs for care for a dependent parent so that she or he may continue working. The amount of the credit equals the cost of care (up to a maximum of $2,400 for one dependent or $4,800 for two or more dependents) times the rate in the credit schedule. Form 2441 is used to claim this credit.

Tax Forms

Not having the appropriate tax forms when you sit down to prepare your parents' return is akin to not having a plumber's wrench handy when you're ready to fix the kitchen sink. You can avoid frustration by making a master list of the forms you need. These forms can be downloaded from the Web at www.irs.gov. A list of commonly needed forms is provided in Table 6.1. Many of the forms can be filled in on the computer and then printed. Note that you may not be able to save the files, and that the "fillable" forms do not perform calculations—you must do some of the work!

If your parents have only interest and dividend income and do not itemize deductions, they are eligible to file their return using Form 1040EZ. Taxpayers who are filing only Schedules A (itemized deductions) and B (interest and dividend income) may qualify to file a Form 1040A rather than Form 1040. However, it is almost as easy to file a regular Form 1040 as it is to file a Form 1040A.

You will need Schedule A if the total of deductible medical expenses, property taxes, mortgage interest, and charitable deductions exceeds the standard deduction. In many cases, you will complete Schedule A, only to find that the standard deduction amount is greater than the total

Table 6.1   Tax Forms You May Need

Form 1040	U.S. Individual Tax Return	Form 2120	Multiple Support Declaration
Form 1040A	U.S. Individual Tax Return	Form 2441	Credit for Care for the
Form 1040 ES	Estimated Payment		Elderly or Disabled
	"coupons"	Form 2848	Power of Attorney and
Schedule A	Itemized Deductions		Declaration of
Schedule B	Interest and Dividends		Representative
Schedule D	Capital Gains and Losses	Form 8283	Non-Cash Charitable Con-
Schedule H	Household Help		tributions in Excess of $500
Schedule R	Credit for the Elderly or	Form 8821	Tax Information
	Disabled		Authorization

itemized deductions. In this event, simply discard Schedule A and use the standard deduction amount.

Schedule B is required if taxable interest or dividend income exceeds $400. Regardless of the amount of interest, taxpayers are required to file Schedule B if they received interest on behalf of someone else or if the interest is excluded under the Education Savings Bond Program.

Mutual fund companies will often report both dividend income and capital gains income on Form 1099-DIV. In this case, the capital gains portion of the return should be reported on line 13 on the front of Form 1040.

Capital gains from the sale of stocks, bonds, mutual funds, and other investments are reported on Schedule D. Several pieces of information are required in order to complete this form accurately. You will need to know the date on which the investment was purchased, the date of its sale, the purchase price (or cost basis in the case of mutual funds), and the selling price. Be sure to add the commission paid to purchase the investment to the cost basis and to subtract the commission for selling from the selling price.

Household employee taxes are reported on Schedule H. The taxes due on withholdings are estimated and paid as a part of the estimated tax payments throughout the year.

Some parents will qualify for the credit for the disabled and retired. This credit is claimed on Schedule R. It is available only if the taxpayer meets the income and age requirements.

Is There an Easier Way?

About 44 percent of taxpayers prepare their own returns. However, you may feel more comfortable if you use a paid preparer to complete your

parents' tax return. If your parents own business interests or rental properties, or if they have a lot of investment transactions, you should consider hiring a professional tax preparer. Or, you may feel confident that
you can complete the tax return using a software product.

Paid Tax Preparers

There are many tax preparation services available in most communities.
Anyone can hang out a shingle and offer tax preparation services.
However, the IRS recognizes the work of some tax preparers as "professional." Enrolled agents, certified public accountants, and attorneys are
allowed to represent your parents before the Tax Court. All three have
met minimum standards as set forth by the Internal Revenue Service, state
accountancy boards, or state bar associations.

The cost of professional tax preparation services will depend on the
difficulty of the tax return, the level of service provided by the preparer,
the preparer's experience and education, and the licenses held by the preparer. Expect to pay a minimum of $100 to have a basic income tax
return prepared. If you choose to file electronically, there may be an extra
charge imposed. A reputable tax preparer will examine your parents' previous year's return and give you an estimate of the cost of preparing this
year's return. However, a preparer can provide a fair estimate only if you
fully disclose the types of income and deductions your parents normally
include on their tax returns.

While you can find a list of tax preparers in the Yellow Pages of your
telephone book, you may want to obtain referrals from family members,
friends, or the other professionals your parents use, such as attorneys or
investment or insurance representatives. You can find a list of CPAs by
calling the Society of Certified Public Accountants in your community or
state. Attorneys can be identified through the community or state bar
association. A list of enrolled agents may be obtained from the IRS.

Tax Preparation Software

An alternative to using a paid tax preparer is to complete the return using
a good software product. There are several companies that sell tax preparation software, and most such packages cost under $50. These software
programs can be purchased through most large department stores, computer products retailers, office supply stores, or Web-based retailers.
Many of the programs offer a "wizard" format that asks you, the preparer, questions. If you answer the questions correctly, the software will
automatically insert the information on the correct form and line and

accurately perform the calculations. The printed return will be in a format that has been preauthorized for filing with the Internal Revenue Service. To maximize the efficiency and accuracy of your parents' return if you use a software product, you should have the previous year's tax return and the tax reporting forms from each income source readily available. The most popular tax preparation software includes TurboTax, Tax Cut, and TaxACT.

Final Thoughts

Filing tax returns is not easy. The task is made more difficult in this case because you will be preparing a tax return for someone else. It's important that you gather the important information and review the previous returns your parents filed. Be sure to take advantage of all exclusions, deductions, and exemptions. Prepare and pay estimated taxes in a timely fashion. And don't hesitate to hire a professional tax preparer or use software to make your job easier.

Once you've filed your parents' tax return, you've completed one of the most dreaded and difficult financial management tasks. Be sure to retain a copy of the filed tax return in your records for a minimum of 7 years. It will be easier the second time around . . . next year.

Part II

Protecting and Investing

7

Insurance

Marlene Osborne's father, Don Fraser, recently caused an automobile accident. While Don was changing lanes, his car struck a new luxury vehicle, which in turn, hit two parked cars. Fortunately, no one was injured. Don's car was "totaled," and within days he received a check for its book value less his $100 deductible. Don was happy with the quick payment, but he was upset that he did not receive enough money to buy what he thought was an equivalent vehicle. Several weeks later, Don received a letter from his insurance company. It notified him that the company had agreed to pay $25,000 on his behalf for the damage to the other vehicles, but that the total claim was $37,500 and that Don would be responsible for the remainder. He called Marlene right away. He simply could not understand how he could owe more money. He has had the same policy with the same company for 25 years. He wants Marlene to call the company and straighten out the problem. After all, he has paid the company lots of money over the years. Now he needs it back. Marlene is not sure where to start. She knows her dad does not have $12,500 to spare.

PROBABLY THERE is no topic in personal finance that is less well understood by the average person than insurance. Insurance policies do not make for easy reading. They are very detailed and are written in a legalistic style. What one section of the policy appears to provide may be changed in another section. Because people rarely have losses that lead to insurance claims, they lack frequent, firsthand experiences that could help them to better understand insurance. As Don and Marlene have found out, years of confidence that losses will be covered can be quickly shattered, leading to dismay, frustration, and even anger.

This chapter will help you understand your parents' insurance coverage. It will focus on what you can do to help them buy appropriate insurance protection and save on insurance premiums. We will first provide a basic overview of insurance. Next, we will describe auto and home-owner's insurance. Then we will discuss techniques that you can use to receive the highest possible reimbursement for losses. Finally, the chapter provides guidelines for adequately and economically covering the possible financial losses that your parents may face.

Insurance Basics

Every time we drive a car, cook a meal, or entertain guests, we run the risk that our actions might cause a loss for ourselves or for others. These losses can be minor or major, and the largest of them can absolutely destroy your parents' financial future. Insurance protects the insured from such financial losses.

What Is Risk?

Risk means uncertainty. It is simply not knowing whether or not something bad will happen. People do not like risk when the outcome can only be negative. Such risk is called pure risk and is addressed through insurance. Speculative risk exists when the outcome can also be positive. Speculative risk is covered in Chapter 8, "Your Parents' Investments."

Risk can be managed. One way to do so is to simply avoid activities that expose us to risk—not skydiving, for example. Another way to manage risk is to minimize the losses that can occur. Installing smoke alarms and wearing seat belts are ways to minimize losses. But losses can still occur. Therefore, most people turn to insurance as a way to manage their risk of financial loss.

What Is Insurance?

Insurance is a means of reducing risk by transferring it to a third party. Insurance protects each individual by replacing all or a portion of an uncertain, and possibly large, financial loss with a certain, but comparatively low, fee called the insurance premium. The rules and obligations of this transfer of risk are laid out in the insurance policy. Insurance allows a large number of individuals to share in the financial losses suffered by just a few individuals.

Insurance policy: The contract between an insurance company and an insured person.

Insurance has two basic elements: the transfer of risk and the sharing of losses. Most people—Don Fraser, for example—focus on the sharing of losses. They want to be covered when a loss occurs. But insurance purchasers benefit whether or not they suffer a loss. The transfer of risk itself provides a benefit. It provides the peace of mind to drive a car, own a home, and simply live our lives with the confidence that some unforeseen event will not bring financial disaster. This is really what we are paying for when we buy insurance. Don was upset because he had paid premiums all those years without a loss. But he had been protected all those years.

How Insurance Works

Let's look at insurance in more detail. An insurance company promises to cover certain losses and, in return, collects premiums. The company invests the premiums and later pays losses when the insureds make claims. To make a profit, the company must be very specific about the promises made in its policies. Insurance companies solve this problem by making the same, carefully worded promises to many people. This makes it easier for them to predict the total dollar amount of losses that will occur. The premiums are then based on the average losses.

You may be asking yourself what this has to do with your parents' money. Let's examine Don Fraser's auto accident and his subsequent insurance problem. Don bought a standard automobile insurance policy. In the policy, the company promised to pay for property damage that Don might cause, with an upper limit of $25,000 on the amount it would pay for such losses. It probably sold thousands of policies with that same limit. Don caused damages that exceeded that limit by $12,500. He is responsible to the owners of the other cars for the difference.

It is too late for Don to do anything about his current situation. But what could he have done? Don's problem is a common one for people his age. The limits on his automobile policy had not been updated as the cost of vehicles increased. Twenty-five years ago, when he bought the policy, the average new car sold for under $5,000. Now the average price exceeds $17,000. And Don damaged three vehicles!

Even though insurance companies are very careful about the promises they make in their policies, they are usually willing to adapt those policies to your specific needs. The premium will be adjusted accordingly. The next sections of this chapter look at the standard coverage in automobile and homeowner's insurance policies and address specific ways to tailor those policies to your parents' needs.

Reading an Insurance Policy

There is no substitute for carefully reviewing your parents' insurance policies. There are several specific things that you should look for and evaluate:

1. **The perils covered.** Perils are the events that cause a loss, such as a fire. Some policies list the perils that are covered; others list only the perils that are excluded.
2. **The property covered.** The property covered under a policy may be listed specifically, or only the excluded property may be listed. When the specific property is listed, any new acquisitions must be added to the policy.
3. **The locations covered.** Where the loss occurs may affect whether it will be covered. For example, cars driven into Mexico are generally not covered by a U.S. automobile insurance policy.
4. **The time period of coverage.** Policies are generally written to cover a specific time period, usually 1 year.
5. **Loss reduction.** Insurance companies often require that the insured take certain steps to reduce their losses. Examples include locking your car, installing smoke alarms, and notifying the police immediately after a theft. Sometimes they give discounts for doing so. They may deny coverage if required loss control efforts are not taken.
6. **The limits of coverage.** All insurance policies have limits. It is easy to increase the limits by letting the company know your needs. The premium will be increased accordingly. You usually don't have to wait until the policy is up for renewal.

Insure against the losses your parents cannot afford and assume (self-insure) the losses that they can reasonably afford. This helps them make the most of their insurance premium dollar and avoid large losses that can destroy their wealth. This advice is true for all families.

Factors That Affect the Cost of Insurance

Certain policy features can lower your premiums without significantly lowering the amount of protection you have. These features include deductibles, coinsurance, and hazard reduction and loss reduction efforts.

Deductibles require that you pay a portion of any loss. For example, automobile collision insurance often includes a $200 deductible. This means that the insured must pay the first $200 of each loss. The insurance company then pays the remainder of the loss, up to the limits of the policy. Most health and property insurance policies also include deductibles. You usually have a choice of deductible amounts. The higher the deductible, the lower the premium will be.

Coinsurance requires that the insured and the insurer share losses proportionately. Health insurance plans commonly require the insured to pay 20 percent of a loss, with the insurer paying the remaining 80 percent. Substantial premium reductions can be realized through coinsurance, but you must be prepared to pay your share of any losses.

Insurance policies sometimes give discounts or charge lower premiums if the policyholder takes action that will reduce the probability or the severity of a loss. Installing dead-bolt locks actually reduces the likelihood of having a loss. Smoke alarms and fire extinguishers in the home do not prevent fires, but they may lessen the severity of the loss.

Automobile Insurance

Automobile insurance is a package policy that combines liability and property insurance to cover four types of losses: (A) bodily injury and property damage liability, (B) medical payments insurance, (C) protection against uninsured and underinsured motorists, and (D) insurance for physical damage to the insured vehicle. Table 7.1 summarizes these coverages. The emphasis is on the liability aspect because that is where the potential for large losses is greatest. Don Fraser's liability coverage paid for the first $25,000 of the damage he caused to the other vehicles. His physical damage coverage paid for the loss of his vehicle.

Liability insurance: Insurance that protects the insured when he or she is held responsible for someone else's losses.

Property insurance: Insurance that protects the insured from losses to his or her own property.

Table 7.1 Coverage Provided By Auto Insurance

Policy Section	Type of Coverage	Losses Covered	Limits
A. Liability	Bodily injury liability	Bodily injury losses suffered by others for which the insured person is responsible.	Usually written as two numbers, such as $100,000/$250,000. The first is the limit per person per accident, and the second is the total for one accident.
	Property damage liability	Property damage losses suffered by others for which the insured person is responsible.	Usually written as one number, such as $50,000, which is the total for one accident.
B. Medical payments	Medical payments/ personal injury protection	Medical and related losses suffered by passengers in the insured's vehicle, regardless of who was at fault.	Usually written as one number, such as $10,000, which is the amount per person per accident.
C. Uninsured and underinsured motorist	Uninsured motorist	Medical and related losses suffered by passengers in the insured's vehicle when the other drive is at fault and uninsured.	Usually written as two numbers, such as $100,000/$250,000. The first is the limit per person per accident, and the second is the total for one accident.
	Underinsured motorist	Medical and related losses suffered by passengers in the insured's vehicle when the other driver is at fault and is underinsured.	Usually written as two numbers, such as $100,000/$250,000. The first is the limit per person per accident, and the second is the total for one accident.
D. Physical damage	Collision coverage	Losses caused by collisions and rollovers, regardless of who was at fault.	Pays the actual cash (book) value of the vehicle less any deductible.
	Comprehensive coverage	Losses caused by events other than collision: fire, theft, vandalism, etc.	Pays the actual cash (book) value of the vehicle less any deductible.

Bodily Injury and Property Damage Liability Insurance

Automobile liability insurance limits are usually stated as three figures, such as the $50,000/$100,000/$25,000 policy covering Don Fraser. The first figure is the maximum that will be paid for *one* person's bodily injury losses. The middle figure represents the overall maximum that will be paid for bodily injury liability losses to *any number* of persons involved in a single accident. The third figure represents the maximum that will be paid for property damage liability losses resulting from an accident. Such losses can include damage to other vehicles, buildings, roadside poles and equipment, and even cargo in the other vehicles.

Liability insurance does not pay for bodily injury losses suffered by the driver of the insured vehicle or for property damage to that vehicle. Passengers of the at-fault driver who are injured may collect under the driver's liability coverage, but only after using up the coverage provided under medical payments (discussed in the next section) and only after payments are made to persons in other vehicles or pedestrians who were injured.

Medical Payments Insurance

Automobile medical payments coverage pays bodily injury losses suffered by the passengers of the insured vehicle, regardless of who is at fault for the accident. Medical payments coverage is subject to a single policy limit, which is applied per person per accident. Once this limit is reached, the passengers can make a claim against the at-fault driver's bodily injury liability coverage.

Watch Out for Subrogation

When Don Fraser caused his accident, the other drivers' policies initially picked up their losses because collision coverage is written on a no-fault basis. This did not absolve Don of responsibility, however. Subrogation rights allow an insurance company to take action against an at-fault driver and that driver's insurance company when it must pay a claim from one of its own customers. Don was responsible for the full $37,500 in losses, and his company picked up the first $25,000 of this amount, with Don being responsible for the remainder. Subrogation comes into play even if the other driver's uninsured or underinsured motorist coverage paid the other driver's losses.

Uninsured and Underinsured Motorist Insurance

Uninsured and underinsured motorist insurance protects the driver and passengers from bodily injury losses (and, in a few states, property damage losses) when an accident is caused by an uninsured or underinsured driver. The limits for uninsured motorist insurance are similar to those for automobile liability insurance. For example, uninsured motorist protection with limits of 50/100 would provide up to $50,000 for any one injured person and up to $100,000 for multiple bodily injury losses in one accident.

Physical Damage Insurance

Physical damage insurance covers losses due to collision, theft, and other perils. There are two types of physical damage insurance. Collision insurance covers losses from a collision with another car or object or from a rollover, regardless of who was at fault. Collision insurance is written with a deductible that usually ranges from $100 to $1,000. If you carry collision insurance coverage on your own car, you are generally covered when you drive someone else's car with permission. Comprehensive automobile insurance covers property damage losses caused by perils other than collision and rollover. Covered perils include fire, theft, vandalism, hail, and wind, among many others. Comprehensive insurance is written with a deductible ranging from $100 to $500.

Many times, the estimate of the loss exceeds the book value of the vehicle. In this event, the book value is paid to the insured, less any deductible. The book value is based on the average current *trade-in value* of cars of the same make, model, condition, and age. It is not based on what it would cost you to pay off your auto loan or buy a similar vehicle.

Buying Automobile Insurance

It is a good idea to shop carefully for automobile insurance because the industry is highly competitive and it is easy to get quotes from different companies. Premiums vary widely because they depend on the pool of customers insured by a company. Your goal is to get the proper coverage while keeping your premiums as low as possible. When you are assisting your parents with their selection of automobile insurance, you can take four specific steps:

1. *Identify what coverage is needed.* Liability and medical payments protection are generally required by state law. Uninsured

and underinsured motorist protection is not overly expensive, perhaps $50 per year. Whether or not you should select physical damage protection depends on the age and value of the vehicle involved. Vehicles that are more than 10 years old and below $2,500 in value may not be worth insuring for physical damage, as they are likely to be "totaled" because of their low book value. The cost of protection over a period of several years can exceed the value of the vehicle. Many people drop this coverage when the vehicle reaches a certain age and set the money aside to help them buy another vehicle or make repairs should they cause an accident. If the other driver is at fault, his or her policy will provide reimbursement.

2. *Select policy limits.* Your parents must conform to the minimum requirements in your state. These minimums are too low for most people's needs, however. Don Fraser's policy had liability limits that were too low given the current market, and he has to pay the difference between the loss and his policy limit. Minimum limits of $250,000/$500,000/$100,000 are commonly recommended today. Similar limits for uninsured and underinsured motorist coverage are also advised. Recommended medical payments limits are a minimum of $50,000 per person.

3. *Decide on deductibles.* Deductibles are chosen for Part D of the auto policy. It is best to select the highest deductible you can afford. This will lower the premium, and the savings can be used to increase the liability limits.

4. *Shop around for the best price.* The elderly often have a steadfast loyalty to one insurance company or agent. This loyalty can be costly, as auto insurance premiums can vary as much as 100 percent for the same coverage.

Homeowner's Insurance

Homeowner's insurance combines the liability and property insurance coverage needed by homeowners and renters into a single package policy. Homeowner's insurance emphasizes property losses because they have the highest potential to be financially significant. As outlined in Table 7.2, there are four types of homeowner's insurance for people who own a single-family dwelling, one type for those who rent housing, and another type for the owners of condominiums.

Retirement Benefits and Liability

Retirees should not assume that just because they have no labor income, they are exempt from liability. In general, retirement benefits are exempt from seizure when a person is held liable for automobile- and home ownership–related accidents. This exemption includes pension plan benefits and salary-reduction plans, e.g., 401(k) plans. It does not include IRAs and general investment accounts that are not part of a retirement plan. As a practical matter, however, retirement accounts are still at risk because all other assets can be taken to pay claims that are not covered by insurance. To keep one's home and other property, retirement funds may need to be tapped. Therefore, high liability limits are still a good idea for retirees.

Table 7.2 Coverage Provided by Homeowner's Insurance

Coverage For	Plan	Perils Covered	Limits
Single-family dwellings	HO-1 Basic Form	Covers 11 named perils: fire/lightning, wind/hail, explosion, riots, damage by aircraft, damage by vehicles not owned by family members, smoke, vandalism, theft, glass breakage, and volcano.	The declared replacement value of the dwelling, with other coverages tied to that amount: 50% for personal property, 10% for unattached structures, 5% for trees, shrubs, etc., and 10% for additional living expenses.
	HO-2 Broad Form	The previous 11 perils plus 7 more: falling objects, weight of ice/snow, collapse, water leakage from plumbing or air conditioning, bursting/cracking/bulging of water-heating equipment, freezing of equipment, and damage to electrical equipment (but not circuitry or chips) from short circuits.	The declared replacement value of the dwelling, with other coverages tied to that amount: 50% for personal property, 10% for unattached structures, 5% for trees, shrubs, etc., and 20% for additional living expenses.

Table 7.2 (continued)

Coverage For	Plan	Perils Covered	Limits
	HO-3 Special Form	Covers the dwelling, unattached structures, trees/shrubs, and additional living expenses for all perils except those specifically excluded (commonly flood and earthquake). Covers personal property for all of the 18 perils except glass breakage.	The declared replacement value of the dwelling, with other coverages tied to that amount: 50% for personal property, 10% for unattached structures, 5% for trees, shrubs, etc., and 20% for additional living expenses.
	HO-8 Older Home Form	Perils 1–11.	The declared actual cash (market) value of the dwelling, with other coverages tied to that amount: 50% for personal property, 10% for unattached structures, 5% for trees, shrubs, etc., and 20% for additional living expenses.
Renter's insurance	HO-4	Perils 1–18 excluding glass breakage.	The declared value of personal property, with other coverages tied to that amount: 10% for trees, shrubs, etc., and 20% for additional living expenses.
Condominium insurance	HO-6	Perils 1–18 excluding glass breakage for personal property.	The declared value of personal property, with other coverages tied to that amount: 10% for unattached structures owned solely by the condominium owner, 10% for trees, shrubs, etc., and 40% for additional living expenses. Also covers up to $1,000 for owner's additions and alterations to the unit.

Basic Homeowner's Insurance Coverages

The standard homeowner's insurance policy is divided into two sections. Section 1 provides protection from property damage losses, including losses caused by (1) damage to the dwelling, (2) damage to other structures on the property, (3) damage to personal property and dwelling contents, and (4) expenses arising out of a loss of use of the dwelling (for example, food and lodging). Additional coverages are usually provided for such items as debris removal, damage to trees and shrubs, and fire department service charges.

Section 2 covers liability losses when a homeowner is negligent or otherwise fails to exercise due caution in protecting visitors. Losses to members of the homeowner's immediate family are not covered. Typically, Section 2 also provides no-fault medical payments and property damage protection that pays small losses suffered by others regardless of who was at fault. An example of such a loss might include damage to a friend's leather coat when it was chewed by your dog. The policy would pay without your friend having to show negligence.

Types of Homeowner's Insurance

There are six distinct types of homeowner's insurance policies: HO-1 through HO-4, HO-6, and HO-8. They are described in detail in Table 7.2. The descriptors used to identify these policies are similar for most insurance companies.

Coverage for Single-Family Dwellings   Coverage for single-family dwellings is generally based on the replacement value of the dwelling itself. The replacement value is often a bit higher than the market value of the property. The homeowner selects the dollar amount of coverage. Most policies now require that the insured select 100 percent of the replacement value. If the insured does not do so, then he or she will be required to pay a proportionate share of (coinsure) any loss. For example, someone who insures a house with a replacement cost of $200,000 for $180,000 (90 percent) would have to pay 10 percent of any loss to the dwelling itself. This is because the homeowner is underinsured by 10 percent ($20,000/$200,000).

Your parents may own a home that was built more than 50 years ago. Older homes require special consideration because the replacement value is often much higher than the market value. Companies will not write standard replacement-cost protection on such dwellings, because insuring the home for more than it is worth provides a temptation to intentionally cause a loss. An older home policy form that provides actual-cash-value protection for the dwelling is available. The dwelling will not be rebuilt to the same standards of style and quality as the original, as those standards may be prohibitively expensive today. Instead, the policy provides that the dwelling will be rebuilt to make it serviceable.

Homeowner's policies often include a clause that automatically increases the coverage each year to keep pace with increases in the cost of its replacement. It is a good idea to insure your dwelling for 100 percent of its replacement cost. Many insurance companies will fully cover a loss even if it exceeds the policy limit by 20 to 25 percent if the dwelling was insured for 100 percent of its projected replacement cost.

Personal Property Coverage Homeowner's insurance on single-family dwellings will automatically cover the contents and personal property for up to 50 percent of the coverage on the home. For example, a home that is insured for $200,000 would have $100,000 of personal property coverage. You may buy additional personal property coverage for an additional premium. Certain items of personal property have specific limits of coverage. For example, standard policies usually provide a maximum of $1,000 of coverage for jewelry. If your parents own jewelry, coins, stamps, silver items, or other unique items, you should let your agent know and either buy additional protection or keep the items in a safe-deposit box.

Actual cash value: The purchase price of property less depreciation.

Traditional homeowner's insurance policies pay only the actual cash value of personal property. For example, a TV might have cost $500 when it was new. If it had a total life expectancy of 10 years and was stolen after 8 years, its actual cash value when it was stolen was only $100 (2/10 of $500). Your parents probably have a considerable amount of personal property that is older than its projected life span and may not be covered at all.

Replacement-cost protection for contents, which pays the full replacement cost of any personal property, may be available for an additional premium. Because the 50 percent overall limit applies even if replacement-cost protection for contents is purchased, you may need to raise the overall limit when replacement-cost valuation is used.

Coverage for Renters Renters do not own their dwelling and therefore cannot insure it. Instead, renters base their insurance amount on the value of their personal property. The elderly often move from a single-family dwelling into an apartment and bring with them considerable personal property. Renters will want to take an inventory of their personal property and come up with an estimate of its actual cash value or replacement cost, depending on which type of coverage is desired.

Coverage for Condominium Owners   Condominium owners face three potential losses: (1) losses to their personal property, (2) losses due to the additional living expenses they face if their unit is unlivable after a loss occurs, and (3) liability losses. A condominium homeowner's policy covers these losses. As with renter's insurance, the base amount of coverage is tied to the value of the personal property in the unit. Standard policies provide $1,000 in protection against losses to the structural alterations and additions that condominium owners sometimes make when they remodel their units. Higher limits can be purchased. The building itself is covered by insurance carried by the condominium association. Condominium homeowner's policies provide supplemental coverage for the dwelling unit if the building is not sufficiently insured by the condominium association.

Coverage for Liability Losses   Standard homeowner's policies typically provide $100,000 of personal liability coverage, $1,000 of no-fault medical expense coverage, and $250 of no-fault property damage coverage. Increasing these limits further protects one's financial assets. The extra cost is small, and the "large loss principle" applies.

Filing a Claim

When a loss occurs, you must take specific steps to properly file a claim.

Notify Your Insurance Agent

This should be done as soon as possible after you become aware of a loss. The agent will provide instructions about whom to contact next (including filing a police report) and what to do to minimize the magnitude of the loss. Failure to follow an agent's instructions for minimizing a loss can result in the denial of all or a portion of a claim. Such instructions are often outlined in the policy as well. Keep the agent and the claims adjuster informed, even if this requires daily or weekly contact until the claim is settled. The tenacious claimant is most likely to collect fully on a loss.

Claim adjuster: The person designated by the insurance company to assess whether the loss is covered and to determine the dollar amount that the company will pay.

File Your Claim

Insurance companies require that claims be made in writing. Your agent or the adjuster may help you complete the necessary forms. Many insurance policies limit the time period during which a claim can be made. They also generally describe the specific steps to be taken. Consult the policy whenever a loss occurs.

Provide Proof of the Loss

The burden of proof for insurance losses lies with the insured party. Without documentation, the insurance company will generally interpret the situation in a manner that is favorable to its interests, not yours. Police reports are essential for auto accident claims.

Your parents probably have considerable amounts of personal property. It is a good idea to have records of their property for insurance and estate planning purposes (see Chapters 14 and 15). Pictures are a great way to establish such records. You can photograph or videotape all valuable property in your parents' home. Write the date of purchase, price paid, description, model name and number, and serial number (if any) of the property on the back of the photograph or verbally record it on the videotape. Prepare a list describing any items that were not photographed or videotaped. When a loss occurs, you can present a *copy* of your documentation to the claims adjuster. Be sure to retain the original.

You should always file a police report when you are involved in an automobile accident or when you suffer a property theft or vandalism. If your parents are in an auto accident, you can help them prepare a narrative giving the time and place of the accident, the direction of travel and estimated speed of the cars involved, road and weather conditions, and the behavior of the parties involved. It is also helpful to include a diagram of the accident scene showing the location of the vehicles before, during, and after the time of impact, plus the location of traffic lights and signs and any landmarks (for example, road construction or repairs). Include the names and addresses of any witnesses.

Sign the Release

Signing the release is the final step in the claims-settlement process. The release absolves the insurance company of any further responsibility for the loss. It is tempting to sign a release in order to obtain reimbursement quickly. But companies can often release partial payment without a final release, so resist the temptation to sign a release until you are sure that the full magnitude of the loss has become evident and you are satisfied with the amount being offered.

> **Release:** An insurance document affirming that the dollar amount of the loss settlement is accepted as full and complete reimbursement.

Helping Your Parents Save Money on Insurance

You should focus your efforts on helping your parents obtain appropriate coverage at the lowest price. Here are some suggestions for reaching this goal.

- *Assume affordable losses.* Insurance is designed to address catastrophes. Common and low-cost losses can be paid for in other ways. Increasing deductibles can yield considerable savings.
- *Select appropriate coverages and limits.* Buy only the coverages that are needed and select policy limits that are appropriate for the largest potential losses. Insure against losses that would be financially unaffordable. Choose high liability limits and pay for them by choosing a higher deductible.
- *Shop around.* When policies are up for renewal, get quotes from several companies. To obtain a quote, simply telephone an agent or company directly. You will be asked some basic descriptive information. You can also use a Web-based quote service such as http://www.quotesmith.com or http://www.insquote.com. Many state insurance departments publish helpful insurance buyer's guides and rate the companies that provide various types of insurance. You can visit http://www.naic.org/1regulator/ usamap.htm to access your state insurance regulator.
- *Take advantage of discounts.* Ask about discounts for buying multiple policies from the same company. Also ask about loss control efforts that can generate a discounted rate.

- *Make sure you are properly classified.* Insurance premiums differ based on your age, marital status, location, and a number of other factors. Your agent may not know of changes that could lower your premiums. It is also important to verify that you are properly classified because claims may be denied if premiums were based on an inappropriate classification.

Final Thoughts

Insurance allows individuals to transfer the risk of financial loss to a third party. Your parents are no less at risk because they are older. In fact, late in one's retirement is no time to relax one's protection against property and liability losses. Your parents' income is not likely to be able to absorb losses, and they probably have valuable assets that could be at risk. This chapter gave some basic steps that you can take to keep your parents well protected. It is important that you shop wisely and choose appropriate insurance to protect them from possible financial losses.

8

Your Parents' Investments

Throughout 2002, Jerome Evans noticed a steady decline in his mother, Emma's, living conditions and appearance. Previously she had displayed holiday decorations in her apartment and occasionally had purchased new items of clothing and accessories. She typically had her hair styled every week, but she hadn't had it done in quite a while. She was losing weight and seemed very sad much of the time. She rarely entertained friends or went out any more. Over the holidays, he noticed that there was little food in her apartment. Jerome had verbalized his concerns periodically and received vague, "I'm okay" responses. Finally, fearing for her health, he pushed hard for an honest answer. He was stunned by Emma's reply. She said that she was broke.

Jerome couldn't understand how that could be. His father had left her $80,000 in a retirement account in late 1999. The money had been invested in a balanced mutual fund divided equally among various stocks and bonds. She had also opened several savings accounts with $135,000 in proceeds from the sale of her house in early 2001. These funds, along with her social security check, should have been supporting her adequately. When Jerome questioned her on the matter, Emma said that she had lost most of the money on some investments. She had moved monies from the balanced fund into a growth stock fund in late 2000. In early 2001 she had bought a variety of corporate stocks with the savings account monies. Since then, her broker had been making trades for her that hadn't worked out very well.

WHILE THEY WERE WORKING, your parents tried to build a nest egg that would support them during retirement. The techniques they need to use now to preserve and draw from that nest egg are different from the ones they used to build it. There is a kernel of truth in the conventional wisdom that retirees should be more conservative with their investments. But the key factor is not that they are now retired. Instead, their investment decisions should be based on how soon they will need the funds and on their wealth level, income needs, and risk tolerance. Short time horizons warrant less risk and longer time horizons more risk. With life expectancies for today's retirees lasting into their early 80s for males and mid-80s for females, even retirees have a long time horizon for investing a portion of their funds.

> **Investing:** Buying or lending assets with the primary goal of generating income in the future.

As Jerome Evans is about to find out, helping your parents with their investments can get complicated very quickly. This chapter is designed to give you a broad overview of the basics of investments tailored for those who are in the process of spending down rather than building up their nest egg. It begins with a discussion of the sources of investment returns. Next, we provide tools to help you understand investment risk, risk tolerance, and sources of investment risk. The investment vehicles used by retirees are then discussed. The final section describes strategies that enable retired investors to reduce their investment risk with minimal impact on their investment returns. If your parents' nest egg exceeds $100,000, you may want to consult an unbiased financial planner who does not have a financial stake in the advice being given.

Investment Returns

The dollar return on an investment is simply the total income it generates. Some of that income, called current income, is "earned" while the investment is held. Interest, stock dividends, and rent are examples of current income. Emma Evans has seen her current income drop because her growth stocks have been paying low dividends. The remaining return comes when the investment is sold; this is referred to as a capital gain (or, sometimes, a capital loss). Should Emma sell some of her stock soon, she might actually have capital losses because of the decline in stock prices she has experienced. Eventually her stocks will probably go up in value, and she will have capital gains. But she needs money now. This is a common problem for retirees. Emma does not have the time to wait out the ups and downs of stock prices.

Capital gain (or loss): The difference between what was paid for an investment and its sale price after subtracting transaction costs.

Several factors must be considered when evaluating investment alternatives. These include the need for current income and the desire for long-term growth. Some investment vehicles tend to generate current income. Others tend to generate capital gains. Some can do both. Table 8.1 summarizes the major groups of investments chosen by retirees according to their tendency to generate current income or capital gains.

Table 8.1 Current Income versus Capital Gain Potential for Selected Types of Investments

Investment Type	Potential for Current Income	Potential for Capital Gains
Savings accounts and money market mutual funds	Interest on the account	None
Certificates of deposit	Interest on the account	None, but interest income can be allowed to accrue and be taken when the CD matures
Bonds/bond mutual funds	Pay quarterly or semiannual interest	Gains possible if market interest rates drop while the bond is held
Income stocks/ mutual funds with an income objective	Dividend income paid quarterly	Modest capital gains possible
Growth stocks/ growth mutual funds	Low dividend payout patterns	Significant capital gains possible, especially over the long term. Dividends can be reinvested in additional shares to grow principal
Balanced mutual funds	Dividend income paid quarterly	Modest potential for capital gains. Dividends can be reinvested in additional shares to grow principal
Real estate	Potential for cash flow that can be eroded by operating expenses; especially in the early years of the investment	Significant capital gains possible, especially over the long term

An investor must also compare the yield (or rate of return) on various investment options. For example, money in a savings account might earn 2 percent interest. A bond investment might be paying 6 percent. It may appear that the bond is the better option. Choosing the savings account would have an opportunity cost of 4 percentage points. However, as you will read later in this chapter, even yields can be deceiving because income is eroded by inflation and subject to taxes.

> **Yield or rate of return:** The return on an investment expressed as a percentage of the original investment on an annual basis. It includes both current income and capital gains.

Taxpayers in the 30 percent federal income tax bracket may get to keep only 70 percent of the income on their investments (even less if their state levies an income tax). Thus, the savings account pays 1.4 percent (2 percent × 0.70) and the bond pays 4.2 percent (6 percent × 0.70) after taxes. Then they must subtract the rate of inflation to get the real, after-tax yield. If inflation is currently 3 percent (close to the long-term average), the savings account really pays –1.6 percent (1.4 percent – 3 percent) and the bond pays 1.2 percent (4.2 percent – 3 percent). The bond still looks better. After considering inflation, savings accounts lose buying power each year. That is why they are not viewed as good long-term investment options.

> When comparing investment options, always compare after-tax, after inflation rates of return.

Investment Risk

All investments, even those that are perceived as fairly safe, carry risk. The greater the risk, the higher the potential return on the investment. Riskier investments offer higher potential rates of return but also carry a greater potential for losses.

> **Investment risk:** The possibility that actual investment returns will differ from what is expected.

Investment risk is like a roller-coaster ride: There are peaks and valleys. The greater the risk, the steeper and more frequent the peaks and valleys. If you can ride them out over time, the return on investment is often higher. But you are in trouble if, like Emma Evans, you need to draw money from your investments when values are down.

Some people abhor risk so much that they avoid it altogether. They "invest" in federally insured savings accounts. These are not truly investments, but simply places to put money for a period of time. They want their money to be safe. As shown previously, however, they find it difficult to get ahead over the long term because taxes and inflation offset most, if not all, of their interest. Therefore, investors must accept some risk, but the amount should be reasonable given their tolerance for risk, their investment goals, and the time horizon for their investment goals.

Your Parents' Risk Tolerance

Jerome Evans's concern over his mother's financial situation was heightened because her investment choices were so out of character. Emma was a conservative woman who had always expressed concern that she would lose her nest egg. Yet she had chosen some fairly risky options for a woman her age. She had violated one of the cardinal rules of investing: Stay within your risk tolerance. Why? Her reasons became clear as she and Jerome discussed her situation. Her concern for her long-term future had caused her to focus on the positive aspects of investment risk and ignore the negative.

The positive view states that the higher the risk associated with an investment option, the greater the *potential* return. This potential for gain is what motivated Emma to accept greater levels of risk. She saw the rising stock market of the late 1990s as a chance to build a more secure future. But risk cuts both ways, as Emma sadly found out.

When you address your parents' investments, you will first need to discern your parents' tolerance for risk. In other words, how much anxiety related to investments can they handle? Jerome knew that his mother had a low risk tolerance. That is why it took her a year to even admit that she was having problems. Investors can be placed into one of four risk tolerance categories.

Conservative Investors   Conservative investors tolerate very little risk. They accept relatively low rates of return in order to be safe. Conservative investors choose certificates of deposit (CDs), government securities, high-quality corporate bonds and stocks, balanced mutual funds (which own both stocks and bonds), and fixed annuities. Conservative investors want to preserve capital and earn a modest rate of return. Their goal is to have an after-tax, after-inflation return of perhaps 1 or 2 percent. They also tend to be focused more on current income (even if they reinvest it) than on capital gains.

Moderate-Risk Investors   Moderate-risk investors seek slow and steady growth in their nest egg through capital gains with modest current income that they tend to reinvest. They can tolerate a fair amount of risk of capital loss. People who are seeking moderate returns often invest in dividend-paying common stocks, growth and income mutual funds, high-quality corporate bonds, government bonds, variable annuities, and residential real estate. Retirees who have no immediate need for a portion of their nest egg can take this approach with those funds. They can accept modestly rising and falling market conditions because they have the time to endure the peaks and valleys.

Aggressive Investors   Aggressive investors seek out risk and focus primarily on capital gains. They know that riskier investments have the highest long-term rates of return, even though those rates can fluctuate from a negative 10 percent in some years to plus 20 percent or more in others. Aggressive investors choose growth stocks, growth stock mutual funds, stocks in new companies and new industries, and commercial real estate. Aggressive investors might focus on a single stock that they expect will rise in the short term. Or they might buy and hold a group of stocks that have good prospects but are currently out of favor. Aggressive investors often see weak markets as a time to buy and strong markets as a time to sell.

Speculative Investors   Speculative investors take a short-term approach to investing in order to capitalize on wild market swings. They are risk seekers. They invest in "junk" bonds, stock options, commodity futures, limited real estate partnerships, undeveloped land, gold, and collectibles. It is entirely possible for a speculative investor to lose all the money he or she has put into a particular investment. It is also possible for such an investor to double or even quadruple the money invested in a month or two.

Which Approach Works?   In one sense, all of these investors can be successful because each has different goals. You should focus on which approach works best for retirees like your parents. The answer depends on several factors:

1. Knowledgeable investors can be more aggressive. Novices need to be more conservative.
2. Active investors can be more aggressive. Those who do not want to spend much time on their investments need to be more conservative.
3. Investors can be more aggressive when they have a longer time horizon. Table 8.2 illustrates the links between risk tolerance, investment goals, and time horizons for various groups of investments chosen by investors.
4. Investors can apply different approaches to different segments of their portfolio. Smart investors take all four approaches simultaneously. They take more risk with a small portion of their portfolio and less risk with a larger share.

Portfolio: The investments owned by an individual or family.

Table 8.2 Realistic Investment Goals and Investment Types for Various Time Horizons

Time Horizon	Goals	Investment Types	Likely Negatives
Less than 2 years	Liquidity Steady value Predictable current income Moderate rates of return	Certificates of deposit Money market accounts or mutual funds Savings accounts Treasury bills	Low rates of return Inflation risk No growth of principal
2 to 7 years	Moderate rates of return Steady current income Steady growth of principal	Treasury notes Short-term bonds Income stocks Balanced mutual funds Long-term CDs Growth and income mutual funds Bond mutual funds	Little growth of principal Moderate current income Some inflation risk Some market swings
More than 7 years	Long-term growth in principal through capital gains Outstrip inflation	Index mutual funds Growth stocks/ mutual funds Real estate Long-term bonds	Volatile market swings Requires moderate to high-risk tolerance

Sources of Investment Risk

Investment risk takes two forms. The first is called *random* (or *unsystematic*) risk. This is the risk that any particular investment may do well or not so well because of matters intrinsic to itself. For example, if a company is not well managed or suffers labor unrest, its value will fall. If you invest in only that one stock, the value of your portfolio will also fall. However, if you invest in five or six different stocks, the odds that all of them will suffer the same fate at the same time are lower. Some of the companies will be well managed, and their stocks will rise in value. They will balance out the ones that decline. Emma Evans addressed random risk by diversifying across several stocks. Diversification is discussed more fully at the end of this chapter.

> **Diversification:** Reducing risk by spreading one's investment portfolio across multiple investments.

Liquidity risk and financial risk are examples of random risk. Liquidity risk results from the possibility that you may have to accept a lower price if you have to sell an asset quickly. Real estate is subject to liquidity risk. Financial risk is associated with the performance of a particular company or piece of real estate. For example, a corporation might experience financial difficulties and fail to pay dividends on its stock or interest on its bonds. Table 8.3 indicates the types of risk that characterize some of the more common classes of investments held by retirees.

Table 8.3 Types of Investments and Their Associated Risks

Type of Investment	Type of Risk				
	Inflation	Interest Rate	Financial	Market Volatility	Liquidity
CDs, money market funds	Moderate	Moderate	Low	N/A	Moderate (CDs)
Annuities	High	Low	Low	Low	N/A
High-rated bonds and bond mutual funds	High	High	Low	Moderate	Low
Stocks and stock mutual funds	Moderate	Moderate	Moderate to high	High	Low
Real estate	Low	Low	High	High	High

The second form of risk is called *market* (or *systematic*) risk. Market risk arises from outside of a particular investment and relates to an entire type or category of investment. Perhaps the economy is in a recession or interest rates are dropping, affecting the entire stock market. Perhaps investors fear that the stock market will decline soon and begin to sell, thereby reducing the market even further. This is what happened to Emma Evans. She put the bulk of her investments into stocks just when stocks were about to decline. Diversification is less effective in addressing market risk. However, it is possible to diversify across investment groups—by holding both stocks and bonds, for example. When stocks are depressed, bonds may be doing well, offsetting the stock declines. Emma failed to diversify in this way when she transferred her balanced mutual fund money into a stock fund.

Inflation risk, interest-rate risk, and market volatility risk are examples of systematic risk. Systematic risk can be further subdivided by its source. Inflation risk is the risk that an investment's return may be affected by inflation. Savings accounts are subject to inflation risk. Interest-rate risk results from possible up and down movements in interest rates in the economy. Bonds, certificates of deposit, savings accounts, and money market mutual funds are especially subject to interest-rate risk. Since retirees tend to invest in these lending investments, they are especially affected by interest-rate risk. The low interest rates of the early 2000s have been hard on retirees. Market volatility risk stems from the change in market prices for similar investments. Stocks are especially subject to market volatility risk, as the market goes up and down hourly.

Types of Investments

We mentioned earlier that investing can get very complicated very fast. One way to keep things straight is to recognize that you can invest money in two ways: by lending money and by owning assets. When you lend money, you receive some form of IOU and the promise of future interest income. Savings accounts, CDs, bonds, and money market mutual funds are all examples of lending investments. You are usually assured of current income when you make lending investments. But regardless of how much profit the borrower makes with your funds, you will earn only the promised interest.

When you own an investment asset, you typically own shares in it. You can buy common stock, buy shares in a mutual fund, put money into your own business, or purchase real estate. Owners have the potential for a substantial return because they typically share in the profits of the investment. But there are no promises. If the investment does not do well, the owners suffer.

> **Equities:** A term commonly used to describe ownership investments, especially stocks.

Both lending and ownership investments can meet your parents' needs. Lending investments tend to be more conservative on average because of the promise of interest income. However, there are some very risky lending investments and some very conservative ownership investments. Let's look in more detail at six classes of investments commonly held by retirees.

Stocks

When you own corporate stock, you own part of the company. Each share is a slice of the corporation's assets and a piece of its future profits. Stockholders expect that the corporation will be profitable enough to pay dividends (current income) and/or that the market price of a share of stock will increase (capital gains). Many stocks enjoy excellent liquidity and usually can be bought and sold quickly through a stockbroker.

Stocks can be classified according to the investment goals they meet. They can be divided into three basic groups. Income stocks are companies that are consistently profitable and tend to pay those profits out regularly in dividends. Growth stocks are companies that are also profitable but that retain their profits in the company in order to fuel expansion. They tend to generate capital gains through price appreciation. Speculative stocks are companies that are not currently profitable but that may become very profitable because they are in new and emerging markets. They are much riskier. Retirees tend to prefer income stocks to supplement their other income streams. People who are saving for retirement tend to prefer growth stocks.

Stocks can be further classified in a number of other ways.

Blue-Chip Stocks   The term *blue-chip stocks* is used to describe companies that are leaders in their industry and have a long history of strong earnings. Their shares are widely held. Examples include Dow Chemical, General Motors, Procter & Gamble, and Coca-Cola. Investing in such companies is considered much less risky than investing in other types of firms.

Value Stocks   Value stocks are stocks that are undervalued by most investors; thus, their current price makes them an investment bargain. Sometimes they are leaders in an industry that is going through hard times. For example, retail company stocks were down in the latter part of 2001. Yet Wal-Mart was seen as a good value because the company was doing well during that period.

Countercyclical Stocks   Some companies maintain substantial earnings during a recession. Such firms are considered countercyclical stocks, as they go against the economic cycle. For example, utility companies generally continue to have good earnings during periods of economic decline. During rising markets, the prices of these stocks tend to rise less quickly than those of cyclical stocks. Retirees who are interested in receiving current income regularly sometimes choose these stocks.

Brokerage Accounts

Emma Evans opened a discretionary account when she bought stocks with the funds from the sale of her home. This account gave her broker discretion to buy and sell securities on her behalf without her prior approval. Discretionary accounts are one of three types of accounts offered by brokerage firms. She could have opened a cash account by making an initial deposit of perhaps $200 and then placing buy and sell orders with her broker. She didn't feel comfortable doing that, so she relied on her broker's judgment. She also could have opened a margin account, which would have allowed her to borrow funds from her broker to buy shares.

Discretionary accounts are offered by full-service brokers, which not only transact purchases and sales but offer a full range of services to investors, including investment research reports and advice to individual investors. In the past 15 years many investors have chosen to use discount brokers, which focus on executing orders to buy and sell securities at a low cost and provide minimal additional services to investors. More recently, online brokers have become popular for their streamlined purchase and sale process and low fees. These latter two types of brokers are best used by sophisticated investors who can do their own investment research. Emma wisely chose a full-service broker, but she then turned over her decision making to the broker—an unwise move in her case.

Bonds

Bonds are the most common type of lending investment. The bond itself is basically an IOU. The initial purchaser of the bond lends money to the borrower, who, in return, makes two promises: to pay interest over the life of the bond, and to repay the investor's principal (usually $1,000) on the maturity date. At any point in time, the bondholder can sell the bond to another investor through a stockbroker. Corporate bonds are the most popular type of bond available to investors. Corporate bonds are simply a company's long-term debt.

It is the promise of regular (usually semiannual) interest payments that makes bonds attractive to retirees. When held to maturity, good-quality bonds have low risk. However, the market price of bonds does fluctuate. Consider a bond that had a 6 percent interest rate when it was issued. If interest rates in the economy are now 8 percent, the 6 percent bond will be less attractive to investors, and its market value will have declined. The bond will have dropped in value to the point where the interest to be paid based on the 6 percent rate will be equivalent to an 8 percent return. Of course, if interest rates have dropped to 4 percent, the 6 percent bond will be more attractive today. This is why bonds are subject to interest-rate risk. The market value of a bond increases when interest rates in the economy are declining and decreases when interest rates in the economy are rising.

Emma Evans made three mistakes when she transferred her balanced mutual fund holding to a stock fund. First, she did so when stock prices were at historically high levels. Therefore, she bought high. Second, when she sold her balanced fund, it contained bonds, at depressed prices. When stock prices are high, bond prices are generally low (because interest rates have generally been increasing). In other words, she sold low. Third, she gave up the regular interest income from her balanced fund.

Buying low and selling high are the keys to successful investing. Sadly, many inexperienced investors get in when the market is peaking and bail out when it nears bottom. Thus, they buy high and sell low. It takes courage to go against the prevailing tendencies.

Mutual Funds

Mutual funds are investment companies that sell shares to investors. An investment company does not sell goods and services to the public. It makes investments. Investing in mutual funds provides the investor with a diversified portfolio of stocks and/or bonds. A mutual fund's professional managers make its investment decisions. The managers choose a portfolio of investments that fits with the stated investment philosophy and objectives of the fund. All these factors serve to reduce but not eliminate risk. When Emma Evans sold her balanced fund shares and bought her stock fund shares, she went against her investment philosophy.

Like stocks, mutual funds pay dividends (usually quarterly). These dividends are made up of the dividends and interest the fund has earned on its investments and the capital gains it has earned from any investments it sold during the last dividend period. Unlike stocks, mutual funds do not retain earnings. All of their profits are paid out in dividends. Emma Evans was not receiving large dividend checks from her stock mutual fund. Corporate profits were low in 2001 and 2002, and the stock market was declining. Her mutual fund had little dividend and capital gain income to pay out to shareholders like Emma. Theoretically, Emma could earn capital gains from selling her shares. But because the stocks owned by the mutual fund have decreased in value, the value of the mutual fund shares has also decreased.

Many people think of IRAs and 401(k) plans as types of investments. However, they are simply types of accounts. You must still decide how to invest the funds involved. Mutual funds provide an excellent way to diversify their investments within these types of retirement accounts.

Mutual Fund Philosophy and Objectives   There are four basic investment philosophies and objectives used by mutual funds. They are listed here in order of increasing risk. Investors can read a fund's prospectus to see whether the fund's investment philosophy and objectives match their own investment philosophy and objectives.

Prospectus: A written disclosure document outlining a mutual fund's investment objectives, the experience of its management, its financial status, the securities it currently holds, and its historical success.

1. *An income objective.* A mutual fund that has an income objective focuses on paying a high level of dividends from the investments in its portfolio. Income funds invest in high-quality

corporate bonds and blue-chip income stocks. There is little growth in the mutual fund share price.

2. *A balanced objective.* Mutual funds with a balanced objective invest in a portfolio that is divided among stocks and bonds. They try to provide a flow of current income through dividends, but they also hold some stocks that are likely to grow in value. This will allow the market price of the mutual fund shares to increase and provide an opportunity for capital gains for the fund's investors. The managers of a balanced fund try to ensure that the market price of the shares maintains its value, thereby avoiding capital losses.

3. *A growth and income objective.* Mutual funds with a growth and income objective also invest in a portfolio that is balanced between stocks and bonds, but they place more emphasis on growth stocks. They may provide a flow of current income through dividends, but they put more emphasis on the opportunity for capital gains for the fund's investors. This means that there is an increased possibility of capital losses if an investor must sell shares when the mutual fund's share price is down.

4. *A growth objective.* A mutual fund with a growth objective emphasizes long-term growth in the value of the securities held in its portfolio rather than a flow of dividends. Such a fund buys and holds growth stocks, which in turn push up the mutual fund's share price. Such funds can provide a very good total return for the investor who is willing to accept more risk. That is because growth stocks have the highest average annual return of all stock investments over the long run, primarily from capital gains. Growth funds may be appropriate for investors who have sufficient income from other sources and longer time horizons.

Unique Features of Mutual Funds   There are several features of mutual funds that make them attractive to investors. Mutual funds allow automatic reinvestment of dividends to buy additional shares of the fund without paying any commissions. Shares in an open-end mutual fund can be bought and sold almost immediately simply by notifying the investment company, which will electronically transfer funds from one account to another or to or from another financial institution. Most mutual funds are part of a family of funds managed by the same investment company. Fund families allow their shareholders to transfer monies in one fund to another mutual fund managed by the same investment company. This switching privilege was used by Emma Evans to move her balanced fund holdings to a growth stock fund.

Types of Mutual Funds

There are thousands of different mutual funds available, so it is possible to find some fund that will fit almost every investor's needs. While funds are classified according to the four objectives described in the text, they are also identified by the types of securities held in their portfolios. Bond funds hold a portfolio of bonds and other investments, such as preferred stocks and common stocks that pay high dividends. Bond funds are generally low-risk, but some bond funds specialize in investing in riskier, high-yielding junk bonds. Municipal bond funds are available for those desiring tax advantages (see the discussion later in this chapter). Common stock funds invest mainly in corporate stocks. They can be either high- or low-risk funds depending on the risk associated with the common stocks that they hold. There are several types of common stock funds, including growth funds; aggressive growth funds; value funds, which invest in value stocks; large-, mid- and small-cap funds, which hold stock in companies of a particular size; and sector funds, which focus on a specific industry, such as automotive stocks. Index funds invest in the same stocks as one of the prominent stock indexes, such as the Dow Jones Industrial Average or Standard & Poor's 500 Index. Index funds track the market as a whole. Their management fees tend to be low because they do not require extensive management decision making. Global funds invest in stocks and/or bonds of multinational companies. Precious metals and gold funds invest in securities associated with gold, silver, and other precious metals.

One very low-risk type of mutual fund is the money market mutual fund. Money market mutual funds typically pay the highest rate of return that can be earned on a daily basis by small investors. These funds usually require a minimum deposit ranging from $1,000 to $5000. It is possible to write checks on the account. Electronic transfers are permitted, but not through automatic teller machines, because money market funds are not bank accounts. These funds are not insured by any federal agency, but they are virtually risk-free.

When you open a mutual fund account, you designate a beneficiary on the account. Should the account holder die, the fund ownership is automatically transferred to the beneficiary without going through probate (see Chapters 14 and 15). Most retirees who own mutual fund shares do so through tax-sheltered retirement accounts, such as IRAs and 401(k) plans. Such plans mesh well with mutual funds' periodic withdrawal plans. Investors can take money out of a mutual fund by using one of five methods: (1) by taking a set dollar amount each month, (2) by cashing in a set number of shares each month, (3) by taking the current income as cash, (4) by taking a portion of the asset growth, or (5) by simply taking a withdrawal of any size at any time. Emma Evans had elected method 3 and has seen her income drop, as the stocks in her stock fund have been doing poorly. If she switched to method 1 or 2 to boost her income, she would have to start eroding her portfolio just when share prices are low.

The Costs of Investing

Brokerage firms receive a commission on each stock or bond transaction. The commission rate declines as the total value of the transaction increases. Emma Evans's broker received a commission each time he executed a trade on her account.

The costs of investing in mutual funds are more complicated. All mutual funds charge an annual management fee to compensate the fund's managers; this is built into the price of the fund's shares. Many funds charge a sales commission, called a front-end load, when shares are purchased. These load funds tend to be sold through stockbrokers or by financial planners. Front-end loads can be as high as 8.5 percent of the amount of the purchase. No-load funds charge no sales commission, as they are sold directly by the mutual fund company by phone or over the Internet. Some mutual funds may also charge a fee (often called a back-end load) when shares are sold back to the fund company. These redemption charges phase out over time, usually by the end of 6 years.

Many funds charge a 12b-1 fee annually to pay for advertising and marketing the fund. These annual charges directly affect the yield from the fund. No-load funds tend to have higher 12b-1 fees to pay for their higher marketing costs. A fund with a 12b-1 fee of 2 percent and an advertised yield of 8 percent would have an actual yield of 6 percent.

There are no hard and fast rules about which types of funds to purchase. What really matters is the fund's performance. Short-term investors should be wary of load funds and funds with redemption charges. Long-term investors should be concerned with a fund's 12b-1 fee, which can add up over time.

Government Securities

The U.S. government issues a number of securities that can be divided into two general groups: (1) Treasury issues and (2) federal agency issues. These securities really represent loans to the U.S. Treasury or other government agency. The interest rates on federal government securities are lower than those on corporate bonds, but they are virtually risk-free, and the interest income is exempt from state and local income taxes. You may purchase U.S. securities directly from the government, through banks, or through brokerage firms.

Treasury securities include Treasury bills, notes, and bonds. Treasury bills, also called T-bills, mature in 13 weeks (3 months) or 26 weeks (6 months). They are sold at a discount from their face amount, and the difference between the purchase price and the T-bill's value at maturity represents the interest. U.S. Treasury notes are issued with 2-, 3-, 5-, and 10-year maturities; they pay interest semiannually. Treasury bonds are long-term U.S. government securities that have a maturity period of 11 to 30 years or more. Interest is paid semiannually. Treasury notes and bonds are popular with retirees because of their safety and their regular interest payments.

In addition to these Treasury issues, more than 100 different securities are issued by various federal agencies. Agency issues are not as widely known and often pay a yield that is 0.5 to 1.5 percentage points higher than comparable-term Treasury securities. They are still extremely safe.

Municipal Bonds

Municipal bonds are certificates of long-term debt issued by state and local government entities. The funds are used to build roads, office buildings, airports, sewage systems, and other civic projects. Interest on municipal bonds is exempt from federal income tax. As a result, municipal bonds almost always pay a lower interest rate than other bonds. Nonetheless, if your parents' marginal tax rate is above 27 percent, it may make sense for them to invest in municipal bonds. You would need to calculate the after-tax return on a taxable bond to make the comparison. To do so you can multiply the return on the taxable bond by 1 minus the marginal tax rate. For example, a taxable bond paying 8 percent to a taxpayer in the 30 percent tax bracket would be 5.6 percent after taxes (8 percent × 1 − .30). In general, the higher your federal tax rate, the more favorable municipal bonds become as an investment compared with taxable bonds. Capital gains on the sale of municipal bonds are taxable. Retirees often hold bonds to maturity, however, minimizing the impact of capital gains. Also, recall from Chapter 6 that the maximum federal income tax rate on long-term capital gains is only 20 percent. Further, most states exempt from state income taxes the interest earned from municipal bonds issued by their own state and municipalities. High-income taxpayers who earn a substantial portion of their income from municipal bond interest may be subject to the alternative minimum tax and should consult a qualified tax adviser for guidance.

Annuities

Many retirees use annuities to generate retirement income. Annuities combine the principles of investment and insurance. They are an investment prior to the onset of the periodic payments. They are insurance once the payments begin. This is because the annuity can be set up to guarantee the payments no matter how long the recipient may live. In a sense, annuities are the opposite of life insurance. Life insurance provides financial protection against dying too soon. Annuities provide protection against outliving one's income.

> **Annuity:** A contract made with an insurance company that provides for a series of payments to be received at stated intervals (usually monthly) for a fixed or variable time period.

Variations of Annuities Annuities may be classified as either immediate or deferred. The deferred annuity builds up funds prior to retirement. Workers, or their employers through a retirement account, pay premiums to an insurance company, which invests the money. Once the annuity begins providing a stream of payments, the annuitant (the person receiving the annuity) can live off the money, often for the remainder of his or her life.

An immediate annuity is another retirement income tool. With an immediate annuity, the retiree deposits funds into the annuity account and asks that payments begin at the end of the first month or year after payment of the premium. For example, Emma Evans could have used a portion of the proceeds of the sale of her home to buy an annuity that would provide her with a stream of income for the rest of her life. Immediate annuities are also often used as a place to put the proceeds of a life insurance policy (see Chapter 9) or a lump-sum pension plan distribution. Some annuities pay a fixed interest rate and therefore make a fixed monthly payment. Others, called variable annuities, pay a variable rate of return and thus have variable monthly payments. The annuitant usually has several choices as to how the funds in a variable annuity are invested by the insurance company. Annuities, especially fixed annuities, often pay a low rate of return. But they are low-risk ways to provide income.

Annuity Payout Options There are five types of annuity payment schemes. The simplest kind of annuity is a *straight-life annuity,* which pays a monthly amount until the annuitant dies. If the annuitant dies after only 10 months, the contract ends and payments cease. If the annuitant lives well beyond the average life expectancy, payments will continue unaffected. Thus, an annuity can serve as protection against your parents' outliving their assets. An annuity can also be written as a joint and survivor annuity. As such, it will pay proceeds until the death of the annuitant and one surviving beneficiary, often a husband or wife.

Many people do not like straight-life annuities because the payments could cease after only a short period of time. They can choose a *guaranteed annuity,* of which there are three basic types. Installment-certain annuities can be set up to guarantee a minimum number of payments, even if the annuitant dies before that number of payments has been made. A cash-refund annuity pays a beneficiary a lump sum if the annuitant dies before collecting at least the premium paid. Or, a period-certain annuity can be set up to guarantee payments for a specified period of time, at the end of which payments will cease. With such a plan, it would be possible for your parents to outlive their income. Once payments begin, the annuitant cannot change the pattern of payments from straight-life to a guaranteed annuity or even among the three types of guaranteed annuities.

Using Annuities for Retirement Income Annuities can provide peace of mind because one knows that one's income will not run out, or, at least, will last a specified period of time. That is why they are attractive to retirees. Like all investments, however, they need to be clearly understood. For example, compared to growth stocks, annuities do not have high rates of return. However, they are safer. Annuities also may have front-end loads and administrative expenses like some mutual funds. It is difficult to compare the rate of return promised by an annuity with that for other investment alternatives. Federal regulations require that every prospectus for a variable annuity include a table outlining the costs associated with the purchase of that annuity.

Real Estate

Retirees invest in real estate for both economic and noneconomic reasons. Some like the feeling of being closely involved with their investments and the pride and satisfaction associated with owning property.

But the ultimate goal of investing in real estate is economic—the maximization of positive after-tax returns.

Real estate investments have three advantages: the possibility of a positive cash flow, the potential for capital gains, and a number of special tax treatments. But there are disadvantages as well. Real estate investments require large initial investments, can be time-consuming to manage, may provide low current income streams, have unpredictable costs, and may be difficult to sell.

Managing Your Parents' Portfolio

Diversify, diversify, diversify is the three-word mantra of all investment advisers. It is good advice, whether you are investing for retirement or investing during retirement. The question is, diversify in what? Table 8.2 suggests a partial answer. You want to diversify according to the time horizon for your investments. Funds that will be needed within 3 years should not be "invested" at all. Instead, they should be in liquid alternatives such as savings accounts, money market mutual funds, or certificates of deposit. CDs can be laddered so that they mature as the funds are needed.

The remainder of the portfolio can be diversified according to your parents' investment risk tolerance, net worth, and need for current income. Table 8.4 provides suggested portfolios for conservative, moderate, and aggressive retired investors. Note that the liquid funds are not included in these illustrations. Thus, the overall portfolios will be more conservative than Table 8.4 indicates. Retirees may want to be more conservative than younger investors.

A similar approach is an investment technique called asset allocation. It takes diversification one step further by providing a technique for periodically adjusting the portfolio so that it stays within one's risk tolerance and the desired allocations among various types of investments are maintained. Figure 8.1 illustrates asset allocation proportions for various investors. In Figure 8.1, a conservative investor might set allocations of 50 percent cash equivalents, 30 percent bonds, and 20 percent stocks. Over time, these allocations will change whenever one of these categories has better success than the others. Let's say that stocks have gone up recently. The proportion of the portfolio that is in stocks will go up relative to the proportions that are in bonds and cash equivalents. Asset allocation requires that the investor reallocate the portfolio to the original proportions annually. To do so, our conservative investor would sell stocks and buy bonds or put money in cash equivalents. The magic of asset allocation lies in the periodic reallocations. The investor will be selling high and buying low. Maintaining the balance is the key.

Table 8.4 Portfolios Diversified According to Risk Tolerance

	Percentage of Total Assets		
	Conservative	**Moderate**	**Aggressive**
Real estate	0%	10%	30%
Growth stocks or mutual funds	10%	15%	30%
Blue-chip stocks or mutual funds	15%	20%	25%
Balanced mutual funds	15%	20%	5%
Quality long-term bonds or bond funds	20%	15%	10%
CDs and money market funds	40%	20%	10%

Asset allocation: Dividing an investment portfolio into preset proportions of stocks (or stock mutual funds), bonds (or bond funds), and cash equivalents, with periodic adjustments made to maintain the predetermined proportions over time.

Figure 8.1 Asset Allocation Illustrated

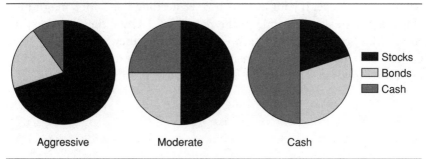

| Aggressive | Moderate | Cash |

Emma Evans's investment portfolio simply does not reflect her investment philosophy. Nor is it diversified. The damage has been done, and there is no point in throwing good money after bad. Jerome can help her by establishing an appropriate asset allocation pattern, then selling stocks and using the proceeds for bonds and cash equivalents.

When Should You Sell an Investment?

Savvy investors understand that knowing when to sell an investment is just as important as knowing when to buy. There are several rules of thumb that you can use to guide your thinking. First, you should consider selling when you have reached your goal for an investment. Perhaps when you bought a stock, you projected that it would go up 25 percent in 2 years, and it has done so. Yes, it may go up even more. But it could drop as well. Stay with it only if you can realistically project gains for the next 2 years. Second, cut your losses quickly. If an investment is doing poorly and is likely to continue to do so, get out. Have the courage to admit that your initial projections were in error. Third, when assessing an investment, ask yourself if you would put more into it if you had extra money to invest. If not, sell it.

Final Thoughts

Retired investors need to be more conservative than younger investors. Nonetheless, younger retirees will need funds for 15 to 25 years into the future. Depending on your parents' age, health status (reflecting life expectancy), income, and wealth level, they may be able to accept more risk. It is also important to consider your parents' sources of income and level of monthly expenses (see Chapter 4). Those with sufficient income for day-to-day spending from pensions and social security can afford to be more aggressive. If your parents foresee needing funds for a major purchase such as an automobile in the next 1 to 3 years, they would want to have additional funds in cash equivalents. As they spend down their cash equivalents for current expenses, they will want to sell stocks, bonds, or mutual funds to replenish the cash equivalent portion of their portfolio.

9

Life Insurance

*B*ill Cargill's father, Jim, passed away 2 weeks ago at the age *of 73. The last few months were emotionally stressful as Bill, his sister, Carol, and his mother, Susan, age 68, focused on his dad's care. Early on, his father had assured Bill that he and Bill's mother had plenty of life insurance. In fact, they had bought several policies in the last 10 years to go along with others they had purchased throughout their marriage. Yesterday, Bill asked Susan about the insurance. She said she wasn't sure of the details, but all the policies were in a drawer. Jack started to go through the papers and found seven policies. It appeared at first that Jim had about $170,000 in life insurance. But as Bill read through the policies, he became more and more confused. Some of the policies covered Jim's life, and some covered Susan's. Two of them appeared to insure both lives. Jim, Bill, Susan, and Carol were all named as beneficiaries on specific policies. Bill knew that he needed to start on making claims against the policies, but he was unsure of where to begin.*

THERE IS AN OLD SAYING that life insurance isn't bought, it is sold. People don't seek life insurance. Someone sells it to them. As a result, people often buy a disjointed set of policies that do not meet their needs. They may have the wrong amount of insurance or the wrong policy features. Jim and Susan Cargill had just that sort of life insurance plan. The individual pieces made some sense, but they were not well coordinated.

This chapter will help you understand your parents' life insurance policies and provide tools for shaping a life insurance program that makes sense at their ages. We begin with an overview of the major types of life insurance, using the Cargills' policies as examples. Then we show how you can take an inventory of the life insurance policies that your parents currently have. From there we will look at the need for life insurance during retirement years. Finally, we will address specific life insurance policy features that are important to retirees.

The Basic Forms of Life Insurance

In addition to their personal grief, survivors may experience severe financial losses. The purpose of life insurance is to provide survivors with a sum of money. Life insurance does this simply and efficiently.

In many ways, life insurance is the simplest form of insurance. You buy a policy for a specific face amount of coverage, say $50,000. If you die while the policy is in effect, your beneficiary receives the face amount (or close to it). There is little debate over the dollar amount of the insurance benefit, as there might be after a house fire. And death is the only peril involved.

Several parties are named in a life insurance policy. The *insured* is the person whose life is insured. Generally, life insurance policies cover the life of this one individual. The *owner* (or *policyholder*) controls the policy and can amend or change it according to the terms of the contract. If the owner of a policy on another person's life dies first, the ownership transfers to his or her heirs, not to the insured or the beneficiary. The *beneficiary* is the person or organization who will receive the benefit payment upon the insured person's death. A *contingent beneficiary* can be named to become the beneficiary if the original beneficiary dies before the insured. Sometimes the same person fills more than one of these roles, but it is possible for four different people to be named.

It is also possible to cover two (or more) persons with one policy. First-to-die policies pay the face amount when the first insured dies. The coverage then expires. Jim and Susan had a first-to-die policy for $10,000. An alternative is a survivorship joint life policy, which pays when the second person dies. They also had a survivorship policy for $50,000 that will remain in effect as long as Susan chooses to pay the premium.

Although insurance companies put fancy names on their policies, there are really only two types of life insurance: term insurance and cash-value insurance. All other forms are variations of one of these two basic types of life insurance. Term insurance is bought for a specific period of time, such as 1 year, 5 years, or 10 years. It must be renewed at the expiration of that period in order to maintain coverage. Cash-value life insurance is designed to be permanent. It does not have to be renewed each year; it stays in effect as long as the required premiums are paid. It also has an investment feature that allows for "cash values" to build up. These can be tapped prior to the death of the insured person. Because of its investment aspect, many people automatically feel that it is the better option. However, cash-value life insurance costs significantly more than term insurance at its inception and is not necessarily the best investment or insurance option available.

Term Life Insurance

Term life insurance is often called pure protection because it focuses solely on providing a cash benefit to the beneficiary upon the death of the insured person. When the insurance is renewed at the end of each term, the premium increases according to the age of the insured person. If the person has a health problem, he or she may be denied a renewal policy or have to pay even higher premiums. However, term policies can be written as "guaranteed renewable." This means that the premium will go up on the basis of age and not because of health-related concerns. Jim and Susan's two $50,000 term insurance policies are 10-year policies taken out about 9 years ago. They are guaranteed renewable, and Susan could renew hers next year at a new premium of $445 per year for another 10 years. With Jim's passing, Susan will receive approximately $50,000 from his term insurance policy.

> **Term insurance:** Insurance that pays benefits only if the insured person dies during the policy's term.

Cash-Value Life Insurance

Cash-value life insurance pays benefits upon the death of the insured, but it also has an investment element that allows the payment of benefits prior to death. The annual premiums for cash-value policies usually remain constant, but they are always higher initially than the premiums for term policies that provide the same amount of coverage. This is because only a portion of the premium is used to provide the death benefit; the remainder is used to build the cash value.

> **Cash-value insurance:** Insurance that pays benefits at the death of the insured and has a savings account/investment feature that can be accessed during life.

The cash value belongs to the owner of the policy and not the beneficiary (unless, of course, they are the same person). While the insured is alive, the owner may obtain the cash value by borrowing a portion of it from the insurance company or by surrendering the policy. At death, the face amount goes to the beneficiary. The face amount includes the cash value. It is rare for the cash value to grow beyond the face amount of a policy.

The life insurance market is highly competitive. Always shop around for the best premium and return on your investment. Web sites such as www.insquote.com and www.lifequote.com can be a big help in this regard.

The rate at which the cash values accumulate in a policy depends on the rate of return earned on the funds invested. Most cash-value policies have a guaranteed minimum rate of return of 2 to 5 percent. Some types of cash-value insurance, such as variable life insurance, pay a "current return" that varies with the success of the investments the insurance company makes. All of Jim and Susan's cash-value policies have built up some cash value. Since Jim's passing, the cash values in his policies are no longer relevant. But Susan "owns" the $29,000 ($11,000 + $18,000) cash value in the two policies that remain on her life.

Cash-value life insurance can be set up so that the owner can stop paying premiums and still continue the coverage. These so-called limited-pay life insurance policies carry a higher premium while the premiums are being paid to reflect the fact that the premiums will cease. Paid-up policies continue to accumulate cash values, but at a slower rate because a portion of future accumulations goes to pay the premiums that are no longer being paid. The $100,000 policy on Jim's life was such a policy.

Participating Policies

Both cash-value and term policies may be written as participating policies that pay insurance dividends, although term policies are less likely to do so. These dividends reflect the difference between the premium charged for the policy and the actual cost to the company of providing the insurance.[1] Policies that do not pay dividends are called nonparticipating policies. These dividends usually remain with the insurance company to earn interest. They can grow to significant amounts over the long term. Jim's $100,000 policy is a participating policy and has accumulated $6,000 in dividends, including interest.

Participating policies: Insurance policies that pay dividends, which can accumulate.

---

[1]Insurance dividends are not considered taxable income. The IRS has ruled that they are simply refunds for overpayment. The interest income on the dividends is considered to be taxable income, however.

The Life Insurance Inventory

Bill's first task was to figure out what life insurance coverage his parents had. He developed the life insurance inventory shown in Worksheet 9.1. This inventory outlines the types of policies each of his parents had, the dollar amount of coverage, the owner, the beneficiary, the current cash value, the annual premium, and comments about the policy. Based on the inventory, the policies will pay approximately $180,000 to Jim's beneficiaries.

A life insurance inventory will be a valuable asset for you as you address your parents' life insurance situation. An inventory should be completed for each parent. The information you will need is readily available in the insurance policy on its "declarations" pages. You can also contact the insurance agent or the company for information. You will want to ask the agent for an "in-force" illustration to determine the current and projected cash value accumulations. Because of privacy constraints, you will need to work through the owner of the policy in order to get this information.

Worksheet 9.1 Life Insurance Inventory—Jim and Susan Cargill

Life Covered	Policy Type	Face Amount	Owner/ Bene- ficiary	Cash Value + Dividends	Premium	Comments
Jim	Term	$50,000	Jim/Susan	N/A	$475/yr.	Expires next year
Susan	Term	$50,000	Susan/Jim	N/A	$395/yr.	Expires next year Renewal for $445 per year
Jim	Cash value	$20,000	Jim/Susan	$12,000	$412/yr.	Purchased 35 years ago Nonparticipating
Susan	Cash value	$20,000	Jim/Jim	$11,000	$336/yr.	Purchased 35 years ago
Jim	Cash value	$100,000	Susan/ Susan	$38,000 + $6,000	Paid up	Purchased 40 years ago $3,000 policy loan Participating policy
Jim and Susan	Cash value	$10,000	Jim/survivor	$1,400	$290/yr.	First-to-die policy Purchased 8 years ago Nonparticipating
Jim and Susan	Cash value	$50,000	Susan/Bill and Carol	$18,000	$780/yr.	Survivorship policy Purchased 22 years ago

What to Look for in a Policy Illustration

Policy illustrations can be very helpful for understanding a cash-value insurance policy. But they can be written to make the policy look better than it really is. Ask the following questions about the "in-force" illustration you receive on your parents' policies:

1. What were the current rates of return for each of the last 5 years? The current rate is usually the rate paid by the company in a calendar year.
2. What assumptions regarding company expenses and dividend rates were used? If expenses are underestimated and dividend rates are overestimated, the cash-value build-up will be unrealistically high. You can ask for the actual expenses and dividend rates for the past few years to compare to the assumptions used.
3. Does the current rate apply to the entire cash value? Often it does not. If it does not, then the true current rate will be lower than that illustrated.
4. Does the illustration show the cash value or the cash surrender value? The cash surrender value reflects what will actually be paid if the policy is cashed in.

Collecting the Death Benefits on a Policy

Once Bill had developed the inventory of his parents' life insurance policies, he helped his mother make claims against the policies on Jim's life. The claims process for life insurance is much the same as that for any insurance claim. The beneficiary must notify the insurance company, provide proof of loss, and request payment. The death certificate for the deceased provides proof of loss and will be provided by the funeral director within a few days after death. When the claim is filed, the insurance company will consult the policy to determine the dollar amount to pay. This process usually takes a week or two, so Susan could receive checks fairly quickly.

There are two main questions that will come up in the claims process for life insurance. The first relates to the exact amount of the payment. Recall that policies have a face amount that serves as the base for this determination. There are certain additions and subtractions that will be made to determine the actual death benefit. The second question relates to the form in which the death benefit is paid. Of course, Susan could simply request a check from the insurance company. But there are several other options that may be attractive to her.

Calculating the Death Benefit

The death benefit of a life insurance policy is the amount that will be paid upon the death of the insured person. Contrary to common belief, the death benefit of a life insurance policy is not taxable income for the beneficiary. Once the death benefit has been paid, however, the income from the death benefit (e.g., interest from a bank account) becomes taxable.

The amount of the death benefit may be higher or lower than the face amount of a policy. Additions may be made because of such items as accumulated dividends or premiums paid in advance and interest from the date of death until the payout date. Reductions will be made for outstanding policy loans or unpaid premiums. Let's consider Jim's $100,000 participating whole-life policy. This policy had an outstanding cash-value loan of $3,000 and accumulated dividends of $6,000. The death benefit would be $103,000, calculated as follows:

$100,000	Face amount
+ 6,000	Unpaid dividends
$106,000	Subtotal
− 3,000	Outstanding cash-value loan
$103,000	Death benefit

A similar calculation will be made for each of the other policies on Jim's life.

Settlement Options

Susan will have several choices, called *settlement options,* regarding the payment of the death benefit from Jim's policies. Usually, the owner indicates a preferred settlement option when taking out a policy. But the beneficiary is usually free to select another option after the death of the insured. There are five settlement options. Options 2 through 5 involve leaving the death benefit on deposit with the insurance company. They are very similar to the various types of annuities discussed in Chapter 8, "Your Parents' Investments." We will use the $103,000 death benefit calculated here as an example to illustrate the settlement options.

> **Settlement options:** The choices the beneficiary has regarding payment of the death benefit.

1. Take the death benefit as a lump sum. Susan would simply request payment and the insurance company would send her a $103,000 check for the death benefit.

2. Take interest income. In this case, Susan would receive interest payments from the insurance company. If the company paid 4 percent interest, for example, Susan would receive $4,120 each year from the $103,000 death benefit. The $103,000 death benefit would not be touched and would continue to earn interest until Susan's death, when it would become part of her estate and would be payable to her heirs. At any point, Susan can switch to the lump-sum option or options 3 through 5.

3. Take income for life. Susan will receive an income for the remainder of her life. The insurance company will base the amount of the income on Susan's remaining life expectancy and the rate of return on the funds. (We used 4 percent for these examples.) This option would prevent Susan from outliving the income. Because payments will cease at her death, there will be no funds remaining to pass on to her heirs. A 68-year-old female can expect to live approximately 16 more years. Based on that figure, Susan can expect annual annuity payments of approximately $8,800. If she expects to live longer than average, she might find this option attractive.

4. Take income for a specified period of time. Susan could elect to receive an annual income for a specified number of years. The insurance company would calculate the level of income that would allow for equal proceeds to be paid each year. For example, Susan might want to receive an income for 12 years, or until she reaches age 80. If the insurance company pays 4 percent interest on the funds, she could expect an annual income of approximately $10,950 per year. At the end of 12 years, all funds, including interest, will be exhausted. Should Susan die before the end of the specified time period, a designated beneficiary would receive the remaining payments. Should Susan live longer than 12 years, her payments would stop after 12 years. In this scenario, she could outlive her income.

5. Take a specific amount of income. Susan could choose a specific amount of income to receive per year from the death benefit. For example, she might choose to receive $15,000 per year from the policy. If the insurance company pays 4 percent interest, she would receive the income for a little over 8 years. Payments stop when the death benefit and interest are exhausted.

Should Susan die before the fund is exhausted, a designated beneficiary would receive the remaining payments. Again, with this option, Susan could outlive her income.

Susan will need to make similar choices for each of the policies on Jim's life that names her as beneficiary. She does not have to make the same choice on each policy. She could use the $103,000 policy to provide a stream of income and take the lump-sum payments from the other policies and invest them elsewhere.

Estimating the Need for Life Insurance

Life insurance is not the most exciting topic. Most people do not want to think and talk about death. And life insurance can get complicated. However, it helps to focus on the reason that life insurance is so important. Simply put, life insurance allows people to meet their families' financial needs after death. What are those financial needs?

Life insurance needs vary over the life cycle. Because no one else depends on their income for economic survival, children and single adults have very little need for life insurance. Marriage normally involves financial responsibility for another person. Having children triggers a sharp increase in life insurance needs. As their children grow older, parents see a reduced need for life insurance. Once the children become independent, the need declines further. Retirement and widowhood reduce the need for life insurance even further and may even eliminate it altogether.

Needs That Occur after Death

Life insurance needs can vary from nothing to more than $1 million. These potential needs include paying final expenses, replacing the lost income of the deceased, repaying debts, and other needs.

Final Expense Needs   Final expense needs include the costs of the funeral and the burial and related expenses. The typical funeral and burial today cost $7,000 to $8,000. Many people would like to pay family members' travel expenses so that they can attend the funeral. Likewise, food and lodging expenses for mourners are often substantial. Other severe and costly disruptions of family life can last up to a month or more. Bill and Susan will want to have a serious discussion of her final expense needs. Susan does not want to burden her children either financially or emotionally with these decisions after her death.

> Taking out a new life insurance policy is an expensive way to provide for funeral and burial expenses for the elderly. Consider prepaying these expenses from other assets.

Income-Replacement Needs   During a family's child-rearing years, the loss of a breadwinner's income is the major financial loss resulting from death. For retirees, reduced social security and pension benefits can result in a loss of income. Salary income will be lost if the retiree was still working part-time. If your parents are married, the surviving spouse is likely to see a reduction in income. Susan will probably have less income after Jim's death. Her monthly social security check will be reduced. Income from Jim's pension may decrease. Fortunately, Jim had life insurance that can help replace that income. If your parents are single or widowed, income loss will be an issue only if they are providing support for others, such as a disabled child or an elderly parent. Susan is now a widow, and no one else is dependent on her income. Income replacement will not be a large consideration in determining her need for life insurance.

You can use Table 9.1 to estimate the amount of life insurance needed to replace a given amount of income. Let's assume that Susan's income will drop by $4,000 per year after Jim's death. Also assume that the death benefit from a life insurance policy on Jim could be invested to earn a 4 percent rate of return. If Jim wanted to replace the income for 10 years, he would have needed $32,440 in life insurance (8.11 from Table 9.1 × $4,000).

Table 9.1 Generating a Stream of Income—Life Insurance Needs

Multiply the amount of annual income by the table figure corresponding to the number of years that the funds will be needed and the rate of return that can be earned from investing the life insurance death benefit.

Years of Income Desired	Rate of Return on Invested Funds			
	2%	4%	6%	8%
5	4.71	4.45	4.21	3.99
10	8.98	8.11	7.36	6.71
15	12.85	11.12	9.71	8.56
20	16.35	13.59	11.47	9.82
25	19.52	15.62	12.78	10.67

Debt-Repayment Needs   Many people want to use the proceeds of their life insurance to pay off various debts at their death. In reality, debts can be repaid if there has been adequate provision for the replacement of lost income. Many families also want to pay off mortgage debts. That may not be the wisest course of action. Mortgage loans are among the lowest-cost loans available, especially considering the tax deductibility of mortgage interest. It might be better to pay off higher-APR loans and adequately replace lost income. Replacing the income stream will provide the funds needed to make the mortgage payments.

Paying off credit card debts, auto loans, and other personal debts can make life easier for survivors. Fortunately, Susan has little debt outstanding. Her home and car are paid for, and she carries only a small balance on one credit card. This pattern is traditional for people in her life-cycle stage. Unfortunately, the debt burdens of retirees have gone up in recent years, so debt repayment may be a consideration when addressing your parents' life insurance needs. However, debt repayment may not be an issue for a single or widowed parent because the estate will pay the debt or, if the estate is inadequate, the creditor will assume the defaulted sum.

Individualized Needs   Many families have special needs that must be considered in the life insurance planning process. Wealthier families might want extra life insurance to pay federal estate and state inheritance taxes (covered in Chapter 15). A family with a disabled adult child might need to replace income for the remainder of the *child's* life. Many people want to pass money on to their heirs or to charities and see life insurance as a mechanism for accomplishing that goal. This will be a tough area for Susan and Bill to discuss because it involves Bill's own financial future. Should Susan use life insurance to provide an inheritance for Bill and Carol, and possibly their children?

What Resources Can Meet Those Needs?

Before deciding whether to keep existing insurance or how much additional life insurance, if any, your parents might need, it is necessary to look at existing resources that might cover losses after the death of a family member. Existing life insurance, financial assets, and social security and other government benefits may partially offset those losses.

Existing Insurance   Most people of retirement age have some life insurance, and this can reduce the need for additional life insurance purchases. Susan has three policies on her life that total $120,000. Her term policy will be up for renewal next year. The other two policies are permanent. One of these policies names Bill and Carol as beneficiaries, thereby providing them with an inheritance. She pays a total of $1,116 per year for her permanent insurance, and her term policy premium will be $415 should she choose to renew it.

Be wary of life insurance that is targeted specifically to the elderly, especially through television advertising. Often, these advertisements mention no level of insurance coverage but promise that "you cannot be turned down." Talk to four or five companies.

Existing Assets   As time passes, families usually acquire some savings and investments. In the event of a family member's death, these could be used to meet final expenses as well as to replace lost income. Many families are reluctant to spend down the assets that took them years to accumulate. But life insurance can be expensive for retirees, and cash-value policies may pay low rates of return. If your parents are married, they can consider their existing assets as resources for the surviving spouse. If they are single or widowed, they will have to consider whether they want the assets to cover their final expenses and debts when they die or to be left untouched to pass on to heirs. These issues are difficult because children have a vested interest in their parents' decisions.

Government Benefits   Retirees usually qualify for some type of government benefit. Social security is the most obvious. Many of today's retirees also qualify for veterans' retirement benefits based on military service all the way back to World War II. Married couples must consider the impact on those benefits of the death of one of the spouses.

Social security retirement benefits are based on the lifetime income of a breadwinner. The social security benefits of unmarried retirees will cease with their death unless they have dependent children or parents. Thus, this income is lost and will not be available to meet life insurance needs after their death. This is usually not a problem, as most unmarried retirees do not support others.

The situation is more complicated for married couples. Each spouse qualifies for benefits based on his or her own work history. If one spouse's benefit is less than 50 percent of the other's, however, he or she may take a spousal benefit of 50 percent of the spouse's benefit rather than the benefit based on his or her own work history. Most of today's retired couples had one primary breadwinner, with the other spouse (usually the wife) providing homemaking services for the family. The result is that most married women of retirement age collect social security benefits based on their husband's account rather than their own. As a result, the couple receives a total monthly retirement benefit of approximately 150 percent of the husband's benefit amount. When one spouse dies, the survivor will see his or her benefit drop by one-third, to 100 percent of the husband's benefit amount. This is the situation that Susan will face now that Jim has passed away.

The situation is similar but more dramatic for couples where both are collecting off their own work history. In such cases, the spouse with the lower benefit is receiving a benefit that is greater than 50 percent of the other spouse's benefit. When the first spouse dies, the benefit again drops to 100 percent of the higher benefit. However, the percentage decrease could be as great as one-half of the couple's benefits.

Veterans' benefits are affected in a similar but more dramatic way because a surviving spouse's benefits are even lower. When the veteran, usually a male, passes away, the widow's benefit is approximately one-third of the veteran's benefit. Add this to the reduction in social security benefits and you can see that the impact of a husband's death on a surviving widow can be significant.

The Bottom Line

Susan's need for life insurance focuses on four areas: her funeral and burial costs, income loss when she dies, repayment of her debts, and her desire to leave money to her five grandchildren. Susan wants to have sufficient resources for her funeral and burial costs. She estimates these costs to be about $10,000. Because no one is dependent upon her for income, she is not worried about income replacement. She does have some credit card debt, but that debt can be paid out of her estate, so she does not need life insurance to cover debts. She does want to leave each of her grandchildren $10,000 to help them with college expenses or to buy their first home. Thus, Susan has a total need for about $60,000 in protection. She has $120,000 in life insurance currently and can continue that level of coverage for another 11 years if she renews her term policy. She is adequately insured; in fact, she may have too much life insurance. How might she restructure her program? To answer that question, we need to discuss some additional features of life insurance.

Your Parents' Life Insurance Program

Designing a life insurance program for your parents is both similar to and different from designing such a program for younger people. It is similar because the *types* of economic losses that are likely to occur (final expenses, lost income, debt repayment, and special needs) and the *types* of resources (existing insurance, existing assets, and government benefits) are the same across the life cycle. But they differ in terms of the specifics. In particular, your parents will have a reduced need for income replacement. In addition, they may have more existing assets to cover losses and therefore will need less life insurance to do so. Each family must look at its own situation.

You must also decide whether life insurance needs will be met with term or cash-value insurance. Term insurance is best for those periods of time when the dollar amount of insurance needed is high. It is less expensive than cash-value insurance at its inception, and when the need drops, the policy can simply be allowed to expire. This is why it is highly recommended for people in their child-rearing years. Cash-value life insurance is best when the amount needed will be consistent over the life of the insured. Final expense needs and the funds to provide for heirs stay relatively consistent and can be met with cash-value life insurance. Let's look more closely at cash-value life insurance.

Tapping the Cash Value

Susan Cargill has $18,000 in cash value built up in her $50,000 cash-value policy. She could tap these funds by applying the policy's nonforfeiture options. Like most cash-value policies, Susan's policy gives her four options.

> **Nonforfeiture options:** The choices available to a policyholder who no longer wishes or can no longer afford to keep a cash-value life insurance policy in force.

1. Susan could simply surrender the policy and receive its cash surrender value. She would receive a check for approximately $18,000 and would no longer have insurance coverage under the policy. She would pay income taxes on the amount of the cash surrender value that exceeded the total premiums she had paid into the policy over the years. The cash surrender value

usually does not exceed premiums for policies that have been in place for only a few years. You can consult the policy's table of nonforfeiture values or contact your parents' insurance agent for information on these matters.

2. Susan could use the $18,000 to buy $50,000 of paid-up term insurance. The time period (term) for her continued coverage will depend upon her age and the exact cash value available. Coverage will expire at the end of the time period. This would be a nontaxable option.

3. Susan could use the $18,000 to continue the policy permanently on a paid-up basis. If she does this, she will no longer need to pay premiums. Based on her age and the dollar amount of cash value available, a new (lower) face amount will be established. Her coverage will never expire. This would be a nontaxable option.

4. Susan could use the policy's automatic premium loan provision to pay the annual premium on the policy. Cash-value accumulations in the future would be reduced, but she could maintain her coverage until the cash value runs out. Note that the death benefit of the policy would also decline as the loan balance increases. This would be a nontaxable option.

> **Cash surrender value:** The cash value of a life insurance policy after subtracting any surrender charges.

Your parents may have cash values in their policies that can be used in these ways. Of course, the policies can also be kept in force by continuing to pay the premiums.

Designing the Program

Your parents' marital status will have an impact on their life insurance program. Let's look at how the situation differs for married versus unmarried retirees.

If Your Parents Are Married   Married retirees will feel a strong sense of financial responsibility for their spouse after death. This responsibility relates directly to the need for income replacement. If the death of one spouse will reduce the survivor's total retirement income, that drop in income will need to be addressed. Jim Cargill anticipated this possibility and carried a fairly high level of life insurance, which will provide income for Susan for years to come. Susan will have to decide on the appropriate settlement option for drawing down those funds.

However, not all families are so well prepared. To find out if your parents are in such a position, you should do two things. First, make a realistic assessment of the income each parent will need should the other pass away. You can follow the procedure discussed in Chapter 4 to do this. Second, go through the life insurance needs assessment process described earlier in this chapter to determine whether your parents are adequately or inadequately insured. You will need to do this for each parent and then decide how much insurance there needs to be on each parent's life to protect the other.

You will find that your parents have either too little, too much, or an appropriate amount of life insurance. If they have an appropriate amount, you need only monitor the situation periodically. If desired, nonforfeiture option 2, 3, or 4 could be chosen to allow your parents to stop paying life insurance premiums on one or more policies. If your parents have more life insurance than they need and they have term policies, they can let those policies expire at the end of the term. Cash-value policies require more thought. One or more of the policies can be surrendered to tap the cash value accumulated. But then your parents will have to decide where to invest the funds.

> If your parents need income more than they need death protection, consider surrendering a cash-value policy to purchase a joint and survivor annuity (see Chapter 8) to provide a stream of income until the second spouse dies. Be sure to compare policies from several companies for both the guaranteed and the current rates of return.

The very nature of life insurance works against parents who have too little life insurance. The premium charged for a life insurance policy is based on the age of the insured person at the time the policy is purchased (or renewed, in the case of term insurance). The cost of new life insurance is prohibitive at advanced ages. Term life insurance is generally unavailable at any price for those over age 65 or 70. Even small cash-value policies can cost several hundred dollars per year. What can your parents do? One option is to simply spend less and save the remaining income in order to build an asset for the surviving spouse. Or they might cut back on their plans for their funeral and burial and for passing funds on to heirs. Probably their poorest choice is to buy an unafford-able amount of insurance at a time in their lives when they are already having budget problems.

If Your Parent Is Unmarried   Unmarried individuals have the low-est needs for life insurance. Let's use Susan Cargill as an example. Her final expenses and the desire to pass money on to her grandchildren add up to $60,000. She currently has $120,000 of insurance coverage across the three policies on her life. Here are some options for Susan:

1. Let the term policy expire and continue the two cash-value policies. Use the $20,000 policy for her funeral and burial. Use the $50,000 policy to provide an inheritance for her five grand-children. Her annual premium payments would be $1,016.
2. Renew the term policy for her grandchildren. Cash in the $20,000 policy and use the funds to prepay her funeral and burial expenses. Cash in the $50,000 policy and use the pro-ceeds to supplement her income via an annuity or other invest-ment account. Her annual premium would be $445. Note that she will have to address the term policy again in 11 years when it once again comes up for renewal.
3. Let the term policy expire. Continue the $50,000 cash-value policy to provide for her grandchildren. Cash in the $20,000 policy and use the proceeds to prepay her funeral and burial expenses. Her annual premium would be $780.

Obviously, there are other options as well. The key for Susan is to meet her goals of having the funds necessary to provide for her burial and funeral and passing on a small nest egg to her grandchildren. Your fam-ily may have similar or different needs and so may require a different pattern. Nonetheless, the steps are the same. Identify needs. Identify re-sources. Use life insurance, as necessary, to meet the unmet needs in the most economical fashion. What would you recommend if you were Bill? What will you recommend for your parents?

Final Thoughts

This chapter was designed to help your parents manage their life insur-ance program. For most families, the need for life insurance is greatly reduced during the last decades of life. For married couples, the primary needs are for funeral and burial expenses, replacement of income lost when the first spouse passes away, and, if desired, providing funds for heirs. For unmarried people, there generally is no need to replace lost income. In both cases, existing assets and insurance are often sufficient to meet these needs.

Three family situations require more careful analysis. The first involves retired parents who are financially responsible for an adult child with a disability. Their need to replace lost income will be based on that child's life expectancy, thereby greatly increasing the need for life insurance. Second, families with estates exceeding $2 million in value will probably have an estate tax liability. These families often use life insurance to generate the funds to pay estate and inheritance taxes. Third, life insurance may play a vital role in maintaining the financial viability of a family business and providing the funds necessary to realign the business ownership after the death of the parent owners. Each of these cases goes beyond the scope of this book. If your family has these or other special considerations, you should consult a financial planning expert. The professional should focus on all financial issues, as life insurance needs are intertwined with the full range of family financial management issues.

10

Medicare, Medicare Supplement, and Long-Term-Care Insurance

*D*an Anderson's mother is 85 years old. In the past 2 years she has battled mild memory loss, some osteoporosis, and volatile blood pressure. Four weeks ago she fell and broke her hip. After a weeklong hospitalization, she was admitted to a local nursing facility for 4 to 5 weeks for continued medical care and rehabilitation. As Dan was reviewing her bills, he noticed several "invoices" for services and statements of her Medicare account. Some said, "do not pay," yet those from physicians often showed a balance due. Dan became very confused about what Medicare paid and what should be claimed against his mother's supplemental health insurance policy. He finally stopped paying the bills until he could find assistance.

Dan is also concerned that his mother may need long-term, skilled care when her rehabilitation is completed. Because she lives on small social security and employer pension checks, he knows that she cannot afford to pay for extended services. She has only $45,000 in the bank and total equity of $85,000 in her home.

YOU CAN PROBABLY UNDERSTAND why Dan is feeling stressed. He knows that he is getting drawn into issues about which he understands very little. Many professional financial advisers claim that they are befuddled by the rules and reimbursement procedures of health insurers for the elderly. It is not surprising that Dan finds himself suffering the same fate.

Understanding the insurance system and processing the reimbursements for your parents' health-care costs will be one of the most difficult financial matters you will assume as a caretaker. Yet it is one for which you have little personal experience. That is because their health-care coverage differs from yours. This chapter provides an overview of the three types of health insurance most elderly persons use to pay for their medical expenses: Medicare, Medigap supplemental health insurance, and long-term-care insurance. A discussion of the eligibility requirements, coverages provided and excluded, premium costs, and out-of-pocket expenses for each of these types of insurance is presented.

Medicare

The U.S. government is the largest health insurer for citizens over age 65. Medicare is the name of the health insurance program provided to citizens who participated in the social security and Medicare programs through mandatory tax withholdings from their paychecks. The Medicare insurance program has two parts. Part A pays for hospitalization costs, and Part B covers the cost of physician and outpatient services. Medicare does not pay for prescription drugs, nor are most nursing home or home health-care costs reimbursed.

Eligibility

To have their health-care costs covered, your parents must first be eligible for Medicare coverage. Any person over age 65 who receives social security payments is eligible for Medicare benefits. In addition, some disabled individuals under age 65 and people with End-Stage Renal Disease may also qualify for coverage. To qualify for social security and Medicare benefits, at least one of your parents must have earned 40 social security credits. Usually this takes 10 years, but your parent did not need to work the entire 10 years consecutively. Even if Dan's mother didn't work outside the home, she is eligible for Medicare benefits because she is receiving social security. She probably qualified because her husband had obtained 40 credits.

Senior citizens who were self-employed most likely participated in the social security system by paying the self-employment tax. The self-employment tax, in effect, is equal to the social security and Medicare tax. Again, 40 credits are needed to qualify for social security and Medicare.

Many people who worked for certain government agencies, public schools, public universities, nonprofit hospitals, or church organizations did not participate in the social security program. In most of these cases, the nonprofit employer had a plan that was a substitute for social security and Medicare. Your parents may be receiving health-care benefits from such a plan. All employees who were hired after October 1, 1986, regardless of whether or not they worked for an exempt organization, were required to pay into the Medicare system. If your parents do not appear to be covered by an alternative plan, they may be able to "buy" Medicare Part A and Part B insurance even if they don't qualify for social security.

Applying for Medicare

By the time you take control of your parents' finances, they will probably already have their Medicare cards and have received benefits over the years. Dan is likely to find his mother's Medicare card in her wallet or purse. It would be wise for him to photocopy the card and keep the copy in his files.

However, if you can't find your parents' Medicare cards, or if you don't know whether they qualify for coverage, you can easily find out by applying for coverage through their local Social Security office. Your parents should apply for Medicare coverage 3 months before reaching age 65. The premiums may increase if your parents fail to file for coverage within 4 months after turning age 65.

What Does Medicare Cover?

The Medicare health insurance program is divided into two parts, Part A and Part B. In general, Part A covers hospital costs, and Part B covers physicians' and outpatient services. Regardless of which part of Medicare pays, all costs must be for medically necessary services.

Medically necessary: Needed to provide for the diagnosis or treatment of a medical condition, and not mainly for the convenience of your parents or their physicians. The service must also meet the standards of good medical practice in the local area.

In addition to determining whether a procedure or service is medically necessary, the Medicare system limits the amount it will pay when making reimbursements. Physicians who agree to *take assignment* have agreed to charge a patient who is covered by Medicare no more than the amount Medicare has agreed to pay. This limits the patient's out-of-pocket cost. Dan's mother will be covered for her hospital stay. She will probably also receive coverage for her stay in the rehabilitation facility. However, she will not be permitted to receive coverage for a much longer stay.

Part A Coverage Medicare Part A covers hospitalization expenses. Hospitalization expenses include costs incurred as an inpatient, including those in hospitals, critical access hospitals, skilled nursing facilities, and hospice, and some home health care.

• *Hospital costs not covered.* Private rooms are paid for only if they are deemed medically necessary. Private-duty nursing services, television, and telephone service are not provided. The maximum coverage for inpatient mental health care is limited to 190 days in a lifetime. See Table 10.1 for Part A coverage details.

Table 10.1 Medicare Parts A and B Covered Expenses and Your Out-of-Pocket Share

Medicare Provides	Out-of-Pocket Share (2003)*
Part A Inpatient Stays: semiprivate room, services and supplies. Doesn't include phone, television, or private room	$840 for first 60 days $210 per day for days 61–90 $420 per day for days 91–150† 100% for each day over 150 days
Part A Inpatient Mental Health Care: limited to 190 days in a lifetime	Same payments as for regular inpatient stays. Can use lifetime reserve days for mental health care 100% after 190 days of mental health care
Part A Skilled Nursing Facility (SNF) Care: semiprivate room, services and supplies (after a 3-day hospital stay)	$0 for first 20 days $105 per day for days 21–100 100% for each day over 100 days
Part A Home Health Care: part-time skilled nursing care, physical and speech therapy, home health aide, durable medical equipment	$0 for home health care services 20% of approved amount for durable medical equipment
Part A Hospice Care: medical and support services, drugs, respite care	$5 copayment for each outpatient prescription 5% of the approved amount for inpatient respite care
Part A Blood: at a hospital or SNF	100% of the first three pints
Part B Medical Services: physicians, outpatient surgery, laboratory tests, durable medical equipment, outpatient physical and occupational therapy, outpatient mental health services	$100 annual deductible.‡ 20% of approved amount over deductible 20% for outpatient physical, speech, and occupational therapy 50% for outpatient mental health care

Table 10.1 *(continued)*

Medicare Provides	Out-of-Pocket Share (2003)*
Part B Clinical Laboratory Service: blood tests, urinalysis, and other tests	$0
Part B Home Health Care: part-time skilled care, home health aide services, durable equipment	$0 for services 20% of approved amount for durable medical equipment
Part B Outpatient Hospital Services: for diagnosis and treatment of illness or injury	Coinsurance or flat copayment— depends on service
Part B Blood: as an outpatient or as part of a Part B covered service	100% of the first three pints

*Medicare preapproves the amount for each procedure. You pay the coinsurance percentage of the approved amount and any amount over the approved amount that your doctor charges.

†Days 91 to 150 are considered your "lifetime reserve days." Once you use all of these 60 days, you pay 100 percent after 90 days of a stay. You may use some of these 60 lifetime reserve days for one episode and the remainder for other episodes.

‡This amount may increase.

• *Part A premium costs.* There is no premium cost for Part A hospital insurance coverage for individuals covered by social security and their spouses. The cost in 2003 for those individuals who did not participate in the social security system but chose to purchase Part A coverage was $316 per month. Dan's mother is probably not paying for her Part A coverage. Those individuals who participated in the social security system but only acquired 30 to 39 credits of coverage may purchase Part A coverage for $174 per month.

• *Part A out-of-pocket costs.* Part A does not pay 100 percent of all hospitalization costs. Medicare participants are required to share in the cost of covered care. These costs are called deductibles and copayments. The amount of the deductible increases each year. The amount of the copayment can increase but doesn't necessarily go up each year. Table 10.1 presents an overview of the out-of-pocket costs you can expect to pay.

Deductible: The "first dollar" of health-care costs that an insured party must pay toward her or his own care before insurance coverage begins. It may start over again with a new year or be charged on a "per episode" basis.

Copayment: The part of health-care costs that the insured pays as his or her share. It may be a flat dollar amount, such as $5 per visit, or a percentage amount, such as 20 percent of all costs over a minimum amount.

Your parents will be required to pay the deductible and copayments for Medicare Part A covered costs each time a new benefit period begins. A benefit period begins the first day your parent enters a hospital or skilled nursing facility and ends when no services have been provided for a period of 60 days in a row.

• *Skilled nursing care.* In most cases, Medicare will not pay for nursing home stays. However, Medicare Part A will cover a limited number of days if skilled nursing facility services are required. The skilled nursing care must be medically necessary, certified by a physician, and provided in a Medicare-approved facility; also, your parent's condition must be improving. Skilled nursing facility costs are covered only if your parents are moved to the skilled nursing facility after a hospital stay of at least 3 days and within 60 days of leaving the hospital. It is likely that Mrs. Anderson's care in the rehabilitation facility is covered under the skilled nursing facility benefit of Medicare Part A. Your parents' share of skilled nursing care costs is outlined in Table 10.1.

• *Home health care.* Your parents may need home health care. Home health care coverage includes part-time skilled nursing care, physical therapy, occupational therapy, speech therapy, home health aide services, and medical equipment such as wheelchairs, hospital beds, oxygen, and walkers. This coverage should be good news to Dan. Once his mother leaves the rehabilitation facility, Medicare will cover up to 100 home health care visits. Mrs. Anderson will have to pay only 20 percent of the cost of a walker, a hospital bed, or bath assistance equipment.

Medicare Part A also covers hospice care, drugs for symptom control and pain relief, and short-term respite care. See Table 10.1 to identify what your parents will have to pay for these services.

• *Part B coverage.* Physicians' services, outpatient care, physical and occupational therapy, and other services not covered under Part A are paid for under Medicare Part B. To qualify for coverage, the services must be medically necessary. In addition, only an amount that is approved by Medicare will be covered. In other words, Medicare preapproves the costs of certain services on a scheduled basis. Any amounts over the approved (or assignment) amount will be the responsibility of your parents. This area is probably the most confusing for Dan. His mother is receiving bills from physicians who are charging Mrs. Anderson for the difference between their normal price for a covered service and the amount Medicare is willing to pay. Table 10.1 highlights the medical services covered under Part B and what your parents' share of the costs will be.

• *Medical costs not covered.*   Generally speaking, eyeglasses, prescriptions, hearing aids, cosmetic surgery, and dental expenses are not covered. Routine physical exams, including foot and eye care, are also exempt from Medicare coverage.

• *Part B premium costs.*   A Medicare beneficiary pays a monthly premium of $58.70 for coverage. The premium increases each year. Your parents must apply for Part B within 3 months before their retirement date or 6 months after the date of retirement. Late enrollment will cost your parents 10 percent for each 12-month period in which they were eligible to enroll but did not enroll. This surcharge is paid for the rest of their lives.

If your parents are receiving social security benefits, the premium will be automatically withheld from their monthly social security checks. Premium payments are deductible as a medical expense (itemized deduction) on your parents' income tax return.

• *Part B out-of-pocket costs.*   Each year, your parents will be responsible for paying the first $100 of the cost of covered physician services. Dan must remember that some of his mother's bills are for this deductible, the first $100 of these charges each year. A complete list of the patient's share of costs is provided in Table 10.1

In addition to deducting the cost of premium payments, your parents can also include all deductibles and copayments as medical expenses on their itemized deduction tax form (Schedule A).

• *Preventive services.*   Medicare Part B covers some preventive services if the beneficiary is at risk. For example, Medicare will pay 80 percent of the approved amount for diabetes monitoring equipment and test strips. Medicare will pay 80 percent of the approved amount for mammogram screening for women over age 40. However, they will cover Pap smears and pelvic examinations only every 3 years unless a woman is at high risk for cervical or vaginal cancer or has had an abnormal Pap smear in the past 3 years. Men over age 50 may receive prostate cancer screenings every year and pay only 20 percent of the approved amount. Annual flu shots are covered. Special rules apply for colorectal cancer screenings, bone mass measurements, and other vaccinations.

Alternatives to Traditional Medicare

To allow Medicare beneficiaries flexibility in accessing medical care providers, Congress recently approved two "alternative" Medicare plans. These alternatives to Medicare Part A and Part B are called the Medicare + Choice program. The program has two options. One of these choices is a Medicare managed care plan that operates like a health maintenance organization (HMO). The other option is a Medicare private fee-for-service plan.

Eligibility to Join an Alternative Plan

Individuals who have both Medicare Part A and Part B coverage may choose to join either a Medicare managed care plan or a private fee-for-service plan. However, these plans are not offered in all areas of the country. Your parents will not be eligible to use either of these alternative plans if they have End-Stage Renal Disease.

Medicare Managed Care Plan

Medicare managed care plans are offered by private health maintenance organizations and are an alternative to the original Medicare program. Your parents must be eligible for Medicare to receive this type of insurance coverage. Instead of paying the physicians and hospitals that provide services to your parents, Medicare pays a set amount of money to an HMO. The HMO is then responsible for providing medical services to your parents. Often extra benefits, such as prescription drug coverage, are included. However, your parents will be allowed to seek treatment only from a limited number of physicians and hospitals. If the medical professionals your parents prefer are not part of the HMO, they will probably want to remain in the original Medicare program. In addition, your parents may be allowed to see a specialist only after receiving preapproval from their primary care physician. Dan's mother may not have the choice of enrolling in a managed care plan. There may be no such plan offered in her city. And, even if one is available, she will have to pay extra to get services from her usual physician if he is not included in the managed plan.

Private Fee-for-Service Plans

In some areas of the country, private insurers offer Medicare coverage. These are called Private Fee-for-Service Plans. As with the Medicare managed care plans, Medicare pays the private insurer a set amount of money each month. Your parents and the private insurance company will pay a fee for each physician visit or service received. Rather than having Medicare preapprove the cost of services, the insurance company decides how much it and your parents will pay for the services they receive. Your parents can visit any physician or hospital that agrees to accept the private insurer's payment. Sometimes, extra benefits may be available.

Cost of the Alternative Plans

If your parents choose to join an alternative plan, they are technically still in the Medicare program. This means that they are still required to pay the monthly Medicare Part B premium. All regular Medicare covered services are provided, and your parents will retain their Medicare rights and protections.

Alternative plans are allowed to charge a monthly premium in addition to the Part B premium. The alternative plan also decides how much your parents will pay for each visit, the type of health care needed, and the frequency with which services are received. They may also be charged for extra benefits such as prescription drug coverage. If your parents belong to a Medicare managed care plan (HMO), they will pay extra for health-care services received outside the plan's service area. Private fee-for-service plans may allow medical service providers to bill you for more than the plan pays for services. If this is the case, the plan generally limits what the providers can charge, but your parents will be responsible for the extra charges.

Enrolling in an Alternative Plan

Most Medicare alternative plans accept new enrollees during the month of November, with coverage beginning the following January. If your parents would like to join an alternative plan, simply call the plan and complete an enrollment form. Your parents can join only one alternative plan at a time.

Alternative plans allow your parents to disenroll from their plans, but only at certain times of the year. You may call 1-800-633-4227 (1-800-MEDICARE) to find out when disenrollment is allowed. Your parents will automatically be enrolled in the original Medicare plan if they disenroll from an alternative plan.

It is possible that an alternative-plan provider may leave the Medicare program. In this event, your parents will be notified; they can then choose another alternative plan or return to the original Medicare program.

Choosing a Medicare Coverage Plan

Your parents have a choice as to whether they use the government or an alternative provider for their Medicare coverage. And, with choices come confusion and the need for more information. You will want to consider many factors when you select a Medicare insurance provider. These factors include the availability of a variety of physicians from which to receive services, the out-of-pocket costs, coverage for any extra benefits and services, and any restrictions on services. You and your parents will want to ask the questions highlighted in the accompanying box.

Questions You Should Ask about Alternative Medicare Plans

- Is there an additional premium cost for coverage?
- What are the copayments for services?
- Are the charges for physicians' services greater than what the plan pays?
- How many out-of-pocket costs might I be responsible for?
- What are the deductibles and coinsurance for inpatient care?
- Are the physicians I'm currently using included in the plan's coverage?
- If my physicians aren't included, am I willing to use a physician who is in the plan?
- Will I be able to see the same physician on most visits?
- Can I change physicians if I'm not satisfied?
- What happens if I need a specialist and your plan doesn't include a specific type of specialist?
- Are the physicians' and other service providers' offices convenient?
- What additional benefits are covered?
- Are routine exams covered?
- Are wellness and preventive visits included?
- Is eye care covered?

- Are hearing aids covered?
- Are prescription drugs covered?
  If so, are the drugs my parents use covered?
  Are only drugs on an approved list covered?
  May we use our regular pharmacy?
  May we purchase the prescriptions by mail order?
  Must we purchase the prescriptions by mail order?
  Are brand-name drugs covered?
  Must we use generic drugs when available?
  Is there an annual limit to prescription coverage?
- Who files claims on my behalf?
- When am I allowed to disenroll?
- How do I disenroll?

Supplemental (Medigap) Health Insurance

For most of the elderly, Medicare provides basic health insurance coverage. However, many Medicare participants pay a significant amount for medical costs in addition to what is covered by Medicare. By some estimates, Medicare only covers 50 percent of an elderly person's total health-care costs. To reduce their out-of-pocket medical costs, senior citizens often purchase supplemental health insurance.

Many private insurers also offer Medicare supplement plans, commonly known as Medigap plans. In the past, because of the vulnerability of the elderly, there were many abuses in the Medicare supplement policy market. Since 1990, however, the government has reformed and overseen the development and marketing of Medigap insurance plans. Private insurers are allowed to offer Medigap policies that provide 10 standard sets of benefit offerings. For ease of comparing policies, these types of policies are labeled A through J. Insurance companies that offer these products for sale give them all sorts of trade or brand names. However, they are required to tell you which level of policy (A through J) the policy is. This allows you to easily compare the terms of coverage.

Medigap insurance: Insurance that pays for some of the health-care costs not covered by Medicare or an alternative Medicare program.

All Medigap policies must offer a core package. The benefits in this core package include payment of the Medicare Part A coinsurance amounts for days 61 to 90 and the lifetime reserve days. All policies must cover hospital expenses for an additional 365 days in the hospital. The first three pints of blood provided through Parts A and B must be covered. Finally, core coverage also includes payment of the 20 percent coinsurance for allowable charges for physicians' and medical services expenses. Dan's mother has Medigap coverage through the local senior citizens' organization. It is an A policy, so she is still liable for the $840 for her hospital stay and the $100 deductible for physicians' service fees. In addition, she will also need to pay the $105 per day for 15 days of her rehabilitation facility care. She will also have to pay the part of the physicians' bills that is greater than the Medicare-approved amount.

Each of the 10 standard policies covers various parts of the costs of hospital and physicians' services. The various coverages contained in the 10 standard policies are outlined in Table 10.2. Obviously, the premium will be higher for the policies that offer greater coverage.

Table 10.2 Coverage Required in a Medigap Policy

Covered Item	A	B	C	D	E	F	G	H	I	J
Days 1–60 in hospital ($840)	No	Yes	Yes	Yes	Yes	Yes	Yes	Yes	Yes	Yes
Days 61–90 in hospital ($210/day)	Yes	Yes	Yes	Yes	Yes	Yes	Yes	Yes	Yes	Yes
Days 91–150 (reserve days) in hospital ($420/day)	Yes	Yes	Yes	Yes	Yes	Yes	Yes	Yes	Yes	Yes
Extra 365 hospital days	Yes	Yes	Yes	Yes	Yes	Yes	Yes	Yes	Yes	Yes
Three pints of blood—Part A	Yes	Yes	Yes	Yes	Yes	Yes	Yes	Yes	Yes	Yes
Three pints of blood—Part B	Yes	Yes	Yes	Yes	Yes	Yes	Yes	Yes	Yes	Yes
20% Part B coinsurance for allowable charges	Yes	Yes	Yes	Yes	Yes	Yes	Yes	Yes	Yes	Yes

Table 10.2 (continued)

Covered Item	A	B	C	D	E	F	G	H	I	J
Physician deductible —Part B ($100/yr.)	No	No	Yes	No	No	Yes	No	No	No	Yes
Skilled nursing facility coinsurance—Part A ($105/day)	No	No	Yes	Yes	Yes	Yes	Yes	Yes	Yes	Yes
Physician charges in excess of assignment amount	0%	0%	0%	0%	0%	100%	80%	0%	100%	100%
Foreign country emergency care	No	No	Yes	Yes	Yes	Yes	Yes	Yes	Yes	Yes
At-home recovery	No	No	No	Yes	No	No	Yes	No	Yes	Yes
Outpatient prescription drugs	No	No	No	No	No	No	No	Yes*	Yes*	Yes†
Preventive care	No	No	No	No	Yes	No	No	No	No	Yes

*Maximum benefit of $1,250/year; $250 deductible per year; 50 percent coinsurance.
†Maximum benefit of $3,000/year; $250 deductible per year; 50 percent coinsurance.

Long-Term-Care Insurance

The average cost of a nursing home currently exceeds $150 per day. Senior citizens and their families are increasingly concerned that the cost of long-term care will deplete any savings the parents have and leave little, if any, money to pass to the children. The provision and sale of long-term-care insurance has become big business. But long-term-care insurance is expensive. A 65-year-old can expect to pay an annual premium of $1,000 to $2,000 for coverage. Furthermore, there may be significant limits placed on the coverage.

Evaluating the Need for Long-Term-Care Insurance

Your parents may or may not be good candidates for long-term-care insurance policies. To adequately evaluate their need for this insurance, you must understand the basic concepts of insurance and the specific details of long-term-care insurance.

In return for an annual premium payment, your parents receive coverage in the event that they need long-term nursing care. The premium must be paid each year. If during that year, your parents require covered care, the insurance company will pay the cost up to an agreed-upon amount. If your parents stop paying the premium, their coverage stops. In this respect, long-term-care insurance is much like auto insurance—if you're insured when the accident happens, you're covered; otherwise, the consequence of not paying premiums is not having insurance coverage. And if you never use the insurance, your premiums were effectively used to cover those in the insurance group who made benefit claims.

You will want to purchase a long-term-care policy only if you think a need for the covered care will ever exist. The likelihood of needing long-term care increases for those over age 85 and those who are likely to suffer from chronic but not immediately life-threatening conditions, such as Alzheimer's disease. If your parents are unlikely to live to age 85 or if they are candidates for dying from acute diseases such as cancer or heart disease, they may not need long-term-care insurance. Mrs. Anderson would seem to be a good candidate for long-term-care insurance. She suffers from chronic, not acute, illnesses, and she's over age 85. But because of her advanced age, if she has not yet purchased a policy, the premium will be beyond the reach of her budget.

Limitations on Covered Conditions   Some policies exclude coverage of certain specific medical conditions or diseases; if your parents enter a facility because they have one of these excluded conditions, they will not be covered. Popular exclusions include alcohol or chemical dependency, nervous system or mental disorders, and specific diseases such as cancer, diabetes, or heart disease. If the policy you are considering excludes coverage for a specific illness, the likelihood that your parents will receive benefits may be greatly reduced. You should proceed with extreme caution before buying such a policy.

Limits on Type of Care Provided   Your policy premium will be lower if the restrictions for qualifying are more stringent. Most policies require that a patient be chronically ill. A chronically ill patient is defined as one who is unable to perform two daily living tasks, such as eating, toileting, transferring, bathing, and dressing. In addition, the insured is expected to be unable to perform these tasks for a period of 90 days. Alternatively, patients who can perform daily living tasks but suffer from severe cognitive impairment or need to be protected from threats to their personal health and safety may also qualify for benefits. For costs to be paid, a licensed health-care provider must prescribe the care. These qualifications are not necessarily easy to meet. As she recovers from her fall and is able to do more for herself, Mrs. Anderson may cease to qualify for benefits.

Limits on When Coverage Begins and How Long It Will Pay   Some long-term-care policies require that the insured receive services for some period of time (usually 30 to 90 days) before reimbursement begins. This period is called an elimination or waiting period. The premium will decrease as the waiting period increases. In addition, the policy may pay benefits for only a certain number of days or months, called the benefit period. Obviously, coverage for a longer benefit period will increase the premium cost. Dan's mom may be able to qualify for services under most policies because she is likely to need benefits for a significant period of time. However, if she is now ready to enter a nursing home, it is too late to buy the policy.

Limits on Preexisting Conditions   Other policies omit coverage if the need for long-term care results from a preexisting condition. Preexisting conditions are those that were diagnosed or treated during a period prior to purchase of the policy—usually 6 to 24 months. Many companies avoid covering preexisting conditions by limiting benefits during an exclusion period. The exclusion period may be 3 to 6 months. This means that your parents will not receive benefits for the length of the exclusion period after they buy the policy. Long-term-care insurance is not for your parents if they need coverage immediately. If Mrs. Anderson decides to purchase coverage, she will probably not qualify for benefits until the exclusion period has elapsed.

Premium Cost for Long-Term-Care Insurance

The cost of long-term-care insurance varies widely and depends upon the company offering the insurance, the benefits included in the coverage, the waiting period before coverage begins, and the age at which the insured purchases the coverage. Many individuals choose to purchase and begin paying premiums on a long-term-care policy as early as 40 years of age because otherwise the premium will be unaffordable when they need the coverage. Obviously, such a person is likely to pay premiums for many, many years before receiving any benefit. And, if the insured ceases making premium payments, the insurance lapses and coverage is no longer provided. In Mrs. Anderson's case, because of her age, the premium for long-term-care insurance is likely to be prohibitive.

Covered Expenses

You will want to examine any policy you are considering purchasing very carefully. Most policies cover only qualified expenses. Qualified expenses generally include the cost of skilled nursing care while treating chronic diseases. The cost of rehabilitating a chronically ill patient is also covered. Maintenance expenses such as cooking and cleaning may also be reimbursed. You may wish to purchase coverage that pays for home health-care expenses. Expenses that can be reimbursed by Medicare are not covered.

Although many providers offer some of these services, and the direct care provider does not necessarily need to be a nurse, many insurers only cover care provided in eligible facilities. In many cases, eligible facilities are those defined as skilled nursing facilities or intermediate nursing facilities. Be sure that any policy you purchase pays for custodial care and does not require the insured to need skilled nursing care to receive benefits, as many insurers will not reimburse the cost of care in a custodial-only facility. Purchasing a policy with this restriction may result in a greater out-of-pocket expense for your parents.

Benefit Payments

Benefits are paid in one of two ways. Some policies pay a per diem rate. That is, the insured will receive a given dollar amount per day of covered service. Other policies pay only for actual expenses. The method of benefit determination has an effect on the premium price.

General Provisions

The insurance company must guarantee your parents continued insurance coverage as long as they continue to pay the premium. However, there is no guarantee that the premium will remain the same. You should look for policies with a premium that stays at the same level for several years or only increases by a reasonable amount each year. Furthermore, it is wise to purchase a policy that will pay more for covered services as the cost increases with inflation.

Tax Deductibility of Insurance Premium

The Internal Revenue Service allows your parents to deduct the premium cost for long-term-care insurance. The maximum amount that can be deducted is determined by the age of the insured. Taxpayers between the ages of 61 and 70, inclusive, may deduct up to $2,510 in long-term-care insurance premiums. Those age 71 and over may deduct the actual premium cost up to a maximum of $3,130. The allowable deductible amount increases each year.

Any out-of-pocket costs for health care are deductible. However, you may not deduct the cost of services provided by a close family member, such as a parent, spouse, or child. The premium cost is deducted as part of the total medical expenses on Schedule A.

Taxability of Benefits

Benefits paid by policies that pay only actual expenses are tax-free to the insured. Those that pay a set dollar amount—for example, $100 per day—are tax-free if the insured patient is terminally ill. Patients who are chronically ill, but not terminally ill, may receive up to $200 per day ($73,000 per year) without paying taxes on the benefits. Any benefits over the $200 per day limit that actually exceed the cost of service are taxable to a chronically ill patient. All long-term-care insurance companies must issue Form 1099-LTC, which shows the amount of benefits paid and whether the benefits were paid on a per diem or reimbursed amount basis.

Related Issues

As your parents get older, you may find that their income becomes very limited, that their need for services exceeds the services that are readily available, or that their assets are depleted. You will need to be creative in finding solutions to these and other dilemmas. Fortunately, public assistance, in the form of monetary, in-kind, or other services, is available to help you and your parents. If you need assistance with any issue related to elder care, you should call your local Area Council on Aging.

Medicare Premium Assistance

Two programs are available to help the poor elderly pay their Medicare insurance premiums. Both are operated under the rules of local Medicaid, public welfare, or social services offices. Both restrict the amount of income a benefit recipient may have and still qualify for the benefit.

The first, the Qualified Medicare Beneficiary Program, pays the premium, deductibles, and coinsurance for the poor elderly who receive Medicare Part A benefits. To qualify, your parents' income must be at or below the poverty level. In addition, the value of their total assets must be below $6,000 per couple or $4,000 for a single person. Mrs. Anderson would not qualify for this program.

A second program, the Specified Low-Income Medicare Beneficiary Program, will pay the Part B premium for citizens with a low income, up to an income that is slightly higher than the national poverty level. Mrs. Anderson may qualify for this benefit. Dan should call his local Social Security office or 1-800-MEDICARE and inquire as to her eligibility. He may also visit Medicare's Web site at www.medicare.gov.

Final Thoughts

Paying for medical care, prescriptions, nursing home services, or home health-care services can quickly deplete the resources of even the most financially well prepared senior citizen. By the time your parents need care from outside providers, you will usually be managing their financial affairs. However, they may request your assistance much earlier when they are deciding what insurance coverage they need. Medicare is considered a first-tier reimbursement program. That is, Medicare pays for the initial cost of medical and skilled nursing care. You may decide that paying for a Medigap policy is well worth the benefits your parents receive. Purchasing long-term-care insurance late in life is very expensive, and the probability of receiving benefits decreases as the number of policy restrictions increases. You may wish to consult with your accountant, your financial adviser, or a geriatric adviser before committing to the purchase of additional insurance. Don't hesitate to request assistance from local social service providers—they exist to help you! You may also want to visit the following Web sites: www.hcfa.gov, www.medicare.gov, www.medicare.org, www.seniors.gov, and www.ssa.gov.

11

Medicaid

*D*an Anderson's mother is 85 years old. In the past 2 years she has battled mild memory loss, some osteoporosis, and volatile blood pressure. Four weeks ago she fell and broke her hip. After a weeklong hospitalization, she received 5 weeks of rehabilitation. Dan and the doctors have now decided that she needs more time in a skilled nursing care facility. He is also concerned that his mother may need long-term care. Because she lives on small social security and employer pension checks, he knows that she cannot afford to pay for extended services. She has only $45,000 in the bank and total equity of $85,000 in her home. His mother has always told him to take her assets and put her on Medicaid, but Dan doesn't know if he can do this in good conscience.

YOUR PARENTS will need many types of insurance coverage to minimize their financial risks. The major economic risk that your parents will be facing will be the staggering cost of health care and long-term nursing care. In the previous chapter, you learned that Medicare health insurance is available to almost every citizen over age 65, and that private insurers offer supplemental health insurance policies, commonly known as Medigap insurance. However, neither Medicare nor Medigap policies were designed to cover the costs of long stays in nursing care facilities.

Medicaid is a national health-care assistance program for the poor, operated cooperatively by the federal government and the 50 individual states. The aged, defined as those who are over age 65, blind, or disabled, are automatically eligible if they meet the financial and medical necessity requirements. Payments for care are made directly to health-care providers, such as hospitals, doctors, clinics, and nursing facilities. Medicaid is often confused with Medicare. Medicare usually does not cover long-term care in a nursing home; Medicaid does. A family's assets can quickly be severely depleted by nursing home costs. That's when people explore Medicaid coverage.

This chapter includes a thorough discussion of what Medicaid covers, how to apply for coverage, and the medical necessity, income, and asset tests that must be met in order to be eligible. In addition, you will learn what assets the "well" parent gets to keep, and how to protect the family's wealth. A brief discussion of the moral arguments for depleting your parents' assets in order to qualify for Medicaid follows.

Medicaid Coverage

Medicaid provides health insurance protection for citizens with low incomes and limited assets. Most individuals who receive government assistance under such programs as Temporary Assistance to Needy Families and Supplemental Security Income qualify for Medicaid benefits. In the case of the elderly, the program will pay the cost of medical care when Medicare benefits, income, and personal assets are exhausted. Unless a patient has significant wealth or income, Medicaid benefits are usually required within a short period of time after a person enters a skilled nursing facility. Your parents are most likely to qualify for Medicaid if they do not have a regular pension benefit in addition to social security or if they have little savings available with which to pay for care.

If your parents qualify for Medicaid coverage, the benefits can be substantial. The basic coverage includes inpatient and outpatient hospital services; doctor, laboratory, and x-ray services; skilled nursing and home health care; and transportation and ambulance services. Medicare provides good coverage for most of the basic services in this list.

Eligibility

Your parents must meet three tests in order to qualify for Medicaid. The first is an income test. Their income must fall below a certain threshold. The second is an asset test. Your parents' assets will be valued to determine whether they have more assets than are allowed by Medicaid. These first two tests are complicated and are discussed more fully later in the chapter.

Once a person receives Medicaid eligibility (sometimes referred to as getting a medical card), Medicaid can begin to cover medical services. This is where the third test comes in. The medical services must be "medically necessary." This means that the patient's treatment plan must be certified by a physician as being necessary to address the patient's medical condition.

There are three levels of nursing home care: skilled, intermediate, and custodial. Although each state has its own rules, Medicaid will often cover the first two of these care levels as long as the care is medically necessary. Coverage of the intermediate-care level may require the patient to have specific functional limitations. Specific functional limitations may include not being able to toilet, feed, or bathe oneself. If your parents are receiving or have received Medicare coverage for a skilled nursing care stay, they will probably meet the medical necessity requirements for Medicaid benefits when their Medicare benefits run out. Dan's mother does not need Medicaid coverage yet as she has not depleted her Medicare lifetime reserve days (see Chapter 10). If her rehabilitation and care require a much longer stay, Dan will need to evaluate her eligibility for Medicaid.

Applying for Coverage

Once your parents decide to apply for Medicaid, you can help them prepare their "case." First, they can either represent themselves or name you as their authorized representative. If they appoint an authorized representative, they must do so in writing. When a representative has been appointed, the Medicaid administrative office must send copies of all correspondence to both parties. As an authorized representative, you are liable for giving incorrect information, whether you intended to do so or not. Medicaid has a right to reclaim any benefits based on incorrect or fraudulent information.

Regardless of the state in which your parents reside, you will make the application to the Medicaid office in the county in which they live or are institutionalized. The county's Medicaid office is required to have a face-to-face interview with either you or your parents. They are also required to visit the applicant's residence if necessary.

The county will decide if your parents are eligible for Medicaid within 45 days after receiving a dated application. To efficiently process the many requests for coverage that they receive, most states ask that you complete an application package before or during your interview with an eligibility technician. You should assemble all of the records listed in Table 11.1 and take them with you to the application interview. If after the initial interview and one follow-up letter you do not provide the information requested within the required period, your parents may be denied benefits because of "failure to cooperate." However, if the applicant is not able or not competent to obtain verifications, the burden of doing so is placed on the Medicaid department. You must request such assistance in writing.

Table 11.1 Information Needed for Medicaid Application and Interview

Item	Examples of Acceptable Documents
Proof of age	Birth certificate
	Census records
	Hospital certificate
	Baptismal certificate
	Insurance policy
	Military records
	Naturalization or passport records
	Notations in family Bible
	School records
Proof of citizenship	Alien registration card
	Consular report on birth
	Immigration document
	INS verification
	Naturalization certificate
	Voter registration card
Proof of identity	Driver's license
	Hospital or doctor records
	State identification card
	Voter registration card
	Work badge
Proof of income	Check stub
	Copy of previous year's income tax return
	Letter from employer
	Social security form
Living arrangements	Rent receipts
	Utility bills
Personal property valuation	Bankbooks
	Insurance policies
	NADA Official Used Car Guide
Real property valuation	County auditor's records
	Real estate dealer's statements
	Tax statements
Proof of relationship	Birth certificate
	Census records
	Divorce papers
	Insurance policy
	Other public agency records

Table 11.1 *(continued)*

Item	Examples of Acceptable Documents
Proof of residence	Bank records
	Driver's license
	Mortgage books
	Rent receipts
	Utility records
	Voter registration

The Date of Application The date you apply for Medicaid is very important and should be planned carefully. It will affect a number of factors, including the "look back" period, the assets that are exempt from consideration, and the patient's liability. These factors will be examined in detail later in this chapter. The date of application is the date you physically return the application to the family services office.

Acceptance or Denial for Benefits Once the family services department determines that your parents are eligible for Medicaid coverage, they will send a "notice of determination." In some cases, your parents may be eligible for assistance for up to 3 months prior to the date of the application. If your parents are denied coverage, the reasons for denying the application must be given in the written notice. You will also be told in the notice how to appeal a rejection, and given a contact person's name.

Appealing a Decision Sometimes coverage is denied. Or once coverage begins, it may be terminated for some reason. Don't be deterred. You have a right to appeal any denial or termination decision. If your parents are denied coverage, they must request, *in writing,* an appeals hearing within *90 days* of the date the Medicaid notice was *mailed to them.* If your parents' coverage has been terminated, they can continue to receive benefits, provided you submit a request for a hearing to the local agency within *15 days.* These appeals are called state hearings.

You can also make an "administrative appeal" if the state hearing results in a negative decision. Your appeals request must be *received* in the appropriate office within 15 calendar days of the date the adverse appeals decision was *mailed.*

The Income Test

Like most government assistance programs, Medicaid is available only to individuals with little income and small amounts of assets. The maximum income limits vary by state and by the marital status of the Medicaid recipient. (When two spouses are living in a nursing facility, their incomes will be evaluated separately.) The "well" spouse's income is not considered when determining the eligibility of the spouse who lives in a nursing facility, provided that the spouse applying for benefits has been institutionalized for at least 30 days.

> If your institutionalized parent is married, you do not want to apply for coverage for him or her until he or she has been hospitalized or in a nursing care facility for at least 30 days.

As you discovered in Chapter 2, your parents' income is probably limited to unearned income: interest, dividends, social security, and perhaps pension benefits. Your parents will meet the eligibility requirements if the cost of their care is greater than their monthly income. Your parents will be allowed to keep about $20 to $40 of their income each month to meet personal care needs. This amount is called a "disregard" amount, and the amount varies by state.

What happens if your parents' income exceeds the cost of care? Again, it depends on what state your parents live in. Many states use an "income cap" method. Others use a "spend-down" method to determine eligibility.

Income Cap Method

An income cap is exactly that. If your parents' income falls below the income cap, they meet the income test. The income cap equals three times the payment standard for the Supplemental Security Income program and increases each year. In 2002, the Supplemental Security Income standard was $545 per month, so the income cap was equal to $1,635 per month. No allowance for medical expenses is provided in an income cap state. If your parents' income is even $1 above the cap, they will be ineligible for benefits. The payment standard for the Supplemental Security Income program changes each year.

> If your parents' income exceeds the income cap, you may want to consider establishing a qualified income trust. A qualified income trust may allow your parents to shelter some income. Speak with an elder law specialist before making this move.

Spend-Down Method

With the spend-down method, income is adjusted for medical expenditures. States that use the spend-down method will evaluate whether an applicant's income, after medical expenses have been deducted, falls below a certain federal standard. If their adjusted income falls below the standard, your parents meet the income test. Note that individuals whose income exceeds the income standard can pay for additional medical and remedial care expenses to establish Medicaid eligibility.

The Asset Test

Medicaid applicants who meet the income test must also meet an asset test. Like the income criteria, the amount of assets an applicant may continue to own varies by state. The value of the assets your parents can keep will also depend on their marital status and the type of assets they own. Depending on their state of residence, single Medicaid applicants are allowed to keep between $1,500 and $5,000 of nonexempt assets. The amount increases, but does not double, for married couples. In addition, each Medicaid beneficiary may keep a few "exempt" assets. For example, a married applicant's spouse will be able to keep a house, but a single applicant will be expected to sell the house in a reasonable period of time and use the proceeds to pay for her or his nursing home care. Some assets, such as burial plots and life insurance policies, are exempt from consideration regardless of marital status. Because she is single, Mrs. Anderson's house and bank account balances would be considered as countable resources.

Regardless of when the asset test is performed, the countable resources are determined as of the beginning of the "first period of institutionalization." This occurs when a person is admitted to the hospital or nursing facility and it is determined that the stay is likely to be at least 30 consecutive days.

> **Countable resource:** An asset that is considered to be available to cover the cost of nursing home care.

Countable Resources

For purposes of Medicaid, "countable resources" include all the assets that your parents own that Medicaid expects to be used to cover the expenses of their care. The value of assets owned by both the applicant and the well spouse are counted. Ownership title and prenuptial agreements are disregarded in this determination. You will remember our discussion of assets in Chapter 3 and, hopefully, you will have prepared a balance sheet that will assist you here. In general, you can assume that all assets will be considered to be countable and that your parents will be able to retain between $1,500 and $5,000 of these assets. You need to ask the family services department what this amount is in your state.

Exempt Property

Some assets are "exempt property" and thus are not included in the definition of a countable resource. Some exemptions, such as a very minimal amount of life insurance and a burial plot, are available regardless of marital status. Others, such as homes and motor vehicles, are excluded from consideration only if the applicant is married to a healthy, noninstitutionalized, "well" spouse.

The Home   Your well parent may continue to live in the home for as long as necessary, and the value of the home will not be considered a countable resource. This exemption also applies if your applicant parent has a dependent child who is under age 21, blind, or disabled and is living in the home. If a sibling of the applicant parent shares ownership of the home and has lived in the home for 1 year, that sibling may continue to live in the home, and its value will not be considered a countable resource. In some cases, if a child of the applicant parent is over 65 and living in the home, it may be exempt.

Medicaid assumes that a single applicant's home is a countable resource. However, it exempts the personal residence for 6 months. This allows time to evaluate the need for nursing care and to determine whether or not the patient will be able to return home. At the end of 6 months, it is assumed that the individual will not be returning home, and the individual must place the home for sale; he or she may receive an additional 6 months' exemption while the home is for sale. The value of the countable resource is the fair market value as determined by a sale to an outside party or by the county auditor.

Some states are more lenient. If you can prove to your state's satisfaction that it is likely that your parent will return home, it may approve an extended exemption. You should make this request in all cases.

Autos   Single applicants are allowed to exempt the value of one automobile up to a maximum of $4,500. Any value in excess of $4,500 is included as a countable resource, regardless of whether the auto is to be sold. If a single applicant's auto is equipped for the handicapped or used for medical transportation on a regular basis, its total value may be exempt. Married applicants are allowed to exempt an unlimited value of a first automobile and $4,500 of equity in a second automobile. If a married couple's second auto is equipped for the handicapped or used for medical transportation on a regular basis, its total value may be exempt.

> If your parent is married, exempt the most expensive automobile for the well parent. Then exempt $4,500 of the value of the second auto.

Life Insurance Life insurance with a face value of $1,500 is exempt from the evaluation of available resources. The face value of a life insurance policy is the amount to be paid to the beneficiary upon the death of the insured. Once the sum of the *face values* of all policies exceeds $1,500, then the total *cash value* of all policies is counted as a resource. The cash value of a policy is the amount the life insurance company will pay if you surrender the policy and don't continue to maintain death coverage.

> Consider transferring life insurance policy ownership to children. Do this only subject to the rules discussed in the section on asset and income protection planning.

Burial Costs and Plots You may exempt burial spaces for your parents, siblings, and grandparents and their spouses. In addition, prepaid, nonrefundable burial expenses are exempt. There is no limit on the value of either of these items. Consider purchasing these in advance of applying for Medicaid.

Household Goods Household goods and personal effects, such as appliances, clothing, and jewelry, are exempt.

Businesses and Family Farms In most states, the value of a family farm is exempt as long as the farm is rented to others for income or farmed by the well spouse. In addition, real or personal property that is used in a trade or business by a well spouse may be exempt. Up to $6,000 of nonbusiness property is exempt if it is essential for self-support. You must remember that the income from these exempt assets will be included in the calculation of patient liability, discussed further on in this chapter.

Unavailable Property Sometimes property is not available for use or sale by the applicant. It may be owned jointly and the other owner is attempting to block a sale. Or there may be a legal order or contract forbidding its sale. In these cases, the value of the property will be exempt. However, income from the property can be considered when Medicaid determines the patient's share of the cost of services.

Property That Is Not Exempt

It is important to emphasize two types of property that are not considered exempt. Jointly owned property, other than the specific items listed in the previous section, is not generally considered exempt. To exempt the property, the applicant must show that the other owners will not cooperate in its sale and that liquidation cannot be forced legally.

In addition, if an applicant holds a life estate in a property, the value of that estate will be included at an amount determined from a life estate table. If the property cannot be sold, it will be exempt. To prove that the property cannot be sold, you must receive verification from two sources that the property is not salable or show evidence that the property was made available for sale but received no reasonable offers.

Are You Expected to Impoverish the Well Spouse?

The short answer is no. The Medicaid rules allow a well spouse to retain ownership of a minimum level of the couple's assets. This exception to the countable resource calculation is called the "spousal impoverishment consideration." In effect, the well spouse is allowed to retain 50 percent of the couple's countable resources. Medicaid expects that the remaining 50 percent will be used to pay for the institutionalized spouse's care before any Medicaid benefits are received.

Of course, allocating the couple's resources in this manner may in fact serve to impoverish the well spouse. To protect against this possibility, Congress enacted safeguards. The well spouse is allowed to keep a minimum amount of countable resources. This minimum amount is established by law and increases each year. The annual adjustments are tied to the Consumer Price Index. In 2003, the minimum amount of countable resources that the spouse was allowed to retain was $18,132.

Once the countable resources exceed two times the minimum, then the well spouse may keep 50 percent of the countable resources. However, in no case is the well spouse allowed to retain more than $90,660 in countable assets. For example, if countable resources equal $200,000, the well spouse can keep only $90,660, not 50 percent of the total, which would be $100,000.

Regardless of the amount retained by the well spouse, the institutionalized spouse keeps the basic exempted amount permitted in his or her state, $4,500 of value in an auto, a very minimal amount of life insurance face value, prepaid burial plans and plots, and personal property.

Within 1 year of qualifying for Medicaid, the institutionalized spouse must transfer to the well spouse enough assets to meet the well spouse's resource allocation. Once Medicaid is approved, the well spouse may acquire or accumulate additional assets. These newly acquired assets cannot be considered to be available to the Medicaid recipient spouse.

Patient Liability

Qualifying for benefits does not release the patient from paying any costs of her or his care. Once Medicaid is approved, the Medicaid department will calculate the "patient liability," or the amount the patient is required to pay toward her or his own care. This process is somewhat laborious, but you should work through it before applying for Medicaid benefits. The following example is used in Worksheet 11.1 to calculate the patient liability.

Katie and Kevin Fitzpatrick have been married for 60 years. Kevin has been placed in a skilled nursing facility. Their children are trying to determine what amount of the costs their parents will have to pay each month.

Kevin's social security benefit is $1,200 each month. Katie receives a monthly check for $600 from social security and $500 per month from an employer pension plan. In addition, they receive interest of about $500 per month from certificates of deposit. They live in Ohio, where the personal needs allowance (PNA) equals $40 per month. The Fitzpatricks' housing costs are $800 per month, and they spend $150 out-of-pocket each month on prescriptions and other medical costs that are not covered by insurance.

Worksheet 11.1 Calculating Patient Liability

Step	Example		Equals
Step 1. Total gross monthly income: social security, pensions, veteran's benefits, interest, and dividends. Don't include the well spouse's income or proceeds from house or investment sales.	His social security Interest Total income	$1,200 $500 $1,700	$1,700
Step 2. Subtract the personal needs allowance: Every state allows a Medicaid beneficiary some amount of income to meet personal needs [called the disregard amount or personal needs amount (PNA)].	His PNA	$40	$1,660
Step 3. Subtract the minimum monthly maintenance needs allowance (MMMNA)* for the well spouse. (Skip this step if single.) The MMMNA equals 150% of the federal poverty level for a family of two and changes each February. Call your Medicaid office for the number to use.	MMMNA	$1,407	$253
Step 4. Subtract the excess shelter allowance. If the total of rent or mortgage, property taxes, homeowner's insurance, and a utility allowance of $244 exceeds 30% of the MMMNA, subtract the difference. The maximum varies by state.	Housing costs Plus utility allowance Equals Less 30% of MMMNA ($1,407) Equals	$800 $244 $1,044 ($422) $622	($369)
Step 5. Add income received in the well spouse's name only.	Her social security Her pension Total	$600 $500 $1,100	$731
Step 6. Subtract monthly medical and remedial care costs not covered by Medicaid.	Uncovered medical costs	$150	$581

Worksheet 11.1 (continued)

Step	Example	Equals
Step 7. Subtract monthly costs for past medical care debt (including that for dependents if Medicaid recipient is obligated to pay)	None	$581
Step 8. Subtract monthly premiums for private health insurance, such as Medigap or long-term-care insurance. This equals the patient's liability.	None	$581 The patient would have to pay $581 of his monthly medical costs.

*The state Medicaid office can increase this amount if exceptional circumstances apply. Exceptional circumstances may include catastrophic illness or home repair/maintenance costs.

Asset and Income Protection Planning

The cost of nursing home care for an ill parent can be devastating. The average cost of care in an intermediate or skilled nursing facility exceeds $4,000 per month. It won't take long for your parents' income and assets to be completely depleted when long-term care in such a facility is required. This section of the chapter presents basic concepts of the Medicaid program that you should understand when planning for Medicaid usage, the methods and techniques that you may consider to protect your parents' wealth for transfer to other generations, and the rules that allow Medicaid to recover your parents' assets after their death.

When your parents need nursing home care, your family will have to make some very difficult planning decisions. You have three choices. First, you can use all their available resources to pay for their care until their assets are depleted, then apply for Medicaid assistance. Second, you can choose to transfer some assets to you and your siblings, which will reduce the assets that are available to pay for your parents' care. Your parents will then qualify for assistance earlier, and you will have protected some of the family assets. Third, if you plan several years in advance, you can have your parents keep just enough assets to meet their living expenses until they require nursing facility care and have Medicaid pick up the entire cost for their care.

Some families develop a plan that avoids the complete depletion of the family's wealth by spending and transferring assets well in advance of the need to qualify for Medicaid. If your parents are considering applying for Medicaid, they should obtain good advice from a qualified elder law professional.

Basic Concepts

Before we begin to examine ways in which you can protect your parents' wealth, you will need to understand a few more basic concepts. Medicaid is designed to pay for long-term care when the applicant can't and Medicare and other insurance won't. Spending and transferring assets in order to protect family wealth and still qualify for Medicaid is contrary to the intent of the program. Therefore, Congress designed rules to minimize the likelihood that a family could avoid using its own resources to pay for care and to penalize those who attempted to do so. Two of these rules involve a "look-back" period and a "penalty" period.

The "Look-Back" Period   The look-back period is a 36-month period of time beginning at the point when the applicant became institutionalized *and* applied for Medicaid benefits. If these two dates are not the same, then the look-back period begins at the later of the two dates. Your parents do not have to apply for Medicaid coverage immediately upon entering a nursing facility. In fact, you will want to carefully plan when they apply for coverage. This decision is discussed more thoroughly in the section on the penalty period.

Many families use trusts to manage parents' assets and financial affairs. In general, the length of the look-back period is extended to 60 months for any monies that were transferred to or from a trust. If your family uses a trust to manage your parents' money, be sure to get professional legal advice before applying for Medicaid.

Medicaid is particularly interested in looking for property that is given away for free or for less than fair market value during the look-back period. The rule presumes that any gifts or transfers for less than fair market value were made specifically to allow the applicant to qualify for Medicaid. However, Medicaid allows an exception to this rule for routine gifts that have been made regularly for a long period of time, such as those made to take advantage of the annual gift exclusion for estate planning purposes. Feel free to challenge Medicaid when it includes gifts that were made under these conditions.

The Penalty Period   Your parents are disqualified from receiving Medicaid coverage during the penalty period. The length of the penalty period depends upon the value of the assets that were given away and the average cost of nursing facility care in your state. It is easy to calculate.

The penalty period equals:

$$\frac{\text{The total value of assets transferred for less than fair market value in the look-back period}}{\text{The average monthly cost of nursing facility care in your state}}$$

There is no maximum limit on the length of the penalty period.

The penalty period starts on the first day of the first month in which a gift was made for less than fair market value. Because these concepts are difficult, let's look at some examples. Betty Wolff is an Ohio resident. On June 1, 2002, she gave each of her four children $12,500 in certificates of deposit, for total gifts of $50,000. On August 1, 2002, she entered a nursing care facility. She applied for Medicaid on September 1, 2002. The average cost of nursing home care in the state of Ohio is determined to be $4,100 per month. Her penalty period equals $50,000 divided by $4,100, or 12 months from the date of the first transfer on June 1, 2002. Therefore, she will not be eligible to receive Medicaid coverage until June 1, 2003.

Betty's case was fairly simple. However, let's consider the situation of Rich Thompson. He lives in Kansas, where the average cost of care is $3,300. On April 1, 2000, he transferred $132,000 to his only child. Mary, his daughter, placed him in a nursing facility 24 months later, on April 1, 2002. She immediately filed an application for Medicaid. Rich's penalty period is 40 months ($132,000/$3,300) from the date of transfer, April 1, 2000. Rich will not qualify for Medicaid until August 1, 2003. Had Mary waited until April 2, 2003, to file the Medicaid application, Rich would have qualified immediately, as the look-back period (36 months) would have extended only to April 2, 2000. The Thompsons would have benefited from four more months of coverage, an amount of $13,200!

Of course, because of emergencies or unforeseen events, not every family will be able to plan ahead and begin disposing of assets before a parent enters a nursing care facility. As your parents age and begin to lose their faculties, however, you will want to give serious thought to beginning some asset transfers.

The average patient enters a nursing home at age 85. Thus, you may want to begin to evaluate your parents' Medicaid qualification status when they are in their late 70s.

Spending Assets

Many situations will call for your parents to "spend down" their assets. The look-back and penalty periods apply to gifts or transfers made to others at less than fair market value. However, the asset assessment does not penalize your parents for spending their assets during the 36 months prior to institutionalization and application. In fact, you will want to consider a large number of possible expenditures before applying for Medicaid. As you evaluate spend-down options, keep in mind that expenditures for the benefit of the well spouse will rarely be questioned. Medicaid will examine expenditures made by a single, institutionalized applicant more closely. Some particular transfers are examined in more detail in the box.

Expenditures to Consider to Reduce Assets

- Pay off home mortgage
- Make all major repairs
- Buy a larger, more expensive home for the well spouse
- Buy a new car for the well spouse
- Pay off all debts (medical debts last)
- Prepay funeral expenses
- Purchase burial lots for parents, children, and in-laws
- Prepay utility, cable television, telephone, and newspaper services
- Prepay property taxes
- Buy the well spouse clothing and personal effects to last a year or two
- Purchase cash or gift cards for groceries, gas, and other day-to-day items
- Purchase an annuity

Annuities   Many families consider taking a portion of their parents' assets and purchasing an annuity. An annuity is an insurance product that pays a periodic income benefit to a beneficiary. In most cases, income from an annuity will be considered when Medicaid applies the income test and evaluates the applicant for eligibility. However, if the annuity was purchased during the look-back period, the amount paid for the annuity may also be considered as a countable resource in the asset test. To determine whether the annuity was purchased for less than fair market value, Medicaid will want to know whether the individual can be reasonably expected to live longer than the guarantee period of the annuity. If so, then there is no penalty. Because some states do not examine the well parent's income as thoroughly as the institutionalized parent's income, buying an annuity for a well spouse may be an idea that is worth considering.

Transferring Assets

Transferring assets to individuals other than the well parent is one of the ways to avoid using all of your parents' wealth to pay for long-term care. In most cases, your parents will transfer their assets to you and your siblings. It does not help to give assets to the well parent, as they will still be counted in the available resources assessment. There is one very important note of caution here. Regardless of intent, neither you nor your siblings nor other recipients of gifts will be required to use these gifts for your parents' benefit later. Once the gift has been made, there is no "take back," and it is likely that many siblings or gift recipients will use the funds for their own purposes before your parents die. Property transfers to consider are included in the sidebar "Assets to Consider Giving."

Assets to Consider Giving

- Life insurance policies
- Investment assets
- Cash
- Home (consider this as a last resort)

As you consider which assets to give to children and other family members or friends, be sure to consider the other implications of the gift. For example, keeping cash assets will allow your parents maximum flexibility in managing their finances. Transferring financial investment assets will lessen their future income taxes, but the new owner will have to pay capital gains taxes on the future sale.

Related Issues

The Medicaid system is complex and confusing. Even if your parents qualify for coverage, their estates may be liable for repaying the benefits once both of your parents die. In addition, many families question whether or not they should apply for and benefit from Medicaid.

Medicaid Estate Recovery

The Medicaid program can reclaim your parents' assets after they are dead. Regardless of whether your institutionalized parent was single or married when he or she received Medicaid benefits, the estate recovery program is designed to recoup the monies Medicaid spent on your parent while she or he was alive. Estate assets, including homes and financial accounts, may be recovered to reimburse Medicaid for the costs of nursing facilities, hospital services, and prescription drug services. Federal law requires states to attempt to recover some of their expenses from the estates of Medicaid beneficiaries. There are rules about what property Medicaid can recover and when Medicaid can recover your parents' property.

Medicaid can attempt to recover assets from any beneficiary who received benefits after October 1, 1993, and who was age 55 or older when the services were received. The beneficiary must also have lived in a nursing or intermediate care facility or received home or community-based services.

Assets cannot be recovered until both of your parents are deceased, and you may be able to obtain a waiver if undue hardship would occur. In addition, and very importantly, only assets that are subject to probate are deemed to be recoverable. Therefore, with careful planning, you can avoid estate recovery by making your parents' home and financial assets jointly owned with rights of survivorship to you or your siblings, or by using payable on death, transfer on death, and direct beneficiary designations (see Chapters 14 and 15).

Once one of your parents dies, consider placing the surviving parent's assets in a trust or changing the title to reflect joint ownership with rights of survivorship with you or your siblings. Also, ensure that all financial assets either name direct beneficiaries or name payable-on-death or transfer-on-death designees.

Moral Decisions

Many families have no choice; they must apply for Medicaid coverage in order to provide their parents with the care they need. However, a large number of families do have the wealth to pay for many months of care. If your family falls into this category, you will have to make a conscious decision as to whether or not to deliberately deplete your parents' assets in order to qualify them for Medicaid. This decision involves examining your personal attitudes about protecting your family's wealth and accepting government assistance, and the details of the income and asset management that will be required in order to qualify for Medicaid. It is important that you and your parents discuss the use of Medicaid and plan well in advance of the need for its coverage.

There are, of course, two sides to this argument. On the one hand, many families feel that they have no obligation to impoverish a well spouse to provide care for an institutionalized spouse. Other families carry the argument a bit further. They feel that their parents are not required to deplete the accumulated assets for which they worked long and hard. They feel that their parents have a right to choose to pass their wealth to the next generation. Some families simply feel that their parents paid taxes for many years and therefore deserve to benefit from the social service programs when they need them.

On the other hand, many families think that the resources their parents acquired should be used for their care. In addition, they may assume that the social service programs should not be used unless a real need exists. Or, the family members may feel that if their parents don't need and don't use Medicaid's benefits, more services will be available for patients who have a serious financial need.

If your parents' wealth level exceeds the exempt amount that Medicaid allows, you will be faced with this decision. Consult with all of your siblings and respected advisers before making any decision to apply for coverage.

Final Thoughts

In the very best case, you will never need to make a decision about applying for Medicaid coverage for your parents. However, as the average life expectancy in this country increases, the likelihood that you will be faced with the need to do so increases. Medicaid is a complicated social service program that, among other things, provides medical insurance coverage for impoverished aged, blind, or disabled citizens. The qualification rules are numerous and complex. Your parents will need to meet income and asset tests. You will need to make decisions regarding the effective management of assets and income in order to qualify your parents for coverage. And, you may also have to examine your moral position about using the program's benefits if they are not truly needed. Once you make the decision to apply for Medicaid coverage, you need to plan appropriately to maximize Medicaid's programs benefits. You may want to visit the following Web sites for more information: www.aarp.org, http://cms.hhs.gov, and www.benefitscheckup.org.

Part III

Consuming

12

Housing

*D*an Anderson's mother, Marian, is 85 years old. In the past
2 years she has battled mild memory loss, a mild form of
osteoporosis, and volatile blood pressure. After breaking her hip
and having a brief hospitalization, she was admitted to a local
nursing facility for rehabilitation. She has since spent several
months in a skilled nursing facility. Dan visits her several times
a week and has come to realize that she will not be able to return
home without assistance. He's not even sure she should return
home. Although his mother has not yet mentioned the subject,
he knows she will be devastated if she is forced to leave the house
she's lived in for 55 years.

THE COST OF HOUSING is one of the largest expenses in the budget of
an elderly person. Also, choosing or changing the home environment is
probably the most emotional issue an elderly person will face. Your role
in assisting your parents with their housing situation is difficult. On
the one hand, you can't appear to dictate where they live or force them
to live less independently. On the other hand, you may be able to more
objectively assess their ability to competently maintain their own home
and provide for their own safety. At some point, your parents may not
be able to afford to stay in their home. Either the costs of upkeep will
have risen faster than their income, or they will need to access the equity
in their home in order to meet their living expenses.

This chapter will help you and your parents make sound housing
choices. You will find information about the types of housing available
to your parents and how to ease the transition should a move be necessary. A thorough discussion of housing finance options is presented,
including the possibility of using a reverse annuity mortgage to allow
your parents to stay in their home while accessing some of its equity for
day-to-day use.

Examining and evaluating any physical moves will go much more
smoothly with advance planning. Even if your parents don't currently

need to make a change, you can read this chapter as you begin to think about the possibilities. In many cases, housing adjustments are required quickly, and if you have thought about them before, then you'll be ready.

Options for Living Space

Housing developers have not failed to notice the growth in the number of older people in the United States. They are busy planning and building many alternative forms of housing for the senior citizen market. These options include smaller single-family homes, limited-mobility condominium options, assisted living arrangements, and of course, intermediate and skilled nursing care facilities. The type of residence your parents choose will be based on the amount of independence they can manage, the types of services they need, the cost of the housing, and whether a specific facility meets their needs.

Staying in Their Own Home

Without a doubt, most seniors would prefer to remain in familiar surroundings for as long as possible. Not only is their home a place where they feel comfortable, but it may also hold a considerable amount of sentimental value. And, because it is likely that their home is paid off, this may be the least expensive option.

Most people are able to live in their own homes until they contract a major illness or experience mobility problems. For others, however, the physical layout or condition of their home may prompt a move. Married couples may be able to remain independent more easily because the spouses tend to complement and help each other. Until your parents are unable to maintain their quality of life in a safe manner, and as long as they can afford to remain in their home, they will probably be happiest there. Marian's ability to maneuver in her home is Dan's greatest concern. Her bedroom is upstairs and her laundry is in the basement of her 60-year-old bungalow.

Even when your parents can no longer maintain the physical structure of their home, there are options that will enable you to keep them there. Help can be hired to mow the lawn, clean the house, and perform minor repairs and maintenance. If the cost of hiring such help is affordable, it may be best for your parents to stay put.

Your parents' needs may range from assistance with the day-to-day chores to having full-time aides available to help them toilet, bathe, or eat. Be sure to inquire about possible Medicare coverage before hiring an individual or home health company to provide these services. If Medicare is paying the costs, the service company must be a Medicare-certified home health care agency. Long-term care insurance generally follows similar rules in determining what providers can be reimbursed.

If you are going to hire home assistance, lock up alcohol, controlled medications, credit cards, and valuables, and inventory these items regularly. Arrange for income checks to be automatically deposited to your parents' bank account, and review bills and records periodically.

In some cases, it will be the physical layout of the house that poses a problem. Perhaps your folks can no longer climb stairs or the laundry room is inaccessible. In such a case, consider the possibility of making physical changes in order to accommodate your parents' changing needs. Is it possible to convert a downstairs dining room, family room, or den to a bedroom? Can a full bath with appropriate bathing facilities be made available on the first floor? What would need to be done to move the washer and dryer to the main floor—perhaps near the kitchen or bath? The cost of making these changes may be minor relative to the selling costs you would incur if you decided to sell the home and find a more suitable residence.

Many adaptations are small and can be done yourself to save money. Consider widening doorways; installing increased lighting, lever faucet and door handles, hand-held showerheads, and grab bars in the bathtub; putting banisters on both sides of stairways; and installing extra phones in the bathroom and bedroom.

More often than not, it's an illness, an injury, or the death of a spouse that prompts the decision to move. In such a case, you need to look at all suitable alternatives—and, there are many. Our discussion of housing options flows from those that offer the senior the most independence to those that provide extensive living and medical assistance. Table 12.1 outlines the types of housing and relevant issues you will need to consider.

Table 12.1 Housing Types and Relevant Issues

Housing Type	Issues
Apartment	Accessibility, cost, location, neighbors, quality of maintenance, size of living space
Condominium	Accessibility, cost, location, monthly maintenance fee, neighbors, quality of maintenance, property taxes, size of living space
Single-family home	Accessibility, cost, location, neighbors, property taxes, repairs and maintenance, size of living space, size and care of lawn/garden
Living with children	Accessibility, expenses, privacy, size of living space
Assisted living/senior housing	Cost, insurance reimbursement, meals, personal assistance, personality and training of staff, recreation programs, size of living space, transportation
Intermediate care	Cost, insurance reimbursement, meals, medical care, personal assistance, personality and training of staff, recreation programs, size of living space, transportation
Skilled nursing care	Cost, meals, insurance reimbursement, medical care, personal assistance, personality and training of staff, recreation programs, size of living space

Moving to a Smaller Space

Many parents may be able to care for themselves quite nicely. It's the big house that they've lived in for years that's the problem. In this event, an apartment, a smaller house, or a condominium may be just the thing. Clearly identifying why their present home doesn't work puts you well on the way to making a list of what you're looking for in a new home.

Selling Your Parents' Home   Before they purchase a new home, your parents will have to prepare their current home for sale. The first step in this process is for your parents to interview three qualified real estate agents and select one to list their home for sale. A qualified real estate agent will be licensed by the state and be active in the local Board of Realtors. Your parents should select an agent who has experience in representing both sellers and buyers in your neighborhood. A real estate agent who is active in the neighborhood will be better able to accurately price your parents' home for sale and is more likely to have a potential buyer for the house.

Most real estate agents ask for a 6-month contract. If your parents' home does not sell within a reasonable period of time, it is probably priced too high. At that point, consider lowering the price. Your parents should consider switching real estate agents if the home has not been sold at the end of 6 months.

Your parents will pay the real estate agent a commission for selling their home. Commission rates vary by geographic location but usually range from 6 to 8 percent of the final selling price of the residence. The amount of the commission should be clearly stated in the contract with the real estate agent. The agent then covers the cost of all advertising and marketing.

Because your parents have probably lived in their home for many years, preparing the home for sale may involve a lot of work. The home will have to be thoroughly cleaned from top to bottom. Your parents will need to discard unused items of furniture, appliances, and clothing. Repairs will need to be made, including putting a fresh coat of paint on the walls, the front doors, and possibly the exterior of the home. You may also need to update the décor in order to compete in the housing market. This includes removing clutter, purchasing a few minor accessories, and removing furniture that tends to crowd a room. Ask the real estate selling agent to provide a list of items that should be addressed before the home is placed for sale.

Searching for a New Home   No matter what type of housing your parents are considering, they should pay attention to all access issues. The housing unit should be easily accessible for both the elderly and the physically handicapped. There should be at least one bedroom and bath on the first floor. Check that the door openings can accommodate a wheelchair. Ensure that the unit includes washer and dryer hookups to make it easier for you or your parents to do their laundry. Ideally, the laundry facilities will be convenient to the bedroom or bath. The kitchen floor plan and the accessibility of cabinets are very important to elders. A one-story home may be the answer to Marian's needs. She may be able to continue living independently if her bedroom, bath, and laundry are on one floor.

In addition to access issues, you will want to examine the lot on which the residence sits. Your parents may need assistance to maintain the lawn and garden. Are the grounds conducive to gardening or bird watching? A neighborhood with a lot of young families may be too noisy. Consider security issues. Also examine the neighborhood for convenient churches, grocery stores, banks, hair salons, and dry cleaners.

Apartments   Any large city will offer an abundance of apartments of all shapes and sizes. Living in an apartment is drastically different from living in a single-family home. Many large apartment complexes house a lot of young single people, and their living styles may not complement your parents' living styles. However, apartments are often conveniently located relative to shopping, public transportation, and public facilities such as libraries, churches, and entertainment venues. It should be easy to find one-story units that are easily accessible, but you will certainly want to evaluate the security of the neighborhood and the individual complex.

Condominium Living   Condominium living often offers the best qualities of two housing worlds. Spacious living spaces are available for ownership in most communities. Owners can usually decorate their condo in any manner they choose, although the condominium association may place restrictions on exterior decorating. However, the main advantage of condominiums is that while owners pay for upkeep and maintenance on a monthly basis, they don't have to arrange for or perform repairs and maintenance.

Smaller House or Garden Home   Most communities have a wide variety of single-family housing, and the smaller homes may be just right for your parents. While a smaller home or a one-story home may be no less expensive than your parents' current home, it may allow them to continue living independently. Smaller homes generally have smaller yards, and you may be able to use low- or no-maintenance landscaping to reduce the upkeep. Moving to a smaller house also allows your parents to begin the "step-down" process of giving away or selling some of their personal property. In addition, they may be able to find a house with all of the living space on one floor or with kitchen and bath designs that are more appropriate for an older resident. Garden homes are much like condominiums in that they have an association that provides for exterior maintenance. The advantage of a garden home is that each residence is an individual structure.

Moving In with Children

For a child, the decision to combine his or her household with that of a parent is very difficult. Both your family and your parents are putting their privacy at risk. Each family has its own living habits, ways of doing tasks, and time schedules. You may not be able to make enough space available to meet your parents' needs. Living together may stress an already tenuous relationship. All of these factors need to be considered before you agree to share living space. Living together with his mother may not be an option for Dan. His work schedule may not permit him to provide enough time for Marian's care.

There may be advantages to sharing living space. Living expenses can be shared, and your parents may be able to provide needed household help. It may be possible for you to add space to house your parents. Sometimes, for economic reasons, combining households is the only choice available.

Should you decide to combine households with your parents, you and your parents should develop clear, but flexible, guidelines for sharing space. These guidelines should address the responsibility for living expenses, the allocation of household space, household chores and maintenance, and time schedules. Some legal documents may be necessary, especially if you are going to co-own a house.

One of the obvious issues in combining households is the amount and allocation of living space. Some families choose to add a private living suite to their home. This "suite" may include a bedroom, private bath, and living room or kitchenette. Others simply allocate a bedroom and let the parents share the kitchen and living space. Still others mesh their lives completely and involve the parents in all of the family's activities, including meals and recreation.

In addition to the financial issues, combining households may raise social issues as well. Social lives may become blurred. Will your parents expect to be included in your social activities? What will your role be in their lives? If you still have children at home, you will need to closely examine the impact that moving your parents in will have on their lives. Disciplining children often becomes a major problem. Include your children in these discussions—they may be the family members who are most affected by the decision. Regardless of which issues your family will face, you will need to set clear boundaries and explicitly discuss your and your parents' expectations.

Consider having a professional family counselor or therapist help you and your parents with the decision-making and transition processes.

Assisted Living Arrangements

The term *assisted living* is used to describe everything from senior housing facilities that offer no communal services to facilities in which extensive medical care is available. Residents are able to maintain independent lifestyles while still having access to a minimal amount of care if needed. Rather than relying on what a facility calls itself, you should conduct an extensive review of the assisted living marketplace before choosing a residence for your parents.

Assisted living facilities are most appropriate for seniors who may need a bit of living assistance, such as housekeeping and a meal or two each day, but who are still fairly independent. These facilities may or may not offer assistance with personal care activities, such as bathing. Most of them offer a furnished or unfurnished room or small apartment, housekeeping and cleaning services, and possibly some personal care assistance. The facility usually provides a recreation program, limited or prescheduled transportation services, and resident monitoring. Your parents will generally not receive any medical, nursing, or rehabilitative care. This type of housing option could provide Marian with the monitoring that she needs while allowing her some independence.

Medical Care Facilities

Medical care facilities, also known as nursing homes, conjure up unpleasant images. However, these facilities range from providing extremely poor, neglectful environments to offering luxurious living spaces. At some point your parents may require medical care in addition to housing. Facilities vary in the level of medical care they offer; however, all provide room and board along with monitoring, personal assistance, and health care for residents.

Your job is to match your parents' needs and personality with a quality facility. Most important, the facility should provide the level of care that your parents require. In addition, the property must be well maintained and clean. The staff must be well trained, appropriately certified, and pleasant.

Custodial Care Facility   Custodial care facilities are the most common medical care facilities and will have the most long-term residents. The living environment may be less clinical and less sterile than that in facilities with a higher level of care. Extensive medical care is generally not included, but assistance with the normal activities of daily living, such as bathing, eating, and toileting, is offered. Recreation and transportation services are usually a staple of this level of care. Marian may need this type of care during a transition period until rehabilitation restores her to full mobility.

Intermediate-Care Facilities These facilities are perfect for long-term residents who suffer from chronic illnesses or from some physical or mental impairment. Most of the residents are ambulatory. You will find that the facilities generally offer recreation programs and physical therapy. Extensive medical care and other types of therapy will cost extra.

Skilled Nursing Care Facilities Patients in a skilled nursing facility require a fairly high level of nursing care as well as extensive personal assistance. Most prescribed medical services and therapies are available in skilled nursing facilities.

Tips for Choosing a Nursing Facility

- Visit facilities before the need is immediate.
- Take an official tour of the residence.
- Visit the facility at least twice more, unannounced.
- Observe the residents—their care, demeanor, and activity levels.
- Examine the upkeep of the grounds, building, furniture, and equipment.
- Eat at the facility to check on food quality.
- Check on the facility's certification with your state's long-term-care ombudsman's office.
- Ask for referrals of patient's family members.
- Request a list of all charges, both base and for amenities, prescriptions, recreation, and aide services.
- Review any contracts with your attorney or an elder care specialist.

Housing Finance

The cost of senior housing varies widely and is dependent upon the type of housing your parents choose, the amount of space purchased, and the type and extent of auxiliary services desired. As you examine the financial costs and financing options, you will need to consider the up-front and monthly costs, the availability of funds to meet your parents' investment needs, and what the return on their investment will be, if any. In addition, you should inquire whether the cost is covered by Medicare, Medicaid, or private insurance.

Rent

Apartment rents are highly dependent upon geographic region, the size of the unit, the location of the property, and the types of amenities included. Rents are usually higher for first-floor units and those that are close to the front of a complex. Keep in mind that while a prime location may be a bit more expensive, your parents may be able to save on transportation costs by walking to their activities or taking advantage of public transit. A location that is convenient to you will simplify your life.

While rental rates vary widely, you should expect to pay $400 to $1,000 per month for a nice one-bedroom apartment. To determine the going cost in your area, review the classified ads in the local newspaper, talk with a real estate agent, or call several rental communities in your neighborhood.

Assisted living programs often include meals and auxiliary services. Therefore, your parents will pay between $1,200 and $3,500 per month, depending on the size of their living space and the amount of personal services they may use. Costs will vary; you can get information concerning average costs from your local council on aging or social service agencies.

There are several financial advantages to renting. Because rents are usually the same for at least a year, it is easy to budget. When your parents need to move into another type of housing, it is relatively easy and inexpensive to move. Your parents will also have no funds tied up in home equity and will be able to invest their funds to generate income if needed.

Home Ownership

While moving to a smaller home or condominium is attractive for many reasons, financially it is not very different from owning a home. Your parents may be surprised to find that the cost of smaller housing is not much less than the fair market value of their current home. However, they may be able to reap the benefits of lower upkeep and utilities costs and smaller insurance and property tax payments if they purchase a smaller property.

Be sure to check with the county treasurer's office about any reduced property tax rates for seniors. Your parents' property tax could be significantly reduced if they qualify for any special programs.

Senior communities are widely available. Within such a community, each resident owns his or her own home. The housing often consists of manufactured housing or reasonably priced and reasonably sized homes. The communities offer social activities specifically geared to the senior market. Homeowners generally pay an annual fee to access the social activities and for the upkeep common areas such as pools, recreation halls, and party rooms.

Condominium ownership has an additional financial obligation because your parents will be required to make a monthly maintenance payment. These payments can be steep and depend upon what services are included. However, repair, maintenance, and insurance costs are reduced because the condominium association is responsible for building and outdoor maintenance. Be aware that condominium associations can assess an extra fee for unusual repairs or maintenance and that your parents will not be allowed to "opt out" of these.

The majority of the elderly own their homes without a mortgage. While this is often a lifelong goal and reduces the amount of income required to meet living expenses it does mean that a significant amount of your parents' assets is not available for investing or producing additional income. Also, the rate of growth in the value of homes may not be as great as that in the stock or bond markets.

Your parents will have to decide whether they wish to carry a mortgage balance on their personal residence. The Equal Credit Opportunity Act prohibits lenders from discriminating against your parents because of their age or marital status. However, when lenders assess credit risk, they do consider the likelihood of repayment and the amount and sources of income your parents have. Because your parents are retired, they may have little regular, periodic income from pensions or social security. So, even though they have significant assets, they may not qualify for as large a mortgage as they desire.

> If a lender does not think your parents can manage the monthly mortgage payment, consider making a larger down payment to reduce the monthly costs.

Reverse Annuity Mortgage

As the U.S. population ages, you are likely to see the use of reverse annuity mortgages increase as well. These mortgages are best for people who own few assets other than for their homes but who are physically able to remain independent or who can live alone with some home health assistance.

> **Reverse annuity mortgage:** A mortgage in which the property owner borrows against the value of a personal residence and receives a monthly payment instead of making a monthly payment.

A reverse annuity mortgage may be useful for your parents. If they were to take out such a mortgage against the value of their home, each month the lender would send them a check. The amount of the monthly payment would depend on the fair market value of the home, your parents' ages, and what type of reverse annuity mortgage they chose. Reverse mortgage borrowers continue to own their homes, so your parents would still be responsible for property taxes, insurance, and repairs. Once your parents leave the home permanently, the home is sold and the lender receives repayment of the amount borrowed and the accrued interest.

There are three types of reverse annuity mortgages. The first type is a single-purpose mortgage. The funds must be used for one purpose, and your parents simply take out one lump sum withdrawal. The single-purpose mortgage may be used if your parents need to make home repairs or improvements.

Federally insured reverse annuity mortgages generally offer a monthly payment that is guaranteed for life or for as long as your parents remain in their home. Some of these mortgages even offer a credit line upon which your parents can draw as they need money. Regardless of the total amounts of benefits and withdrawals, your parents or their estate can never owe more than the value of the home at the time the loan is repaid.

Proprietary reverse annuity mortgages are not backed by the government and are hard to compare. They generally carry the largest upfront costs. Because these loans are not federally insured, the terms of the loans vary widely. Be sure to compare all the terms of the loan if you choose to use a proprietary reverse annuity mortgage.

Reverse annuity mortgages offer many advantages. The homeowner can live in the home for as long as he or she likes. The fixed monthly income allows for ease in budgeting. No monthly payment is required to repay the loan. Finally, the income from a mortgage is not taxable, making it less likely that your parents' social security benefits will be taxed.

Because reverse annuity mortgages offer a monthly benefit, if your parents take out such a mortgage, they may not qualify for social service program assistance. Or, if they don't use the monies each month, their total assets will grow, which may also disqualify them from other benefits.

You may wish to consider alternatives to getting a reverse annuity mortgage from a financial institution. Home equity loans will appear attractive, but they require an interest repayment each month. If your parents need a reverse annuity mortgage for cash flow, they will probably not be in a position to repay the interest on a home equity line of credit. Some family members may be able to finance a reverse annuity mortgage themselves. For example, three or four children may be able to contribute to the monthly payment. In return, when the parent dies, the home is divided equally among them as repayment for the loan. You will need to be cautious about having proper legal agreements in such situations.

Reverse annuity mortgages are fairly new and can be quite complex. Be sure to obtain competent financial advice from an accountant, financial adviser, or attorney before entering into such an agreement.

Shared Housing Costs

From a financial standpoint, moving in with you may be the least expensive housing option available to your parents. However, this option generally exacts the highest emotional costs. You will have to determine how housing costs are going to be shared. In addition to housing and utility costs, you need to consider how other living costs are going to be covered. For example, who is going to pay for food, clothing, and transportation?

Some families decide to build or buy a larger home in order to accommodate an aging parent. In this case, is the equity from the sale of your parents' home going to be contributed to the down payment on the new home? Or are the proceeds going to be invested in order to generate income for your parents? Who will own the new home? How are you going to protect yourself legally and financially in the event of their deaths?

Life Care Plans

Life care plans or some variation thereof have become popular in the past two decades. These plans are associated with assisted living and nursing facilities or properties that offer several levels of care. The general idea is that your parents contract with the facility to provide care for the remainder of their lives. As their need for care increases, your parents will not have to move to another facility, but instead will "step up" to the next level of care.

There are two costs associated with life care plans: an up-front entrance fee and monthly fees. Most life care communities require entrants to "purchase" a unit, pay a significant up-front fee, or transfer assets to the facility in exchange for a lifetime of care. These fees range from $50,000 to $300,000 and are used for the long-term operational costs of the facilities. In many cases, the up-front fee is nonrefundable. Some facilities will refund a portion of the entry fee if your parents move or die after only a brief stay. Because the entry fees are very high, you will want to have a professional geriatric counselor or attorney examine any contract before your parents sign it.

In addition to an entry fee, residents are charged a monthly fee for day-to-day expenses or rent. The monthly fee normally increases annually and can be quite steep. At the base level, most facilities include at least one meal a day in their package. Some include minor medical exams or regular visits from a social worker in their fees. As your parents need increased care and services, the cost will increase. Because the cost of these plans and the services they offer vary widely, you will need to study the contract carefully before your parents sign it. Pay particular attention to whether there is a cap on price increases and how any increases are calculated. Don't sign a contract that does not clearly disclose this information.

There is a tax advantage to these life care facilities. Most such facilities allocate the entry fee and monthly fee between medical care costs and room and board services. Be sure to inquire as to what percentage of the fees is normally considered to be for medical care. Remember that the deduction can be taken only in the year the fees are paid.

Take advantage of the itemized deduction for the portion of the entry and monthly nursing home fees that is attributed to providing medical care for your parents.

Insurance Reimbursements

Nursing care facilities are quite expensive. The cost of a custodial care residence begins at $80 per day. Care in a skilled nursing facility averages $153 per day in the United States. Rates vary widely across geographic regions and are often dependent upon the type of facility and the amenities available.

As we discussed in Chapters 10 and 11, Medicare will not cover the cost of nursing home stays unless the patient requires skilled nursing care. Even if your parent qualifies for skilled nursing care, Medicare will only pay for the first 100 days of care.

Because the cost of care is so expensive, many families take advantage of the Medicaid program. Medicaid may pay for custodial, intermediate, and skilled nursing care if your parents' income is insufficient to pay for the services and they have exhausted their assets. You may wish to review Chapter 11 about Medicaid, the type of care it covers, and how your parents can qualify for benefits.

The IRS does allow a deduction for the cost of stays in a skilled nursing facility. However, it does not allow a medical deduction for the room and board portion of the cost of care in a nursing facility.

Final Thoughts

Do not wait until your parents are forced to make a housing change to begin exploring living options. There are many housing options available for seniors, each with its own advantages. You will want to match your parents' specific needs with the housing option that is best for them. Explore housing options with your parents while they are healthy and can gather information and tell you what they might like. They should consider options that are convenient for their caretakers as well.

The cost of housing for your parents will vary widely. The cost depends on both the amount of living space and the services that are included. Many housing options include medical services. These services may enable your parents to receive Medicare or Medicaid reimbursement for some or all of the costs. If the cost includes medical services, some part of the cost will be tax deductible.

Regardless of your parents' particular needs, you will want to spend a great deal of time searching for just the right place. Any option that includes medical services will need to meet a higher standard of quality. You can receive assistance and education concerning senior housing from many community social service agencies, such as the Area Agency on Aging, and senior citizens' centers. Or you can visit www.eldercare.gov or www.aoa.dhhs.gov.

13

Fraud

Jared Johnson's widowed father, Marvin, is 81 years old and lives alone in the small home in which he and his wife raised their family. Marvin is in pretty good mental and physical health for his age, but he gets lonely since he has stopped driving. Jared has noticed that Marvin seems to be on the phone whenever he comes over and that Marvin gets a lot of calls from solicitors while Jared visits. Marvin loves to watch TV; he especially likes to watch infomercials and is always talking about all the interesting gadgets and offers that are being pitched. Marvin gets lots of packages in the mail filled with inexpensive things he has ordered. He also seems to have numerous new magazine subscriptions. Last month, Marvin wrote three bad checks. He asked Jared to help him figure out how that had happened. Jared saw that his dad had been making a number of payments to unfamiliar companies and that a number of large automatic payments were being made from his account. Jared asked his dad about these payments and about all the gadgets and magazines. Marvin was very evasive and tried to change the subject. He said that most of the stuff was free anyway. Jared was able to fix the checking account overdrafts but was concerned about the broader issue.

JARED'S CONCERN is well founded. Marvin shows all the signs of being a victim of "elder fraud." He is reluctant to discuss the situation, he is spending money on things he doesn't seem to need, he is getting lots of solicitation calls, he is making payments to unknown entities, and he is having financial difficulty. Do you see these signs in any of your relatives? The elderly are particularly susceptible to fraud because of their isolation, loneliness, lack of sophistication in certain areas such as Internet usage, possible cognitive impairment, and simple trust in others.

Elder fraud: Fraudulent activities and marketplace abuses focused specifically on the elderly.

Fraud has a specific definition under the law. It involves a deliberate misrepresentation (or concealment) of important facts that is intended to induce someone to take an action that causes her or him financial harm. All these elements must be present for an action to be prosecutable as fraud, and thus it is difficult to prove fraud.

Shady dealers know how to tailor their pitches so that they stay clear of the formal definition of fraud. They use language that tells the literal truth but gives a false impression. They state opinions rather than facts in order to stay clear of the "factual misrepresentation" element of fraud. Over the years a number of laws have been written at the federal, state, and local levels to combat specific activities that fall just short of being fraud. Nonetheless, fraud, scams, rip-offs, and other marketplace abuses continue to plague the elderly. This chapter is intended to help you protect your parents from these activities and to recognize them and obtain redress when they do occur.

Laws Governing Elder Fraud

All fraudulent acts are against the law. However, proving fraud is difficult. In addition, enforcement of the basic fraud prohibition requires that the individual victim file a lawsuit to obtain restitution. Fortunately, the law goes beyond the general prohibition against fraud and addresses marketplace abuses in general. In addition, many laws have been enacted that address specific practices that victimize consumers.

General laws related to marketplace abuse have been enacted at the federal level and in all 50 states and the District of Columbia. Some local governments have also enacted general consumer protection ordinances. The Federal Trade Commission (FTC) Act outlaws "unfair" and "deceptive" acts or practices in commerce. Perpetrators of such acts or practices can be prosecuted in the federal courts or by the FTC itself. Usually, the FTC will act only when it sees an activity that is significant in terms of the number of persons harmed or the dollar amount of that harm. The FTC does not have the resources to address individual situations. Furthermore, its jurisdiction applies only to wrongdoers who engage in a practice across state lines.

All 50 states have passed consumer protection statutes, sometimes referred to as "little FTC acts," that outlaw unfair and deceptive acts. These laws can be brought to bear against perpetrators who operate within the particular state. They apply to all marketplace activity. Some states have been more active in this regard than others. Most states have an agency that attempts to resolve consumer complaints without resorting to legal enforcement. But they have legal enforcement powers, too. States can be very effective against scam artists who have a physical presence in the state. They are less effective in dealing with perpetrators who target their citizens from outside the state. In recent years, the FTC and the individual states have increasingly coordinated their efforts against those who run scams across state lines.

In addition to the general protection provided by the FTC and each state's consumer protection statutes, there are literally hundreds of laws addressing particular sales practices. Practices including mail-order sales, door-to-door sales, home improvement contracts, pre-need funeral contracts, magazine subscription sales, and other such practices that affect the elderly have been addressed. As an example, many states require hearing aid sellers to give purchasers a time period, perhaps 30 days, to back out of a hearing aid contract. Many local communities require door-to-door sellers to obtain a permit. Information about consumer protection laws can be found at the Federal Trade Commission Web site (www.ftc.gov) and on specific state and local agency Web sites via the list of members of the National Association of Consumer Agency Administrators (www.nacaanet.org).

Recognizing Scams

Scam artists use many ways to entice their victims into parting with their hard-earned money. They are pros who work their craft on a daily basis. Consumers are amateurs by comparison. But there are some telltale signs that an offer is not what it might appear to be. Here is what to look for:

- An exceedingly low price for a product or a verbal guarantee of enormous profits to be made on an investment.
- Assertions that the offer is available only to a limited number of specially chosen people.
- An unwillingness to put the offer in writing.
- An insistence that the offer be kept secret from family and friends.

- Very short time limits on the offer and a requirement that money be sent right away to ensure that it will not expire.
- Insistence that the customer send a wire transfer of funds or make a cash payment to someone who will come to the consumer's home to get the money.
- A chance to win a prize if the customer makes a purchase by a certain deadline.
- Requests for bank account numbers.

Scam artists want their victims to act quickly on insufficient information. No one has repealed the old adage that something that seems too good to be true usually is. In fact, scams are intentionally outrageous. The perpetrator seductively appeals to the victim's desire to make a killing. Victims can get drawn in by their own greed. The elderly are targets because they often are having financial difficulties and the offer appears to provide a solution to their problems.

Common Scams against the Elderly

All of us can be the targets of shady dealers. However, the elderly are targeted for certain scams that are tailored to their financial situation and life-cycle stage. These scams include fraudulent charities, identity and credit card theft, sweepstakes, and home improvements. All of these scams prey on the vulnerability of the elderly to loneliness, trust of perceived authority, guilt, and willingness to be complacent. We offer descriptions of the most common of these scams and then suggest ways to minimize or eliminate the threat of your parents' becoming victims.

Charities

Fraudulent charities use strong emotional appeals to target the elderly. They often focus on images of children or tailor their pitch to coincide with natural disasters or national tragedies, such as the attack on the World Trade Center. They focus on the problem without saying exactly what the charity is doing about it. The pitch is carefully worded to avoid specifics but gives an impression of a caring, devoted approach. The emotional pull makes it difficult to think logically. Consumers who question the pitch or deny the request are made to feel guilty.

Often the charity has a name that is similar to that of an established, well-known organization. Sometimes the pitch implies that the group is affiliated with police, firefighters', or veterans' organizations. The callers pressure people to make on-the-spot gifts. If they balk, they are given a pledge card to fill out. Later, requests for payments are sent that look like a bill and allude to the "promise" to help.

Identity Theft

Identity theft refers to any situation in which someone obtains personal information about someone else and uses the information for financial gain. In extreme cases, the perpetrator uses an individual's social security number and other data to open accounts in the victim's name. A small apartment is rented to serve as a mail drop, and all accounts are opened using that address. The fraudulent bills and account statements go to that address, so the victim has no idea that her or his identity is being used.

Identity theft usually begins with a thief's stealing a purse or wallet, stealing mail, or writing down identity information when a purchase is made at a store. The thief uses this information to obtain a credit report. The thief then applies for credit cards, auto loans, and other debt using the victim's name, social security number, and employer information and his or her own address. A thief may even make loan payments for a while to take maximum advantage of the credit available. Victims usually find out that their identity has been stolen when the thief doesn't make payments on the loans.

Credit Card Fraud

Credit card theft is similar to, but not as extensive as, identity theft. The thief may steal a credit card number from a variety of sources—often directly from the victim! Thieves will watch over your parent's shoulder at store checkout registers, pick up discarded or lost credit card receipts, or get the number from them directly during a telephone solicitation. Con artists often pretend to sell a product or service through telephone marketing and get the credit card number from the buyer. Unscrupulous merchants may charge your parents an amount larger than that agreed upon after your parents have left the store.

Sweepstakes Scams

The thrill of winning often tempts the elderly to participate in sweepstakes or prize scams. Generally, the elderly person is notified of her or his big win through the mail or via a telephone call. Invariably, the winner must provide a credit card number or a direct cash or check payment in order to claim the prize. This payment may be for alleged shipping and handling costs or as a "goodwill" gesture to claim the prize. Of course, the prize never materializes.

Home Improvements

The home improvement industry is a multibillion-dollar industry. And, it provides the perfect cover for a con artist victimizing the elderly. Most home improvement scams are "sold" door-to-door or through telephone marketers. The home improvement provider promises to make repairs around the house, blacktop the driveway, clean a chimney, replace windows, or carry out other home maintenance projects. The provider requires a deposit in order to buy materials and promises to return to complete the project. Most often, the buyer never sees the repairperson again. In a few cases, the repairperson shows up but uses inferior materials or does not complete the job.

The Notorious Bank Examiner Scam

An alarming telephone call arrives. The caller claims to be a bank official or "examiner" and informs your parents that their bank accounts have had some unusual or suspicious withdrawals. The "bank examiner" will tell your parents that the bank is investigating a dishonest teller who is making withdrawals from their account. Your parents are invited to help prove the case by giving the examiner a sum of money from their account; the amount can range from $500 to several thousand dollars. The examiner will supposedly "mark" the bills and record the serial numbers. Your parents are assured that they will get their money back after the investigation is over. Of course, they never see the bank examiner or their money again. Or, if the scammer thinks your parents will fall for the scam again, he or she may return the money in the hopes of hooking your parents for a larger amount the next time. The bank examiner scam works through fear—fear that the victim is losing money to the dishonest teller. The scammers provide the solution to the fear they have caused by promising to replace the lost money. They move through the scam quickly so that their victims stay confused and unable to think clearly.

Protecting Your Parents

You cannot be everywhere at once. And, because your parents can become victims very rapidly, you may not see warning signs until they have already been taken. However, as your parents age, you may suggest that they take precautions against becoming a victim.

Preventing a Loss

The first line of defense against becoming a victim of a scam or fraud is to be aware of what the typical scams are. These were discussed earlier in this chapter. Perhaps you should share this information with your parents. You may also encourage your parents to role-play responses to telephone solicitations or suspicious phone calls. Second, you may need to reduce direct marketers' access to your parents. A number of states have instituted "no-call lists" that telephone solicitors must follow. Contact your state's consumer protection agency or local senior center to see if your state has such a law.

> Write to the Mail Preference Service and ask that your parents' name and address be placed on a list of persons who do not want direct mail solicitations. This will also stop most mail from nonsweepstakes marketers, including catalogues and charities. The address is: Mail Preference Service, Direct Marketing Association, P.O. Box 9008, Farmingdale, NY 11735-9008.

More drastic management practices may be needed in order to reduce the likelihood of your parents' falling victim. Your parents may agree to not purchase any item costing more than $50 or $100 without talking with you first. Or, they may agree to consult you before purchasing home improvement services. Some ideas for protecting them against all scams are presented in the sidebar "Techniques to Avoid Becoming a Victim."

Techniques to Avoid Becoming a Victim

- Switch telephone service to an unlisted number and limit the number of people who have the new number.
- Close all credit card and retail accounts that are no longer used or rarely used.
- Limit expenditures to only one credit card account.
- Lower the limit on open credit card accounts.
- Review all credit card statements and compare them with actual receipts.
- Ask the bank and financial institutions to send you duplicate bank statements.

Techniques to Avoid Becoming a Victim (*continued*)

- Limit the amount of funds in easily accessible savings and checking accounts.
- Require two signatures on checks exceeding a specific amount of money, with you as the second signator.
- Notify the bank to call you if it sees any unusual account activity.
- Teach your parents to hang up on telephone marketers.
- Teach your parents to request that written materials be sent before agreeing to any phone solicitation.
- Get a post office box to which all mail is sent.
- In extreme events, have your parents' mail sent to you for screening before they see it.

What Happens If Your Parents Are Victims?

You will not be able to protect your parents completely unless you isolate them totally from the world. And that is not the answer. If your parents are victimized, you will need to respond to the situation on several fronts: emotional and legal.

Emotional Response to Victimization

Addressing your concerns for a loved one who has been the victim of a scam while also helping him or her to maintain a sense of independence and security is a delicate job. Most important, don't blame the person for becoming a victim. This does nothing to rectify the situation and may decrease the likelihood that he or she will ask you for help in the future. You must also help the person without taking away her or his independence and control of her or his own affairs. For example, even though it might be wise for you to manage your parents' mail, the suggestion might be perceived as an involuntary loss of control. Consider some of the control mechanisms suggested earlier in this chapter and choose to implement the ones that offer the most control and provide the most appropriate response to the victimization.

Legal Response to Victimization

Once you become aware of the loss, it is important for you to notify your local police department and the state's attorney general's office. This increases the chances that the con artist can be stopped and limits the losses to other elderly individuals. These criminals thrive on silence. It is also helpful, especially in the cases of home improvement and sweepstakes losses, to notify the local Better Business Bureau and chamber of commerce. You will also want to speak with your parents' financial and credit card institutions. They may be able to provide you with some assistance in preventing future losses.

Getting Help

The following agencies can provide both preventive and redress services for your parents.

- Better Business Bureau
  To contact a local Bureau to make a complaint: www.bbb.org
  To obtain a business reputation report: www.bbb.org/reports/
- National Consumer Law Center:
  www.nclc.org/consumer/repair.html
- The Administration on Aging:
  www.aoa.dhhs.gov/aoa/eldractn/homemodf.html
- The Federal Trade Commission: www.ftc.gov/bcp/conline.html
- National Charities Information Bureau: www.give.org
- American Institute of Philanthropy: www.charitywatch.org.
- National Association of Consumer Agency Administrators:
  www.nacaanet.org
- North American Securities Administrators Association
  (NASAA): www.nasaa.org
- U.S. Securities and Exchange Commission (SEC): www.sec.gov

Final Thoughts

Elder fraud is a growing problem in the United States. Your role as caregiver makes you the front line of defense for your parents. Watch carefully for signs that one of your parents has become a victim. When you know of a particular situation that offers the potential for fraud, you will want to look closer for the telltale signs of a scam. Prevention is the key. However, when a scam does occur, don't be afraid to ask for help from law enforcement agencies and consumer protection organizations. And, finally, you should recognize that being a victim of fraud carries an emotional toll. Your

Part IV

Transferring Estates

14

Estate Planning

Carol Stoll's mother and father, Emily and John Hardman, own a 1950s four-bedroom home, three individual retirement accounts, two autos, two financial investment accounts, and 100 acres of farmland. Their home, like many people's, is filled with furniture, appliances, and personal items. Carol's parents estimate the total value of their estate to be about $1,500,000.

Carol has two brothers. Tom, age 30, became disabled as a result of a car accident 4 years ago. He relies on his parents for a place to live and for some minor daily living assistance, such as transportation. He is unable to work. Both Carol and her older brother, Steve, have three children.

At the present time, Carol's parents have a 20-year-old will in effect and have signed no other legal documents. In addition, they have not spoken with their accountant about potential estate tax liabilities.

Carol's father recently spent 3 weeks in the hospital and found out that he is terminally ill. While her parents are not ready to have Carol manage all of their financial affairs, they have turned to her to assist them in developing and implementing an appropriate estate plan.

YOUR PARENTS may have more wealth than you ever dreamed possible. Or, they may have very little. Most people think that estate planning is only for the rich, or for those with their own businesses. While it is true that the rich and self-employed business owners need estate planning, most other individuals do too. Regardless of the dollar value of your parents' estates, you may need to help them develop and implement an adequate estate plan.

The purpose of a good estate plan is to minimize the work needed to finalize one's financial affairs, avoid misunderstandings and disagreements between heirs, and keep the costs of transferring the estate to a minimum.

Adequate estate planning involves accurately calculating one's net worth (for estate tax purposes), carefully choosing asset ownership mechanisms, and thoughtfully executing a will and other appropriate legal documents. Effective estate planning requires action. The plan must be completely implemented before the person dies or its benefits will be minimized.

This chapter is designed to introduce you to the basic issues of estate planning, including appropriate legal documents, the probate process, estate tax systems, some elementary planning tools, and related issues. Your planning may also incorporate giving away your parents' money now or using trusts to avoid probate, although these measures are not always appropriate or necessary. Estate planning is highly technical and most often requires the assistance of qualified legal practitioners. However, the fundamental concepts provided in this chapter will help you understand the issues that can arise.

Probate

Each state has its own laws regarding probate, and estates are probated in the decedent's county of residence. The estates of decedents who hold real property in multiple states will be probated in each of the states in which property is held. Probate property is the property owned by a decedent at death that will be transferred to her or his heirs via a will or in accordance with state law. Property that is transferred at death using contractual methods or certain ownership forms is nonprobate property.

> **Probate:** The legal process by which estates are settled, including the distribution of assets.

Avoiding Probate

Much ado has been made about avoiding probate, and some of the reasons given for avoiding probate are quite valid. Probate of a simple estate takes about 6 months. Complex estates or those of large value may take 2 years or longer to probate. In addition, although many states do not require an estate to employ an attorney for probate purposes, most executors prefer to have an attorney involved. Having an attorney involved usually translates to increased costs of probate. Sometimes the most important factor for individuals is the lack of privacy surrounding the probating of an estate. Information concerning the value of the estate, the names of the heirs, and other such information automatically becomes public knowledge once the estate is opened in probate court.

Executor: The person who is responsible for probating the will, paying the debts of the decedent, and distributing the estate's assets.

For a variety of reasons, whether privacy, simplicity, or cost reduction, you or your parents may want to bypass the probate process altogether. This will be difficult. In order to accomplish such a goal, you must understand the forms of ownership and contractual terms that transform probate property into nonprobate property. Your parents must transfer property ownership or complete beneficiary designation forms before their deaths. Otherwise, the property will transfer to heirs via the probate process.

Nonprobate Property

Individuals can effectively manage the distribution of their assets by using various forms of ownership and contractual agreements. Using these tools minimizes the costs of implementing an estate plan and probating an estate. Table 14.1 lists various types of property and categorizes them as probate or nonprobate property.

Forms of Ownership Distributing one's estate outside of probate can be accomplished completely through the use of forms of ownership. There are three basic forms of ownership. Joint tenancy with right of survivorship provides for direct transfer of a jointly owned asset to the survivor upon the death of one of the owners. Tenancy in common and sole ownership do not avoid probate unless special techniques are applied. In addition to forms of ownership, trusts can be used in estate planning. Trusts will be discussed later in this chapter.

Table 14.1 Probate and Nonprobate Assets

Probate Assets	Nonprobate Assets
Owned individually by decedent	Owned jointly with rights of survivorship
Share owned as tenants in common	Life insurance with nonestate beneficiary
Life insurance without beneficiary	Annuity with nonestate beneficiary
Annuity without beneficiary	Retirement account with nonestate beneficiary
Retirement account without beneficiary	Bank accounts with "payable on death" designee
Life insurance with estate beneficiary	Investment accounts with "transfer on death"
Annuity with estate beneficiary	designee
Retirement account with estate beneficiary	Assets in trust

Joint tenancy with rights of survivorship (JTWROS) is a mechanism for not only owning property during life, but also transferring property at death. Ownership must be held in equal shares (50 percent/50 percent for two owners, 33 percent/33 percent/33 percent for three owners, etc.). Any property held in this fashion will automatically transfer to the surviving owner(s) in such a way that the surviving owners' shares are equal after the transfer. For example, if a parent and two adult children each own 33.33 percent of a certificate of deposit as JTWROS and the parent dies, each child automatically becomes a 50 percent owner of the certificate of deposit. Retired individuals should be careful about transferring assets into joint accounts with children or other individuals, as the other joint owners have the right to use or transfer the funds without the permission of the original owner. Despite this, Carol's parents might consider owning their home with Tom as a joint owner with rights of survivorship. This will ensure that he receives the house after both of his parents die.

Alternatively, some individuals who own property together hold it as tenants in common. Unlike the situation with JTWROS, the ownership of tenant in common shares does not necessarily have to be equal. Also, transfers to the surviving owner(s) are not automatic. Upon death, the court transfers the decedent's interest in the property to his or her heirs through probate pursuant to the decedent's will or pursuant to state law if the decedent left no will. If Tom and his parents own the house as tenants in common, with each holding an equal share (⅓, ⅓, ⅓) and John dies, Tom will still own only one-third of the home. John's third will pass to his heirs. The heir is most likely to be Emily; thus, after John's death, Emily may own 67 percent and Tom 33 percent of the home. If Carol and Steve inherited shares in the house from Emily at her death, they could force Tom to sell.

Sole ownership simply means that only one person holds title to the property, whether it be a bank account, a piece of real estate, or a set of china. Most personal property, such as clothing and jewelry, is held as a sole owner. Any property held as a sole owner will transfer through the probate process. The heir to a specific piece of property is named in your parents' wills or, if they have no will, is governed by intestate succession.

Sometimes automatically transferring property to an heir at death is desirable, but your parents may not wish to co-own the property with the heir. In this situation, sole ownership of property with a named beneficiary or a payable or transfer on death designation is appropriate.

Named Beneficiaries and Payable on Death and Transfer on Death Designees Transfers of property that the decedent held as sole owner can also bypass the probate process if the account has a named beneficiary listed (such as in life insurance and retirement plans) or if a *payable on death (POD)* or *transfer on death (TOD)* designation is used on an account (such as a checking or savings account). By law, qualified retirement plans, individual retirement accounts, and deferred compensation plans must be held as sole owners. Therefore, it is important that individuals choose appropriate beneficiaries at the time they establish such accounts. Carol's parents can easily avoid probate by naming Carol, Steve, and Tom as beneficiaries on their IRAs.

A payable on death or transfer on death designation is simply an instruction to the financial institution to transfer the account to a named individual or individuals after the death of the owner. Completing a payable on death form allows for the transfer of the asset outside of probate, thus securing privacy, decreasing the time between death and transfer, and lowering the cost of probate. Carol's parents can also use these techniques on their accounts at financial institutions to transfer the assets directly to Carol, Steve, and Tom. Employing this technique would ensure that the property would not be probated.

Probate Property

Probate property is any property that transfers to heirs via instructions in a last will and testament. Basically, probate property is all property other than nonprobate property. When no will exists, it is property that is transferred via the laws of intestate succession. Any asset that is owned individually and has no named beneficiary or payable on death designee will pass through the probate process. The decedent's share of any asset that is held as tenants in common will also pass via probate.

Legal Documents to Be Used in Estate Planning

You are probably reading this book because you are currently facing issues concerning the management of your parents' financial affairs, or you expect to. Your parents may have requested your assistance, or you may be required to take over for them if they have become unable or unwilling to handle their own money matters. Regardless of the circumstances, if you are to have the legal authority to manage their money during their lifetime or after their death, or to make health-care decisions, they will need to sign certain legal documents. The six documents of com-

Table 14.2 Legal Documents and Purpose

Type of Document	Purpose
Power of attorney	A legal document allowing the holder to make financial decisions on behalf of the maker
Health-care power of attorney	A legal document allowing the holder to make medical decisions on behalf of the maker
Living will	A legal document offering advance directives for medical care
Will	A legal document outlining the terms of distributions of assets. Also used to name executors and guardians of dependents
Codicil	A legal document in which minor changes to a will can be made
Letter of last instruction (not a legal document)	A document that may contain funeral instructions, contact information for friends and relatives, or other nonlegal, nonfinancial instructions

mon interest can be divided into two groups: those that you will need before your parents' deaths and those that you will need at the time of or after their death. The former include a *durable power of attorney,* a *health-care power of attorney,* and a *living will.* The latter include the *last will and testament, codicils,* and *trusts.* A letter of last instruction is not a legal document, but it plays a very useful role in estate planning. Appropriate legal documents provide you with the power to conduct business for your parents. They also give professional advisers some direction and protection so that they can aid you in managing your parents' affairs. These documents are discussed next and are outlined in Table 14.2.

Power of Attorney

There are different types of powers of attorney: durable, limited, and springing. Each has a specific purpose. One provides broad powers, and the others limit the discretion that the person holding the power of attorney can exercise. Your parents will want to understand all the types of powers in order to choose the one that is most appropriate to their situation.

Power of attorney (POA): A legal right given to one person to act on behalf of another.

Durable Power of Attorney   A *durable power of attorney* is a legal document created by another person (in this case, your parents) that allows you to conduct their affairs and make decisions on their behalf. In effect, your parents make you their backup decision maker. This means that you would be able to change investments, sell their home, and make other major changes to your parents' financial situation. You don't have to use the power even though it is available to you. Along with this privilege comes the responsibility to act in a prudent manner. You will certainly want to obtain advice from appropriate professionals before making significant or permanent decisions.

It is important that your parents sign this document prior to losing the ability to make decisions, because the document must be signed while they are still competent. Several originals of this document should be signed, as financial institutions may request an original if you attempt to use the power. The physical document can be kept on file at your attorney's office. The attorney can release the document to the person named in it when the need arises. Either Carol or Steve should have a durable POA for each parent. They can use it if the need arises in an emergency or if the time should come when their parents are unable to manage alone.

Limited Power of Attorney   In some cases, a *limited* power of attorney may be in order. The POA can be limited in terms of time or in terms of the authority granted. For instance, if a parent is in rehabilitation after replacement knee surgery, he may wish his son to manage his affairs temporarily. Or, the POA may be granted for an expanded period of time, but the type of decisions or other powers available to the holder of the POA may be limited. This type of POA would have been appropriate while Carol's dad was in the hospital.

Springing Power of Attorney   If your parent is hesitant to give power of attorney privileges, you should at least get a *springing* power of attorney. This document "springs" into effect once a specified event occurs. The specified event is usually mental incapacity. The grantor typically defines mental incapacity as two mental health professionals declaring in writing that they deem her or him to be mentally disabled. This type of POA should only be used in instances where the distrust is valid. However, in that case, your parents should consider giving POA to a third party, such as an attorney or an accountant.

Signing as POA   It's important that you sign all documents correctly when using a power of attorney. Carol would sign, "Emily Hardman, by

Carol Stoll, Power of Attorney." Signing in this manner commits the grantor, rather than you, for the contractual commitments.

Health-Care Power of Attorney

The health-care power of attorney (HCPOA) gives the holder the right to make medical decisions on the signer's behalf. It carries totally different powers from the power of attorney discussed earlier because the powers are limited to medical issues. It is very important that you or the person having this right discuss with your parents their preferences regarding medical care. In addition, your parents should feel comfortable that the holder of the HCPOA concurs with their preferences or will at least carry out their wishes. If you feel that you would be unable to carry out your parents' wishes regarding medical care, you should have someone else hold the HCPOA. Preferably, at least two individuals should hold the HCPOA for a person, although only one may be needed to make decisions. This covers the situation in which the holder of the HCPOA is not available to make quick decisions in an emergency. While Carol and Steve's parents are both alive and healthy, one of the children and the spouse should have the health-care power of attorney for the other spouse. Upon the death of one parent or the incapacity of one or both, Carol and Steve might each have a health-care power of attorney for their parents.

Living Will

A living will has nothing to do with the transfer of assets upon the death of your parents. Rather, it provides direction for when they wish medical treatments to be terminated or limited. While an HCPOA allows the holder to make health-care decisions, the living will instructs health-care providers and the HCPOA about the type and extent of medical care they should provide if your parents are unable to speak for themselves and their illness is terminal with no hope for recovery. Typical topics covered under a living will include the use of extraordinary means to maintain life, mechanical feeding mechanisms, and the use of medication to reduce pain. In addition, the document should cover when treatments should be withdrawn, including the discontinuance of respirators and feeding tubes. Most health-care providers, including doctors and hospitals, ask patients if they have a living will, and if so will request a copy of it for their files. Carol should insist that her parents sign a living will to lessen the likelihood that she or Steve will have to make decisions or invoke their HCPOA. You may wish to visit www.partnershipforcaring.org for a link to your state's living will guidelines.

Last Will and Testament

In the event that your parents die without wills, their property will be distributed according to the law of their state of residence at the time of their death. Even if the state's distribution laws are acceptable, heirs and family members are put in a difficult position if no will exists. The lack of a will increases the likelihood of family battles and hard feelings. It is often more costly to probate an estate without a will because the process is more time-consuming. And, family members are left to second-guess what the deceased person's true wishes really were. The cost of preparing a basic will is minimal compared to the cost incurred after death when no will exists.

Will: A legal document directing the distribution of a person's worldly goods upon his or her death.

A will outlines the distribution of one's assets and the process by which the estate will be distributed. Most wills contain several standard sections: a testament that the maker is of sound mind and freely writes the document; the naming of an executor; and a distribution plan that outlines the maker's assets, names his or her heirs, and allocates his or her estate among the heirs. This last section is of most interest to the heirs. A guardian can be named for minor children should they be orphaned as a result of the writer's death. Parents with adult children with special needs may also want to name a guardian. Carol's parents need to give serious thought to who will take care of Tom when they are gone. Even though he may not need a legal guardian, he may need additional financial resources.

There are two methods of distributing one's material wealth. In many cases, where there are only a few heirs and there is very little in the way of personal property, it is appropriate to leave a percentage share of assets to each heir. This method is called the percentage method. Sometimes, especially when heirs include grandchildren or nonfamily members, people leave a certain amount of money or a specified item of personal property to a person. When an item or amount is specified, the distribution is of a pecuniary nature.

In addition to deciding on the allocation method, your parents will need to decide how much goes to each heir. Some parents strive for fairness. They consider the life situation of each child or heir and allocate their assets accordingly. Of course, many people equate fairness with equality. In such cases, every child, regardless of her or his particular circumstances, receives an equal share or dollar amount. Regardless of your parents' outlook, it is important that they pay particular attention to the needs and resources of all of the children and heirs. Carol's parents may rightly decide to leave a greater portion of their estate to Tom. If they feel that Tom may have difficulty managing the money, they can set up a trust for his benefit and name a trustee to manage the funds. Trusts are discussed later in this chapter.

The will also names the executor or personal representative, the individual who will serve in a legal capacity to carry out the terms of the will. A backup, or contingent, executor is often named; this person is required to perform the executor's duties only if the primary executor is unwilling or unable to serve. It is very important that your parents choose an executor who is willing and able to serve. They should consider factors such as geographic proximity, knowledge and experience, and whether or not the executor pays attention to detail. Some states require that the executor or at least one of two coexecutors reside in the state of the deceased's residence. Issues such as paying the executor and whether bonding the executor is required are usually based on state law and are also addressed in a properly written will.

> **Personal representative:** A term often used synonymously with executor. Some states either use this term exclusively or use it to identify the person who is responsible for the executor's duties when the decedent had no will.

Your parents should review their will every 3 to 5 years or whenever family or financial circumstances change. A codicil (described later in this chapter) can be used to make minor changes to a will. Because of Tom's disability, Carol's parents probably need to rewrite their will.

Wills should be kept in a safe place. They need not be readily accessible to the executor or heir; however, a close relative, friend, or the executor should be aware of where the original and any copies of the will are kept. Most counties allow (for a small fee) individuals to file their wills with the court for safekeeping. Your parents may request that their attorney keep the original, keeping only a copy in their residence or safe-deposit box. Because safe-deposit boxes may not be opened for some time after a person's death and may be subject to inventory procedures by the county, funeral instructions are best left in a letter of last instruction (discussed later in this chapter) rather than in a will.

Sadly, well over 60 percent of Americans do not have a will. A person who has no will dies *intestate*. Each state has its own laws of intestate succession. Under most states' laws, the spouse of a decedent will receive a portion of the estate automatically, and any minor children will also inherit a portion of the decedent's estate. If no spouse or children survive the decedent, the law will probably transfer the assets to parents, brothers and sisters, and other living relatives, in that order.

> **Intestate succession:** The process of distributing a decedent's estate if there is no will.

Few individuals would be totally satisfied with the state's method of distributing their estate. Under the laws of intestacy of most (but not all) states, a spouse will receive 50 percent of the estate and the children will share equally in the remaining 50 percent of the estate. Some states provide that only a third of an intestate estate will be given to a surviving spouse and that the children will share the remaining two-thirds of the estate. Or, a surviving spouse may receive all of the estate below a certain value and one-half of any value over the threshold. You should examine the laws of your state if your parents refuse to make a will.

Codicils

From time to time, people want to make minor changes to their will. When they do, it seems so easy for them to take the will out of its envelope, pencil a change or two in the margin, possibly initial the change, and replace the will in the filing cabinet or safe-deposit box. There's only one major problem: These changes aren't legal and must be disregarded when the will is probated.

> Never make changes directly to an original will. These changes are not legal and will not be carried out. Execute a new will or codicil.

To make legal, minor changes to their will, your parents should prepare (or have an attorney prepare) a codicil. The codicil should be dated and signed. In addition, two parties must witness the signing of the codicil. The codicil should be kept with the original will, and your parents may wish to keep copies in their home filing cabinet. It is possible for codicils to render an entire will invalid if a changed clause conflicts with other, unchanged sections of a will. Because Carol's parents' wills are old, their estates have grown in size, their children have become adults, and Tom was not disabled at the time the wills were written, they should write new wills rather than employing codicils.

Trusts

Like a will, a trust is a legal document. Trusts offer many benefits, including control of assets, avoidance of probate, and minimization of estate taxes. All trusts share some commonalities. However, different types of trusts may be used to acquire different benefits. In any case, you should use an estate attorney to draft the trust agreement.

> **Trust:** A legal entity created for the purposes of owning, managing, and governing the distribution of income and assets.

Parties to a Trust   A trust involves three main parties: the grantor or donor, the trustee, and the beneficiary. A trust can have more than one trustee and in many cases will have more than one beneficiary. A list of the parties to a trust and the roles they play is outlined in Table 14.3.

Living and Testamentary Trusts   Trusts can be written to become effective during life. A trust that becomes effective during life is called a living or *inter vivos* trust. In order to become effective during life, the trust

Table 14.3 Parties to a Trust

Party	Role
Grantor	Creates and funds the trust
Trustee	Responsible for operating the trust and overseeing implementation of its provisions; may be an individual or an institution
Income beneficiary	Receives the income from the trust's property. May be the same person as the principal beneficiary
Principal beneficiary	Receives the principal or "corpus," the original property placed in the trust. May be the same person as the income beneficiary

must be funded; that is, asset ownership must be transferred from the grantor to the trust. A trust made and funded during the grantor's life can "act" just like an individual. Your parents can be the grantor or donor, the trustee (manager), and the beneficiary for as long as they live. The income from these trusts "flows through" to your parents' tax return, and in most cases no specific trust tax return is required.

A testamentary trust is one that is created via a will and funded from probated assets. Testamentary trusts and unfunded living trusts require a properly prepared will if they are to be effective. Therefore, one should consider one's will and a revocable living trust to be "married" documents; that is, you shouldn't have one without the other.

Revocable and Irrevocable Trusts   Many people are afraid to use trusts because they do not want to lose control of their assets. However, a donor does not lose control because he or she sets the rules that the trust must follow with respect to management and distribution of the assets. A revocable trust allows the grantor to retain control of the assets within the trust and to change the terms of the trust, including the beneficiaries, at any time.

An irrevocable trust means the donor can no longer change the terms of the trust once it is signed. Revocable trusts become irrevocable upon the donor's death. Both revocable and irrevocable trusts have their place in estate planning; you will use the one that is appropriate given the goals you wish to reach.

Control after Death   Many estate plans incorporate a trust in order to provide the donor with control over the disposition of the trust's income or assets, even after her or his death. Control is often needed in order to minimize estate taxes or to care for a beneficiary who is incapable of managing his or her financial affairs. The trustee, who may be the grantor or a third party, will manage the trust assets. The trust maker can direct that the beneficiary receive only the income from the assets. Or, the maker can order the assets to be distributed to beneficiaries at a later date, perhaps when they're old enough to manage the funds wisely.

Both living and testamentary trusts can be used to achieve this goal. Carol's parents may want to consider using a trust for the funds they leave for Tom's benefit. However, they should not use a trust instrument without first receiving qualified legal advice.

Avoiding Probate   Trusts are often employed to avoid probate and provide for a more efficient, less costly transfer of assets at death. Using trusts to totally avoid probate is effective only if all of your parents' assets are retitled to the trusts before they die. Otherwise, the assets that are held outside the trust will transfer through the probate process. Trusts can also be used to transfer specific assets outside of probate. Testamentary trusts become effective via the will, so they are not effective tools for avoiding probate. Both revocable and irrevocable trusts can be used to avoid probate.

Letters of Last Instruction

A person's will is not usually located or read prior to her or his funeral. Therefore, any funeral instructions or requests to notify friends or relatives of the death that are included in the will are found too late. A *letter of last instruction* solves this problem. The letter is *not* a legal document. Family members are not bound by the instructions. However, they are often relieved to find such a document so that they may comply with their parent's wishes.

The letter of last instruction may contain funeral plans. A list of friends and relatives to be contacted upon the death is often attached. This list is helpful if a decedent's family does not know the individuals whom the decedent wished to notify. Letters may also provide the location of the will or other important legal documents. Some include personal notes for survivors that often provide comfort. Others provide material to be included in the obituary.

If your parent has a letter of last instruction, it is important that you know where it is. The letter of last instruction should never be kept in a safe deposit box or at an attorney's office. Banks and offices have a way of being closed on the day of a person's death, and in such an event, the letter may be useless by the time it is retrieved. Your parents may wish to make copies for you and your siblings or a close friend.

Be sure to date the letter of last instruction, seal it, and leave it in a convenient desk or dresser drawer. A child, close relative, or friend should be told where it is.

Estate Taxes

The United States assesses a tax upon the value of an individual's estate at the time of his or her death. The Internal Revenue Service taxes estates with a net taxable value over $1,000,000. Effective tax rates range from

41 to 50 percent of the net taxable value of an estate. As with the income tax system, it is important to understand what items are taxed, which costs can be deducted, and how to minimize overall estate taxes. A significant portion of estate planning deals with the tax implications of various alternative plans.

Generally speaking, the fair market value of any asset owned or controlled by a decedent on the day of her or his death is included in the decedent's taxable estate. Deductions for final expenses such as funeral and burial costs, medical expenses, and estate settlement costs reduce the value of the taxable estate. And, a decedent may make a transfer of an unlimited amount of assets to a spouse or a qualified charity. Finally, there is an estate tax credit in the amount of $345,800 to offset the tax. This tax credit equals the tax on a $1,000,000 taxable estate. This means that each parent can transfer up to $1,000,000 of assets to nonspouse, noncharitable entities at his or her death without the estate's incurring a federal estate tax.

Most couples' estate plans have the first-to-die spouse leave everything to the second-to-die spouse. This scenario allows the couple to avoid paying estate taxes when the first spouse dies. However, this scenario often creates a situation in which there is an estate tax when the second spouse dies. If Mr. Hardman leaves his complete estate (50 percent of $1,500,000) to Mrs. Hardman, there will be no estate tax upon his death. However, when Mrs. Hardman dies she is likely to incur a tax because the value of her estate is likely to exceed $1,000,000.

Reducing an estate to minimize or eliminate the estate and gift tax is a job best left to experienced estate planning practitioners. However, it all boils down to one fact: The less property a decedent owns or controls at death, the lower the value of the taxable estate and thus, the lower the estate taxes.

A good estate plan will balance the client's ongoing income needs with the need to minimize the value of the estate to be transferred. Several factors should be considered as estate tax avoidance mechanisms are evaluated. First, you should evaluate your parents' need for income above the regular, periodic income they receive. For example, some people have considerable wealth, but low cash flows (farmers, for example). Others have substantial income flow from pensions and social security, but rather normal wealth levels (retired schoolteachers, for instance). An individual with a fixed pension benefit well in excess of her annual living expenses may be a better candidate for giving an income-producing property such as dividend-paying stocks than one who relies on the dividends to make ends meet. Second, consider an individual's net worth. A person with a net worth (see Chapter 3) or total investment and savings assets that greatly exceed his lifetime needs may be able to safely reduce his estate by making gifts. Third, the age and health of an individual should be considered. A 95-year-old or terminally ill patient is more likely to benefit from reducing the size of her estate and is less likely to deplete her assets before death. Fourth, one cannot forget to consider the age, wealth level, income, and tax bracket of the potential gift recipient. Increasing the wealth or income of recipients or heirs is not always helpful, as it may place their estate in a taxable situation or increase their income tax rates.

Minimizing Estate Taxes

Avoiding probate and avoiding estate taxes are not the same. Many mechanisms for avoiding probate are useless for reducing an estate's tax liability. For example, although holding property as JTWROS avoids probate, it can increase the estate tax on the property. One-half the value of property that is jointly held with a spouse is assumed to be in each spouse's estate. However, the full value of property held jointly with rights of survivorship with a nonspouse is presumed to be in the estate of the first to die. Note, however, that this presumption can be nullified with adequate proof to the contrary. Adequate proof may include business agreements with valid evidence of ownership by others and earlier gift tax returns and statements of completed gifts.

Trusts and Married Couples   Minimizing estate and gift taxes is a valid reason for using trusts in an estate plan. For married individuals, both living and testamentary trusts can adequately minimize estate and gift taxes. Because most couples make wills leaving all of their assets to each other at death, estate taxes are avoided at the time of the first spouse's death. However, the spouse who is second to die often leaves an estate that is larger than the exclusion amount and therefore incurs an estate tax. To avoid this situation, your parents may want to consider using living, revocable trusts if the total value of their taxable estates is greater than the exclusion amount ($1,000,000 in 2003). Using a pair of trusts, often known as A/B trusts or credit shelter trusts, allows your parents to exclude two times the exclusion amount in effect during the year of the first spouse's death. These mechanisms also permit the surviving spouse to have access to the income from the deceased spouse's trust property and to access the trust principal for living expenses in the event of an emergency.

For this technique to be most effective, your parents will need separate trusts. In most cases, your parents should fund the trusts during life. No trust should be funded at its inception with assets greater than the exclusion amount currently in effect. As the exclusion amount increases, they may want to fund one or both of the trusts more heavily, but only up to the level of the exclusion amount.

Trusts and Single Individuals Credit shelter trusts are useful only for married couples. For a single person, an irrevocable living trust to which assets have been transferred during life can reduce estate taxes. The assets in an irrevocable trust avoid estate taxation because the assets have been gifted out of the donor's estate provided the donor does not retain control of the trust.

Trusts and Retirement Plan Assets Unfortunately, a person may not transfer retirement plan assets to a trust during her or his life without incurring income tax liabilities at the time of transfer. In other words, to give retirement plan assets and reduce the value of one's estate, it is necessary to withdraw the funds from the qualified plan, pay income taxes, and then make the gift or transfer. While this option appears unattractive on the surface, the taxpayer's income tax on the retirement plan withdrawal may be lower than the estate tax imposed on the plan at his or her death. Taxpayers must compare the cost of current income taxes with the estate and income taxes that will be assessed on the retirement plan assets at death.

Giving Plans

In the rush to deplete the value of a gross estate, an individual or family may make a concerted effort to give away assets. However, except for those gifts that qualify for the annual gift exclusion (discussed later in the chapter), the value of all gifts made during life is included in the decedent's gross estate at the time of death.

A gift is an irrevocable transfer of property with economic value that is made during the life of a donor. To be considered a gift, the gift needs to be completed; that is, the donor or giver cannot retain any control over the property being given after the transfer. For example, when a grandmother tells her favorite granddaughter that she may have a piece of jewelry upon her death, the grandmother has not made a completed gift. In fact, if the bequest is not made in the grandmother's will, the granddaughter has no legal right to the piece of jewelry. The jewelry would actually have to be given to the granddaughter and be in the granddaughter's possession to consider the gift complete.

The gift tax is coordinated with the estate tax in this country. However, an individual may give, or transfer, up to $11,000 in property to any number of individuals each year without incurring a gift tax or needing to file a gift tax return. For example, Emily could give each of her three children, six grandchildren and an unlimited number of friends up to $11,000 each year.

The amount of a gift over $11,000 in a single year to one recipient is called an excess gift. Gift tax returns are required to be filed if an excess gift has been made. Until the total amount of excess gifts in one donor's lifetime reaches $1,000,000, the donor is simply reporting the excess gifts. A tax is imposed when the total amount of excess gifts exceeds $1,000,000.

> **Gift tax exclusion:** The amount of the annual gift that an individual can make to one other person without incurring a gift tax.

Gift splitting is a concept that allows married couples to double the amount of the annual gift tax exclusion, *even if* the property is owned by only one of the donors. For example, grandma and grandpa wish to gift $18,000 to a grandchild for a down payment on a home. The cash will come from an account that is solely owned by grandma. If grandpa chooses to join in the gift, the transfer is considered "split," and the entire transfer qualifies for the exclusion. This part of the law allows married couples to gift up to $22,000 to each recipient (donee) each year and still be under the gift tax exclusion.

The recipient of a gift does not pay income taxes on the value of the gift during the year in which it is received. However, if a recipient sells a piece of property that was a gift, she or he will recognize a taxable capital gain on the difference between the selling price and the donor's purchase price. This makes transferring a home from a parent to a child risky because the child may have to pay capital gains tax upon the sale unless the child lives in the property for at least 2 years before selling the residence. In addition, in the attempt to minimize estate taxes, some individuals transfer investments with sizable capital gains to others as a gift. By doing so, the donor will succeed in lowering the value of her or his gross estate (if the gift is valued at less than $11,000 per donee per year), but the recipient may incur a sizable capital gains tax liability upon the sale of the asset. All gifts need to be analyzed by comparing the amount of estate taxes saved with the amount of capital gains tax paid by the recipient. In addition, the effect that the income from a transferred asset will have on the income tax situation of the recipient in the future must be considered. Even if the gift won't produce a capital gain upon sale, it may produce taxable interest and dividends if invested. This latter consideration takes into account the difference in income tax rates between the donor and the recipient.

Gifts to Charities   Many individuals have charitable interests, and the need to reduce estate taxes provides the perfect opportunity to address these interests. Gifts made to qualified charities, during life or at death, are excluded from gift and estate taxes. Any gifts made during life can also be claimed as a current deduction on the donor's income tax return.

Related Issues

Estate planning can be complex and time-consuming. Adequate planning allows individuals to distribute their assets in accordance with their wishes, and also to consider the effect of estate taxes on any transfer plan. In addition, many individuals wish to bypass the probate process in order to save time and money and preserve privacy. Several related issues should be considered during the estate planning process. These include the inclusion of life insurance proceeds, the imposition of income taxes on the distribution of retirement plan assets, the use of life insurance trusts to replace gifts or tax liabilities, and the retention of an attorney for assistance in developing and implementing an appropriate plan.

Giving Life Insurance

Life insurance benefits pose a particular threat to an estate plan. Life insurance death benefits are often forgotten when the gross taxable estate is estimated because life insurance is not a tangible, currently used asset. The total face value (or life insurance proceeds) of all life insurance policies owned by a decedent on his life will be included in the gross taxable estate.

> To avoid estate taxes on life insurance proceeds, have someone other than the insured own the life insurance policy. When no spouse is living, planners will suggest that the insurance policy be transferred to a child, a grandchild, or an irrevocable trust.

To eliminate the advantage of transferring life insurance policies to third parties at the very last minute, the IRS determined that gifts of life insurance made within 3 years of the date of death are included in the value of the insured owner's gross estate. Also, the total face value of a life insurance gift is included, even if the cash value was less than the $11,000 annual gift exclusion.

How to Handle Retirement Plan Assets

Qualified retirement accounts and individual retirement accounts pose interesting, but complex, problems in estate planning. Recall that these accounts can only be solely owned. Therefore, unless a beneficiary is named, they will pass to the estate upon the death of the owner and will be transferred to the heir(s) via the probate process. The probate process can be easily bypassed if individuals identify direct beneficiaries on their retirement accounts.

Retirement plan assets are unique because not only are they included in the value of the gross estate for estate tax purposes, but the heirs also incur an income tax upon their withdrawal. This "double taxation" can be minimized with adequate planning and the naming of a direct beneficiary. However, if no direct beneficiaries are named, the estate receives the plan assets. In this case, the estate may be forced to withdraw the account's funds, pay income taxes on those funds, and then distribute the proceeds as directed by the will or intestate succession. Income tax rates on an estate's income are more accelerated than those for individuals.

There is generally no income tax assessed on an heir for receiving inherited property. However, because retirement plan assets were accumulated on a tax-deferred basis, the IRS never received income taxes on these funds as they were earned. To remedy this situation, heirs must pay income taxes as they begin to withdraw the funds from the inherited IRA, 401(k), or other retirement plan. The rate at which the beneficiary must withdraw inherited retirement funds depends upon whether the beneficiary is a spouse or a nonspouse.

In any case, if the decedent was 70½ or older at the time of death, the required minimum distribution for the decedent for the year of death must be taken if the decedent had not already done so before death. This required minimum distribution is discussed in Chapter 4. It equals the account balance on December 31 of the year before death divided by the withdrawal factor corresponding to the owner's age during the year of death.

Withdrawal Options for Spouses   Spouses who inherit an individual retirement account may roll the account over to an IRA of their own or elect to treat the IRA as their own. They may then name new beneficiaries. Or, if the decedent was not yet 70½ at the time of his death, a spouse may elect to withdraw the full account by December 31 of the fifth year following the year of the decedent's death.

Spouses who do not choose to roll over the account or withdraw the funds within 5 years must begin withdrawals no later than the year in which the decedent would have turned age 70½. If the decedent had already reached age 70½, then the spouse must begin to take distributions on an annual basis beginning the year following the year of the decedent's death. The spouse will take minimum distributions based on his or her own life expectancy according to the IRS's life expectancy table. If the life expectancy of the decedent was longer than that of the inheriting spouse, the latter may take distributions over the remaining years of the decedent's single life expectancy.

Withdrawal Options for Nonspouse Beneficiaries   Nonspouse retirement plan beneficiaries are treated a bit differently. They must begin annual distributions by December 31 of the year following the year of the decedent's death. The minimum distribution is calculated by dividing the balance in the account as of the end of the year prior to the decedent's death by the life expectancy for the beneficiary during the year after the year of the decedent's death. In subsequent years the denominator is simply reduced by 1.

If the decedent was not yet 70½ as of the date of death, then nonspouse beneficiaries may choose to withdraw the entire amount by December 31 of the fifth year following the decedent's year of death.

Withdrawal Options for Estate Beneficiaries   Retirement plan assets in accounts with no named beneficiaries will be transferred to the decedent's estate and pass to the heirs subject to the provisions of the will. Withdrawals must begin immediately. If the decedent was over age 70½ at the time of her or his death, then withdrawals must be made at a rate consistent with the decedent's life expectancy at the time of death. In each subsequent year, the divider is simply lowered by 1.

> Because of the mandatory withdrawal rules for nonspouse beneficiaries of individual retirement accounts, it is wise to use these assets first to fund charitable bequests.

The required withdrawal rate for estate beneficiaries is much greater when the decedent was not yet 70½ at the time of death. In this case, although no distribution is required until the fifth year after the year of the decedent's death, 100 percent of the account must be withdrawn by December 31 of the fifth year following the year of death. In this event, the estate would pay the income taxes, and possibly at much higher rates than individual beneficiaries would have incurred. The heirs will have one opportunity to avoid the high income taxes if the estate is the beneficiary of a retirement account. Under proposed regulations, if the heirs in the will determine a beneficiary before the end of the year following the year of death, then the beneficiaries can withdraw the plan assets over their own life expectancies. By lengthening the term of withdrawal, income taxes can often be reduced.

It is usually most advantageous to designate your parents' youngest heir or the heir with the least amount of annual income as beneficiary of their retirement plan accounts, making those accounts part of that heir's share of the estate. Because the youngest heir will have the longest life expectancy, the income tax rates and subsequent income tax liability should be lowest. This may not hold true, however, if the youngest heir is in a higher income tax bracket than other heirs.

Life Insurance Trusts

Many individuals make charitable gifts as a vehicle for reducing their estate tax liability. Others allow the government to assess a significant tax on their estates by not reducing the size of their estates before death. In either case, the size of the estate available to their heirs is significantly lower than it might need to be with appropriate planning. A life insurance trust can be used to replace funds that were given to charities or paid to the IRS.

A life insurance trust is like any other trust in that it has a donor, trustee, beneficiary, and principal. The difference is that the asset or principal owned by the trust is a life insurance policy insuring the donor's life. Upon the donor's death, the life insurance proceeds are paid to the trust. The trustee then distributes the proceeds to the beneficiaries.

In effect, the life insurance proceeds "replace" the amount of the charitable gift or the taxes paid by the estate. Of course, the super wealthy cannot purchase enough insurance to replace the amount of taxes they pay, but for the average family, a life insurance trust is a viable tool in an estate plan.

Several considerations are important to the successful use of life insurance trusts. First, if the donor is placing a policy he or she already owns in the trust, this should be done at least 3 years prior to death. Second, the trustee and the donor cannot be the same person. Third, the trust will pay the life insurance premium. In many cases, the donor gifts the premium to the trust, making sure that the premium is less than the annual gift exclusion amount times the number of beneficiaries of the trust. The trust then makes the premium payments. Finally, the trust must be a living and irrevocable trust.

Obtaining Professional Assistance

Many families are penny-wise and pound-foolish when it comes to obtaining professional estate planning advice. While the new estate tax laws have effectively exempted many families from paying an estate tax, the cost of having an inadequately prepared will, or no will at all, can be high. Family squabbles not only delay the distribution of assets and drastically increase the cost of settling an estate, but may also cause hard feelings and lasting separations.

Couples with estates valued at over $1,000,000 should definitely consult with an estate planning attorney or an accountant who is well versed in estate and gift taxation. Those who have heirs with special needs, complicated distribution plans, or charitable intents should not hesitate to meet with an attorney. Emily and John Hardman need to consult with an attorney with respect to protecting their son Tom's needs.

The best method for identifying possible estate planning advisers is through personal references from family, friends, or other professionals. A word of caution is in order here. Your parents' situation may be significantly different from that of your friends or colleagues. Don't hesitate to interview two or three professionals before selecting one who meets your needs.

The range of fees for estate planning attorneys is wide. You will probably pay a minimum of $150 per hour to obtain qualified, reputable assistance. An estate planning expert may charge several hundred dollars an hour for dealing with complicated or large estates. Be sure to inquire about what billing method the attorney uses. Any reputable attorney will be able and willing to offer an estimate of what it will cost to prepare the basic documents discussed in this chapter for you.

Final Thoughts

The most important consideration in estate planning is usually the direction of the distribution of an estate. This can only be done if appropriate legal documents such as wills and trusts have been put into place during the decedent's life.

Those who wish to avoid probate can use tools such as joint ownership, named beneficiaries, and payable and transfer on death designations to transfer property directly to heirs. Trusts allow for the direct transfer of assets to heirs and can often aid in reducing estate taxes.

Estate taxes can significantly reduce the amount of property that is transferred to heirs. In most cases, it is important that the estates of spouses be coordinated so that the total estate tax, not just that of the first decedent, is minimized or eliminated. Many people who wish to reduce or eliminate estate taxes employ gifting programs and trusts.

Most planning (especially for estates over $1,000,000 for individuals or $2,000,000 for couples) should be completed with the help of a competent adviser, such as an attorney, accountant, financial planner, or financial counselor. However, even if your parents' estates are smaller, it may be well worth your money to pay for a consultation or two with an appropriate financial professional.

15

Settling Your Parent's Estate

Carol Stoll's father died 2 years ago. At that time, her parents' net worth was $1,500,000. Her parents had given $11,000 to each of their three children and two in-laws every year for the 5 years prior to his death. Other than that, they had not yet implemented the estate plan recommended by their attorney. Carol's mother, Emily, died 2 weeks ago. Carol estimates her mother's estate to be worth $1,650,000 today. Included in this amount is a life insurance policy owned by Mrs. Hardman with a face value of $100,000 and several individual retirement accounts (IRAs). She promised Carol the death benefits of this policy in return for "taking care of her." Costs for her funeral, estate administration, and final medical bills will probably total $50,000. Carol also expects the estate to pay a hefty estate tax bill.

Carol has two brothers. Both she and her older brother, Steve, have three children. Tom, age 32 and the youngest, is disabled and unable to work. Tom was the named beneficiary on the life insurance policy.

Her mother did have an updated will. Carol was named the executrix. Mrs. Hardman owned her home jointly with Tom with rights of survivorship. The IRAs named the three children as equal beneficiaries. The remainder of her estate was to be transferred in accordance with the terms of her last will and testament.

LOSING A PARENT is difficult. Right now Carol is overwhelmed with grief and inundated with a long list of things to do—and the courts now expect her to begin the process of "closing" her mother's estate. With proper estate planning, probating her mother's estate would have been much easier.

This chapter provides you with a road map for probating your parents' estates. The discussion proceeds in chronological order—first things first. You will find a thorough discussion of the steps involved in transferring nonprobate assets, probating a will, filing the appropriate tax

Figure 15.1 Sample Estate Settlement Calendar

Within 2 weeks after death	Contact social security and pension plan administrators Obtain original will Make 10 copies of the will Obtain 10 copies of the death certificate Prepare a written inventory of the estate Hire an attorney if necessary
Within 1 month of death	Open a checking account for estate Open the estate Obtain letters testamentary or letters of administration Request an EIN Publish notice of probate Verify all deadlines for probate and tax filings Prepare accounting books
Within 2 months of death	Hire an accountant if necessary Prepare home for sale if necessary Sell other assets (autos, personal items) if necessary Get appraisals for assets of decedent Pay debts and final bills of decedent Obtain releases from all creditors Begin to transfer nonprobate property
Within 8 months of death	Prepare final tax returns
Within 9 months of death	Pay taxes due
Within 18 and 36 months of death	Obtain tax release from Internal Revenue Service for Form 706 Make final property distributions Make full accounting to heirs and beneficiaries Obtain releases for property transfers from all heirs Notify court that probate is complete

returns, and closing the estate. A sample probate calendar is outlined in Figure 15.1. Don't be afraid to hire professional assistance if you need it. The probate process does not go on forever, but it will require your patience and attention for several months. Following the road map will not completely eliminate the work or hassles of finalizing your parents' financial matters, but hopefully it will make the job easier.

First Steps in Estate Settlement

Planning the funeral is not technically a part of settling an estate. In fact, you normally will not begin the estate settlement process until after your parent is buried. However, you will need to address a few issues immediately. These include obtaining death certificates, canceling credit card accounts, notifying social security and pension plans of the death, and gathering financial documents.

Obtaining Death Certificates

You will need several copies of your parent's death certificate in order to effectively transfer your parent's assets to the heirs. The funeral home director will provide these to you for a nominal fee. Having plenty of them on hand will make your life easier. You will want to request at least 10 copies of the death certificate from the funeral home director.

Closing Credit Card Accounts

Unless a credit card was held jointly with a surviving parent, you should call and cancel any and all credit cards your parent held at death. Canceling the credit cards will protect the estate against unwanted and illegal use of the cards until the final bills can be settled.

Notifying Social Security and Other Pension Plans

The funeral home director often notifies social security of your parent's death. However, you should either do this yourself or confirm that the funeral home director has done so. It is also important to notify any pension plan payers of your parent's death. In many cases, a surviving spouse is eligible for continued benefits, and the pension plan administrator will need to have additional information. However, if your parent was single at the time of death, pension benefits will usually stop.

Gathering Financial Documents

It is very important for you to gather documents concerning your parents' financial affairs immediately upon their deaths. This task will be easier if you ask your parents about the location of their financial statements before their death. The documents you will need include recent bank and investment account statements; retirement plan information; tax returns from the 3 years preceding death; most recent credit card, installment loan, and mortgage loan statements; titles to autos and homes; and insurance policies. If you don't know where the will is, you must make a serious attempt to locate the most recent valid will. Contact the bank at which the decedent rented a safe-deposit box and arrange to have it opened and inventoried. (County probate courts may require the box to be inventoried.)

What Does "Settling an Estate" Mean?

Settling an estate refers to the process of identifying and distributing any property a person owned at the time of her or his death. The personal representative or executor for the estate conducts the process. In that role, you will need to ensure that nonprobate assets are transferred, the will is probated, and any estate or inheritance taxes are paid. The process generally takes from 4 to 18 months. Estates with a large amount of property such as real estate and those that are required to file a federal estate tax return are likely to take longer to process.

> **Personal representative:** The person charged by the probate court with assembling, managing, and distributing an estate's assets. This person is normally named in the decedent's will. In the absence of a will, the responsibility often falls to a family member. If the estate does not need to be probated, then this is the person in charge of the decedent's property.

You should begin settling your parent's estate within a week or two of his or her death. You will want to consult with an attorney if you feel you will need legal advice or assistance. And you should begin taking an inventory of the estate.

Retaining an Attorney

At some point early in this process, you will need to determine if the services of an attorney are desired. You may wish to use the services of an attorney even if there is no probate estate. Few courts require the estate to employ an attorney, but most probate courts encourage personal representatives to do so. This lessens the stress for the court because it is used to working with attorneys, and because attorneys are more efficient at completing the probate process with less hassle to the court. In many cases, however, a personal representative who is detail-oriented and possesses a healthy dose of common sense will not need an attorney.

> **Probate estate:** The portion of an estate that the decedent passes to heirs according to the provisions in the last will or by intestate succession if no will exists.

An attorney will be worth her or his weight in gold, however, if there are problematic claims made against the estate. In addition, if the estate is large, holds a significant amount of tangible property (not just stocks and bonds), or is required to file an estate income tax return, you will want to consider retaining an attorney to assist the personal representative. Personal representatives who have little time on their hands, or who are unable or unwilling to take time from their work or other activities to carry out their duties, may also wish to consider hiring an attorney.

If you choose to employ an attorney, hire one who is experienced in estate and probate procedures. It is important to note here that whether or not an attorney is retained, the court holds the personal representative responsible for carrying out all transactions, meeting deadlines, and accurately completing the probate process. A personal representative certainly has the right to sue an incompetent attorney, but doing so just presents another hassle and additional stress.

The range of attorney's fees for estate settlement is wide. Some states regulate the amount and/or manner in which attorneys can charge for estate administration. Attorneys may charge by the hour, charge a flat rate for processing the estate, or charge a percentage of the amount of the probate estate. Generally speaking, it is best to pay an hourly fee for the services you use. The hourly fee can range from $150 an hour to several hundred dollars an hour if the estate is complicated or large. Few attorneys charge a flat fee for estate administration unless the estate is small and relatively easy to handle. Historically, many attorneys have charged a percentage of the value of the probate estate for their work. This method sounds fair, but at times it can be very costly, especially if the estate is large but relatively simple to administer. An example of a large, simple-to-administer estate would be an estate that held a home and two large brokerage accounts.

You will want to inquire as to the cost of having the attorney's paralegal complete as much of the work as possible. Paralegals who are experienced in estate administration and who work under an attorney's supervision can be quite reasonably priced.

Regardless of the billing method, reputable attorneys should be able to provide an estimate of the charge for administering an estate. They will also be able to provide an approximation of how long it will take to probate the estate. Because you will be working with your attorney closely for several months, it is important that you find one with whom you can communicate easily and whom you trust.

Making an Estate Inventory

As soon as is practical, you should begin taking an inventory of your parent's property. The property may physically stay where it has been, but you need to identify each tangible and intangible piece of property that your parent owned. The balance sheet described in Chapter 3 can provide a good starting point, but it will need to be updated. All property owned or controlled by your parent at his or her death will need to be listed. Property includes real property, such as homes; tangible property, such as automobiles; and intangible property, such as certificates of deposit, brokerage accounts, savings and checking accounts, and cash on hand. In addition, your parents may have owned life insurance, and any policies should be listed also. Chapter 9 provides an example of a life insurance inventory.

Where do you find the information about their property? You can look around and begin making a list of the tangible property. The most obvious pieces are their home and their autos. Their furniture, jewelry, and other personal effects must also be included. Don't forget to include boats, snowmobiles, and jet skis in the inventory.

The intangible property may be more difficult for you to find. Your parent probably had a checking and savings account. In addition, your parent may have had investment accounts, life insurance and annuity policies, and retirement savings accounts. Look first in your parent's file cabinet or personal papers drawer. Find the most recent statement for each account. Call any financial institutions for which you find a statement, notify them of the death, and ask for the most recent statement of the account. The financial institution will require you to put the request in writing, supply a copy of the death certificate, and show evidence of your role as the personal representative for the estate.

You may also find clues on Schedule B of your parent's tax return. Schedule B identifies the sources of interest and dividend payments. A listing for interest received from Main St. Bank will be a clear indicator of an account at that bank. Likewise, dividends reported from XYZ Corporation will tell you that your parent owned some stock in that company.

You will also have to open any safe-deposit boxes that your parent rented. Many people store titles to property and financial statements in a safe-deposit box. However, most states prohibit heirs or family members from opening, examining the contents of, or removing any items from the box until a third party, such as the personal representative, a banker, or a county auditor, takes a complete inventory. States are obviously afraid that assets may be removed and not be properly accounted

Worksheet 15.1 Estate Inventory Worksheet

Item	Value	Probate Property Recipient	Nonprobate Property Recipient
House	$175,000	To be sold Carol, Steve, and Tom 33% to each	
Life insurance proceeds	$100,000		Tom
Checking account	$20,000 (after estate expenses of $50,000)		
IRA 1	$175,000	Carol, Steve, and Tom 33% to each	Carol, Steve, and Tom 33% to each
IRA 2	$300,000		Carol, Steve, and Tom 33% to each
IRA 3	$75,000		Carol, Steve, and Tom 33% to each
Automobile 1	$25,000	Tom	
Automobile 2	$15,000	To be sold 33% to each	
Investment Account 1	$100,000	33% to each	
Investment Account 2	$300,000	Tom	
100 acres farmland	$300,000	To be sold 33% to each	
Personal property	$15,000	Divided among the three	

for. The bank manager will be able to help you arrange for an inventory to be completed.

Be as thorough as you possibly can when identifying your parent's property at death. You will be allowed to reopen or amend the probate findings should an asset later come to light, but this will be time-consuming and costly and will create a huge headache for you. Worksheet 15.1 shows Mrs. Hardman's estate inventory.

Transferring Nonprobate Assets

Probate refers to the legal process of reviewing and validating the will and distributing property transferred by will in accordance with its terms. However, not all property that your parents owned at death will be transferred through the probate process. Many of your parent's assets will be owned jointly with another party (typically a spouse or child), name a direct beneficiary, designate a payable on death or transfer on death recipient, or be held in a trust. Review the information in Table 14.1 if you are confused about what property is nonprobate property and what property transfers via the probate process.

One of several parties may assume the responsibility for transferring nonprobate assets. Typically, the personal representative of the estate will do so. However, the joint owner, beneficiary, payable on death designee, or trustee may do so.

Transferring nonprobate assets is relatively simple and quick. In order to transfer a nonprobate tangible asset, such as a jointly titled home or automobile, you will need to have the title. For intangible assets, such as bank accounts or insurance policies, you will need to have the account or policy number to make a claim on the account. If you do not have the title, account number, or other proof of your parent's ownership, you will need to request replacement titles or inquire as to the existence of accounts with the financial institution's representative. Without the proper account information, you will probably need to show a *letter of administration* (see the "Probate" section later in this chapter). In any case, the financial institution, Bureau of Motor Vehicles, or Clerk of Courts office will be happy to assist you.

Jointly Owned Property

The most common type of jointly held property is property owned as *joint tenants with rights of survivorship*. Any assets owned jointly with rights of survivorship will bypass probate and be distributed directly to the surviving owner. This means that upon the death of one owner, the surviving owner(s) automatically becomes the new owner(s). Most married couples own their home in this fashion. Although it may not always be wise, many unmarried older people choose to title their homes and bank accounts in this manner with a child. Mrs. Hardman chose to own her home with her disabled son, Tom. This ensured that he would automatically receive the home upon her death.

Homes A deed recognizes the owner of a piece of real estate and is recorded at the County Recorder's Office in your local community. The county recorder will return the deed after recording it. You can find out how a property is currently titled by contacting the County Recorder's Office. The Internet makes this even easier, as many counties, especially the more populated ones, have recorded their databases online. You will need the property address in order to access the information.

Once you have the correct information, you will be able to determine how to transfer the property to its new owner. If the home was jointly held with rights of survivorship, you will not have to file any paperwork for the new owner to take possession.

When your last surviving parent has died, it is more likely that he or she owned the home individually. In this case, the home may be sold according to the terms of your parent's will and the income paid to the estate. The sales proceeds will then be transferred according to the probate process, which is discussed later in this chapter.

Mortgaged Property   In some cases your parents will still have a mortgage on their real estate. The property is the "security" for the mortgage. If the real estate was owned jointly, it is most likely that the joint owner's name is on the mortgage as well as the deed. The new owner can satisfy the mortgage in one of several ways. The new owner or the estate may continue to make payments on the mortgage or simply pay it off. In some cases, the new owner will refinance the property. To do this, the new owner will have to qualify for a mortgage.

Bank and Investment Accounts   Parents will often title checking and savings accounts, certificates of deposit, or investment accounts jointly with a spouse or child. You can easily determine if an account at a financial institution is held jointly with rights of survivorship by examining the bank or financial institution's monthly statement. The names on the account will often be followed by *"Jt Tn."* Alternatively, the financial institution will be able to tell you. You will need to contact each financial institution and present the institution with a valid copy of a death certificate and a tax release (described later in this chapter). You will also want to provide each institution with the name, address, and phone number of the new owner of the account. The financial institution may want you to present your request in writing. Once it reviews the request and the death certificate, the financial institution will either remove the decedent's name from the account or transfer the account to the surviving owner. Again, this process should take no more than 1 hour of your time for each account.

Assets with Named Beneficiaries

Only individuals can own certain types of assets. Typically, life insurance policies, retirement accounts, and annuities are owned in this way and are handled differently from joint ownership properties. These assets have a named beneficiary. The proceeds of a policy or the funds in an annuity or retirement plan will be transferred directly to the named beneficiary upon the death of the owner.

The named beneficiary has no rights of ownership until the insured dies. Even so, it is relatively easy to make a claim for the death benefits of the life insurance policy or for funds in an annuity or retirement account. Typically, the personal representative of the estate will make the claim. However, it is also possible for the named beneficiary to make the claim directly. The party making the claim must present a valid death certificate with the claim in order to effect the transfer. While making the claim may take only an hour, it may take anywhere from one day to several weeks before the funds are completely released to the beneficiary.

Some retirement accounts and annuities will not pay a lump sum to a named beneficiary. Rather, the contract calls for a monthly or other periodic payment to be made to the beneficiary. In this case, the personal representative or the named beneficiary will need to file a claim in order to begin receiving benefits. As with life insurance, the insurance company or retirement plan will have a claim form that needs to be completed and filed. A death certificate should also be presented with the claim.

Sometimes there is a disagreement between the beneficiary designation on the annuity, insurance policy, or investment account and what a person has verbally promised another party. Recall that Carol Stoll's mother told Carol that she could have the proceeds of her life insurance policy. In all such cases, the beneficiary designation will prevail. Tom will receive the death benefit from the policy and has no legal obligation to Carol. The general rule is that contracts (nonprobate property) supersede wills, which supersede verbal promises.

Payable on Death and Transfer on Death Designees

Your parents may have bank and investment accounts that are not jointly held with another party. But there is another way for an individual's accounts to bypass probate. Most financial institutions do not use the term *beneficiary*. Instead, they employ "pay on death" or "transfer on death" clauses. In practice, these clauses are equivalent to beneficiary clauses. The funds in a bank or investment account with a "payable on death" or "transfer on death" designee will be paid to the designated individual or parties upon the death of the owner.

Trust Property

Many individuals create a trust and transfer the ownership of their assets to the trust. They do this for management, estate planning, or privacy purposes. All assets owned by a trust will be distributed according to the terms of the trust, not the terms of a will.

Trusts that are created prior to death are called living trusts or *inter vivos* trusts. Upon the death of the grantor, or trust creator, the assets in the trust are distributed according to the terms of the trust. It is easy to identify property that is held in trust. The title of the owner will be given as "Jane Doe Trust," and there is likely to be a creation date and a "for the benefit of" or "FBO" clause in the title. The terms of the trust may appear to be a lot like those in a will. The major difference, however, is that the assets may be transferred by the trustee almost immediately after the death of the grantor. In addition, creditors do not have any rights to claim against trust assets unless they hold a lien against a piece of property titled to the trust.

You as the personal representative of the estate should work with the trustee in distributing the assets according to the trust's terms. As with the transfer of property held as joint tenants or with a named beneficiary, a death certificate will be required to transfer the property. In addition, a copy of the trust document, validly executed, will also be required. The trust document may already be on file with the financial institution, as many such institutions request a copy of the trust document when the account is opened.

Creditors' Rights to Nonprobate Assets

At present, no state allows a creditor to access nonprobate property of a decedent to pay the decedent's debt. However, several states are examining proposals that would allow creditors to do just that. You should check with an attorney regarding this matter before transferring the assets to the surviving joint owner. An attorney will be able to tell you what the rights of creditors are in your state.

Transferring Probate Assets

The probate process is a way of identifying and distributing the assets of a deceased person when no joint owner, named beneficiary, or payable on death designee exists. Almost all estates hold some property that must be transferred through the probate process. Each state has its own probate laws, and, while they are similar, they will vary a bit. Most states allow "small" estates—those with *probate assets* under a given threshold (usually between $20,000 and $100,000)—to bypass the probate process.

Passing Property by Affidavit

When the value of a probate estate is below the state's threshold, the probate court may exempt the estate from the formal probate process. However, the decedent's property must still be transferred according to the terms of any existing will. If no will exists, then the property must be distributed according to applicable state law. The assets cannot be transferred automatically. The property of a small estate that is exempted from probate can be claimed by affidavit. The legal title to the property can then be passed directly to the heir.

Affidavit: A sworn statement that the value of the estate is under the threshold and that the attesting party is entitled to the property.

Probating an estate involves many activities, including opening the estate, transferring assets by affidavit, distributing the assets, and filing the appropriate paperwork. Many persons confuse the probate process or "going through probate" with the requirement to file and pay estate taxes. These are two separate activities, although the personal representative will have to show proof of tax filing and payment to the probate court before it will close the estate.

Opening the Estate

The first step in probating an estate is termed *opening the estate*. Every county has a probate court. Look in the phone book under the county government information to ascertain the location of the court. Either the personal representative named in the will or an heir, if no will exists, files a written probate application with the county in which the parent resided at death. This should be done fairly quickly—no later than 1 month after your parent's death.

Appointing the Personal Representative

Once the court finds the probate application acceptable, it will appoint the personal representative. Normally, the personal representative is the person designated in the will of the decedent. In the event that a person dies without a will, the responsibility for probating the estate generally falls to a close relative, such as you, the child. It will be most efficient if you and your siblings choose someone who is in close proximity to the county in which your parent lived. However, probating an estate often takes considerable time, effort, and accuracy, so you will want to ensure that the person who is assuming the responsibility is willing and able to serve. Regardless of how the personal representative or executor is chosen, the duties of both are the same. To avoid confusion, we will use the term *personal representative.*

A document called *letters testamentary, letters of administration,* or *letter of authority* is issued by the probate court. This document allows the personal representative to act on behalf of the decedent's estate. It will need to be presented when opening a checking account for the estate, transferring any title to a piece of property, or selling an asset of the estate.

Serving as a personal representative of an estate takes a lot of time and energy. The personal representative may need to take time away from work or other activities to fulfill the obligations of estate settlement. Ordinarily the personal representative can be paid a reasonable fee for services rendered. State statutes address this issue specifically. While receiving a fee is perfectly acceptable, a personal representative may choose to waive the fee if she or he is also an heir.

Obtaining an EIN

An EIN (Employer Identification Number) is an identification number that the IRS uses for nonhuman entities such as trusts and estates. You will be required to apply for an EIN for the decedent's estate if the estate is to be probated or if an estate tax return is required. You apply for an EIN from the Internal Revenue Service using Form SS-4.

Opening an Estate Checking Account

You should open a checking account in the name of the estate: *Estate of Emily Hardman, Carol Stoll, Personal Representative.* It is from this account that the bills of the estate will be paid, and any income to the estate will be deposited in this account. You should transfer enough cash into this account from checking, savings, money market, and other liquid accounts to pay for the funeral, pay the decedent's debts, and cover other operating costs, such as utilities on the home.

Publishing Notice of Probate

Once the estate is opened, the court relies upon the personal representative to publish notice of probate. This publication notifies the general public that someone has died and that an estate has been opened, and it instructs the public how to file any claims (such as debts owed) against the estate. Notices are generally published in the local newspaper. At the time the notice is published, the personal representative or attorney must also notify the heirs, beneficiaries, and any known creditors that the estate is open and the probate process has begun.

Dealing with Creditors

You should have called every creditor of the decedent and cancelled all credit card accounts at the time of death. Although interest charges stop on the date of death, any outstanding balances on credit card accounts should be paid from the assets of the estate as soon as possible. However, before you pay the credit card debts in full, ask the credit card company if the decedent had credit life insurance as part of the credit card agreement. Credit life insurance benefits will be used to pay the remaining balance, and the estate may not be responsible for it. Request a waiver of any late charges if your payment was late as a result of the death of your parent.

Managing the Decedent's Property

Managing the decedent's property is one of the most important jobs of the personal representative. It is also the area with the most pitfalls and in which errors are most likely to occur. Managing the decedent's property consists of three tasks: identifying, valuing, and distributing the property.

Identify the Property   As discussed earlier in this chapter, you should begin assembling your parent's property as soon as possible after his or her death. Complete a thorough inventory and include the value, the method of transfer (probate or nonprobate), and the names of the heirs in your inventory.

Value the Property   In addition to identifying all of your parent's property, you will have to place a *fair market value* on the property as of the date of death. This step is relatively easy for intangible assets such as financial accounts, but it is more difficult for tangible property such as homes and autos. It must be done for all property owned by your parent at death, including property that will transfer outside of the probate process.

The value of the intangible assets is simply the balance on the date of death. Call each financial institution that held an account owned by your parents and request that it mail you a statement of the value of the account, including accrued interest, on the date of death. At the same time, you will want to have the name on the account transferred to the estate's name, such as "Estate of Emily Hardman, Carol Stoll, Personal Representative."

Assessing the value of tangible property such as real estate and autos may take a bit more effort. You can find the fair market value of most autos from a car dealer, who will use the "blue book" value. Or, you can easily find the value from one of several credible Web sites such as www.edmunds.com. Using a Web site tool requires you to know the year, make, model, and options of the vehicle. You will be given the average dealer, retail, and "sold on your own" price. Using the middle value is fairly safe. Be sure to print out and retain a record of this value for the estate's files.

There are two methods of valuing real estate. If the property is to be sold, you can use the actual selling price of the home as its fair market value. In many cases, however, a family member may either keep the home as a share of the inheritance or buy it at a price below fair market value. In these cases, you should have a qualified real estate appraiser examine and value the property. The real estate appraiser considers many factors when valuing the property, including the condition of the real estate and the prices of recent home sales in the neighborhood. The cost of a real estate appraisal will vary by geographic region, but you can expect to pay between $150 and $400.

For ease, and because most families divide personal property such as jewelry, artwork, and household furnishings among themselves, many personal representatives will value the personal property at a flat rate. The flat rate should be reasonable and based on garage sale or resale value. In some cases, however, if there are a large number of items or if the estate includes collections or valuable artwork and jewelry, you should hire an outside appraiser. As with a real estate appraisal, a professional experienced in considering all the relevant factors will determine the value.

Distribute the Property   The heirs are almost always anxious to receive the property they are inheriting. The personal representative, however, has a fiduciary responsibility to ensure that the probate process is followed properly. You may be able to transfer a bit of the property, and certainly the personal property, fairly early in the process. However, a complete distribution of your parent's property should not take place until the personal representative is certain that the debts and tax liabilities of the decedent and the estate are paid in full, and an accounting has been made to the beneficiaries and the probate court. If no property remains after the decedent's debts and the estate taxes are paid, then regardless of what the will states, no heir will receive any probate property. As discussed earlier in this chapter, unsecured creditors do not have a claim against nonprobate property, and heirs will receive nonprobate property of which they were a joint owner with rights of survivorship, a named beneficiary, or a payable on death designee.

How do you know how your parent wished the estate to be distributed? If your parent completed the estate planning process outlined in Chapter 14, he or she should have a valid will. Some wills include clauses identifying specific pieces of property and who is to receive them. Bequests of specific items or specific dollar amounts are called *pecuniary transfers* and are to be made before any other distributions. Most wills also have clauses that outline how the remainder or residual of an estate is to be transferred. Clauses such as "my son, Steven Hardman, is to receive 25 percent of my estate" are called residual clauses. Pecuniary bequests will be made first. Steven Hardman will receive his share from any remaining property.

Paying Estate, Income, and Inheritance Taxes

Taxes are a fact of life, and they are not to be ignored at death. An estate is responsible for paying the appropriate tax liabilities of the decedent and his or her estate just as it would have to pay any other debt. Filing the appropriate tax forms and paying any tax liability is part of the probate process. However, because the process of dealing with taxes is so detailed, a thorough discussion is provided later in this chapter.

Closing the Estate

Once the personal representative demonstrates to the probate court's satisfaction that all property has been identified and valued, all creditors of the decedent and the estate have been paid, and all tax liabilities have been cleared, he or she may make any final distributions and notify the court that probate is completed. The court will then issue a determination that the estate is closed. If a personal representative or heir later discovers the existence of another asset, the estate will need to be reopened;

the asset identified, valued, and distributed; and the estate reclosed. Going through this process is tedious, and no personal representative would want this to happen.

Essential Elements of Inheritance, Estate, and Income Taxation

Over the past few years, much media attention has been focused on the changes in the estate and gift tax laws. In the United States, the estate and gift tax laws are at times intertwined. Many states also assess an inheritance or death tax. Most states' inheritance taxes are coordinated with federal law, or "pick up" where the federal tax ends. In addition to the tax on transfers at death, you will be required to file a final income tax return for a parent who dies during the year and an income tax return for an estate or trust that was opened and received income such as interest and dividends during the tax year. An outline of the relevant forms, their purpose, and due dates are included in Table 15.1.

Table 15.1 Federal Estate Tax Forms and Filing Dates

Form	Due Date	Purpose
706	Nine months after death	Report and pay estate tax
709	The earlier of April 15 of the year following a gift in excess of the annual gift exclusion or 9 months after death	Report and pay any tax due on excess gifts
1040	April 15 of year following death	Report and pay income tax for decedent from January 1 to date of death in year of death
1041	Day 15 of fourth month after close of tax year	Report and pay income tax for estate from date of death to end of tax year
1310	With the Form 1040 or 1040X	Apply for a refund in the decedent's name
2758	Day 15 of fourth month after close of tax year; if a second request, Day 15 of seventh month after close of tax year	Request an extension of time to file a Form 1041 for an estate
4768	Nine months after death	Request a 6-month extension for time to file Form 706
8736	Day 15 of fourth month after close of tax year	First request for an extension of time to file a Form 1041 for a trust

Table 15.1 *(continued)*

Form	Due Date	Purpose
8800	Day 15 of seventh month after closeof tax year	Second request for an extension of time to file a Form 1041 for a trust
K-1 (Form 1041)	With Form 1041	Report beneficiaries' share of estate's or trust's income and deductions
SS-4	Filed immediately upon opening an estate	Apply for an EIN (employer identification number) for the estate

The tax laws concerning estate taxes and the income of estates and trusts are quite complicated. A simple overview is given here. You should not hesitate to get professional advice in these matters. If you are at all uncomfortable with the subject of taxes, consult with an accountant or attorney who is well versed in estate administration and planning.

State Death, Inheritance, or Pick-Up Taxes

Few states allow persons to pass from this world without paying a tax. Some states call these taxes death or estate taxes. Some use the term *pick-up tax* because the tax rate is set equal to the credit allowed against the federal estate tax. Others use the term *inheritance tax*.

A list of the states assessing death, inheritance, or pick-up taxes is given in Table 15.2. Because each state's rules vary, you may need to consult with your accountant concerning the taxability of your parent's estate.

Table 15.2 States with Death, Inheritance, or Pick-Up Taxes

Pick-up tax only	Alabama, Alaska, Arizona, Arkansas, California, Colorado, Delaware, Florida, Georgia, Hawaii, Idaho, Illinois, Kansas, Maine, Massachusetts, Michigan, Minnesota, Mississippi, Missouri, Montana, Nevada, New Mexico, New York, North Carolina, North Dakota, Oregon, Rhode Island, South Carolina, South Dakota, Texas, Utah, Vermont, Virginia, Washington, West Virginia, Wisconsin, Wyoming
Inheritance and pick-up tax	Connecticut, Indiana, Iowa, Kentucky, Louisiana, Maryland, Nebraska, New Hampshire, New Jersey, Pennsylvania, Tennessee*
Estate and pick-up tax	Ohio, Oklahoma

*Connecticut and Louisiana are phasing out their inheritance taxes.

Inheritance or death tax: A tax assessed by the decedent's state of residence for which the heirs are technically responsible. Because the heirs would have to pay the estate tax out of their inheritances, most estates pay any inheritance taxes due before final distributions of property are made.

Estate Taxes

Federal law limits the total amount of property an individual or couple may transfer to others during life and at death without incurring a tax. This limit is called the exclusion amount. An estate with a gross estate greater than the exclusion amount will have to file a tax return and may be liable for estate taxes.

Exclusion amount: The value of assets that may be transferred to heirs without incurring an estate or gift tax.

Simply add up the amount of the gross estate as described in step 1. The amount of the exclusion will depend on the year in which a person dies. Any estate with a value exceeding $1,000,000 (the exclusion amount in 2003) is required to file a return. The exclusion amount will increase through the year 2009 and is unlimited for those taxpayers dying during 2010. The exclusion amounts are included in Table 15.3.

Table 15.3 Applicable Estate Exclusion Amounts and Estate Tax Credits

Year	Applicable Exclusion Amount*	Credit
2003	$1,000,000	$ 345,800
2004–2005	$1,500,000	$ 555,800
2006–2008	$2,000,000	$ 780,800
2009	$3,500,000	$1,455,800
2010	No tax	No tax

*The exclusion is increased to $1.3 million if the decedent owned a family-owned and closely held business or farm. To qualify, the value of the business interest must exceed 50 percent of the adjusted gross estate. The maximum business tax deduction is $675,000, but then the maximum nonbusiness exclusion is $625,000. This exclusion is repealed after 12/31/03.

exclusion in out years?

Calculating the Estate Tax   Like the income tax system discussed in Chapter 6, the estate tax has its own structure. Each step must be completed in turn to calculate the estate tax that is due.

STEP 1. CALCULATE THE GROSS ESTATE

A decedent's gross estate consists of the fair market value of all of the assets he or she owns on the date of death or on the alternative valuation date, which is 6 months after death. This is an "all-or-nothing" proposition. If one asset is valued on the alternative date, then all assets must be.

> A valuation date 6 months after death may be appropriate when a large percentage of the estate is held as stocks and bonds and the value of these assets has dropped significantly since the decedent's death.

In addition to the assets that one automatically includes on a balance sheet, such as a home, investments, and retirement plans, the gross estate also includes the value of personal property such as jewelry, automobiles, and art and the face value or death benefit of any life insurance the decedent owned on her or his own life.

The value of life insurance is often forgotten at the time of estate planning and tax minimization planning. The rules concerning the taxation of life insurance benefits are confusing. For estate tax purposes, the face value (death benefit) of any life insurance owned by and insuring the decedent is included in her or his gross estate. In effect, even though the face value of life insurance is not taxed to the beneficiary for income tax purposes, it is taxed to the estate upon the transfer at death if the policy is owned by the decedent. In addition, the cash value of any life insurance owned by the decedent but insuring the life of another person is included.

The IRS requires that you consider all gifts made during life when determining the gross estate. The first $11,000 of value of annual gifts given to any number of individuals is exempt. However, any excess is added back into the gross estate. In other words, if your single parent gave you a car worth $20,000 during 2003, then $9,000 would come back into the estate for purposes of calculating the estate and gift tax. Your parents could give both you and a sibling $11,000 every year, and nothing would be added back. Your parent could also give every grandchild $11,000 each year and nothing would be added back to the estate. However, once the total gifts to an individual exceeds the $11,000 limit in one calendar year, the excess amount will be added to the value of the estate at the time of death. The property is not actually returned to the estate, but the value of the excess gift is included in the gross estate for tax purposes.

Finally, the IRS will add back the value of certain property that was transferred in the 3 years prior to death even if the transfer fell under the annual gift exclusion amount. These certain properties include transfers of life insurance policies on the decedent's life, relinquishment of retained life estates, and some revocable transfers. In addition, the gift tax that was actually paid on excess gifts made within 3 years of death is added back.

> **Retained life estate:** What occurs when a person transfers the ownership of property to another person, but retains the right to income, possession, or enjoyment of the property until his or her own death.

STEP 2. CALCULATE THE DEDUCTIONS

Some deductions from the gross estate are allowed before the tax rate is applied. These include such obvious items as the outstanding balance on any debt owed at the date of death, including mortgages, credit cards, automobile loans, and personal liabilities. In addition, funeral expenses, last medical bills, outstanding household bills such as utility payments, and legal and accounting bills to settle the estate are deductible.

The Internal Revenue Code does allow for certain transfers of property to be deducted from the gross estate. These transfers include all those made to a decedent's spouse (either at death or during life) and gifts or bequests to qualified charities. A qualified charity is one organized under Section 501(3)(c) of the code and government, religious, and educational institutions.

STEP 3. CALCULATE THE TAXABLE ESTATE

The taxable estate is equal to the value of the decedent's gross estate less the total of all deductions for outstanding liabilities, funeral and estate administrative expenses, transfers to the spouse of the decedent, and charitable bequests. It is upon this taxable estate that the estate tax is calculated. The tax rates are quite steep and can significantly lower the amount of the remaining estate to be transferred to heirs.

STEP 4. CALCULATE THE TENTATIVE ESTATE TAX

It is now time to calculate the estate tax due on your parents' estate. The federal estate and gift tax brackets start at 18 percent and increase to

Table 15.4 Estate Tax Rates

Taxable Amounts Over	But Not Over	Tax	Plus Rate on Taxable Amount over That in First Column Between
$ 0	$ 10,000	$ 0	18%
$ 10,001	$ 20,000	$ 1,800	20%
$ 20,001	$ 40,000	$ 3,800	22%
$ 40,001	$ 60,000	$ 8,200	24%
$ 60,001	$ 80,000	$ 13,000	26%
$ 80,001	$ 100,000	$ 18,200	28%
$ 100,001	$ 150,000	$ 23,800	30%
$ 150,001	$ 250,000	$ 38,800	32%
$ 250,001	$ 500,000	$ 70,800	34%
$ 500,001	$ 750,000	$ 155,800	37%
$ 750,001	$ 1,000,000	$ 248,300	39%
$ 1,000,001	$ 1,250,000	$ 345,800	41%
$ 1,250,001	$ 1,500,000	$ 448,300	43%
$ 1,500,001	$ 2,000,000	$ 555,800	45%
$ 2,000,001	$ Unlimited	$ 780,800	49%

50 percent for the largest estates. Because of the exclusion amount (see the discussion in the next section), the effective tax rates range from 41 to 50 percent. The tax rates are outlined in Table 15.4.

Estate and gift tax rates are progressive; that is, the rate increases on incremental increases in the value of the estate. For this reason, the calculation is similar to that used in calculating the income tax. As shown in the sidebar "Estate Tax Calculation Example," Mrs. Hardman's estate's tentative federal estate tax is $493,300.

STEP 5. CALCULATE THE ESTATE TAX CREDIT

Each estate is allowed three credits against the taxes due. A credit is similar to having a coupon at the local grocery store. The price (or, in this case, the tax) is determined, and the value of the credit is directly offset from the tax.

Every estate is permitted a credit of $345,800 in 2003. This credit is equal to what the estate tax would be for a net taxable estate of $1,000,000. That is why it is often said that each estate enjoys a $1,000,000 exclusion. This is also why gross estates valued at less than $1,000,000 are not required to file Form 706. Both the exclusion and credit amounts are presented in Table 15.3.

Estate Tax Calculation Example

Step 1. Gross estate $1,650,000
Step 2. Deductions for expenses   (50,000)
Step 3. Taxable estate = step 1 minus step 2 $1,600,000
Step 4. Calculate tentative tax
    a. Taxable estate (from step 3) $1,600,000
    b. Less lower end of tax bracket
       (Table 15.4)   (1,500,000)
    c. Equals amount at tax bracket rate $ 100,000
    d. Tax bracket rate (Table 15.4)   0.45
    e. Multiply step 4c by step 4d $ 45,000
    f. Tax on $1,500,000 (Table 15.4)   448,300
    g. Tentative tax = step 4e plus step 4f $ 493,300
Step 5. Calculate estate tax credit
    a. Credit amount in 2003 (Table 15.4) $ 345,800
    b. Calculate credit for state death tax
       1) Amount of taxable estate (step 3) $1,600,000
       2) Less flat adjustment of $60,000   (60,000)
       3) Equals adjusted taxable estate $1,540,000
       4) Calculate tax before reduction rate
          (Table 15.5):
          $[(1,540,000 - 1,540,000) \times 7.2]$
          $+ 70,800 =$ $ 70,800
       5) Less reduction rate:
          $[70,800 \text{ (step 5.b.4)} \times .50 \text{ (year 2003)}] =$ (35,400)
       6) Equals maximum credit for state death
          taxes paid $ 35,400
    c. Calculate total credits
       (step 5.a. plus step 5.b.6) $ 381,200
Step 6. Calculate tentative tax
    (step 4 minus step 5.c.) $ 112,100
Step 7. Amount of gift taxes previously paid   0
Step 8. Final tax liability (step 6 minus step 7) $ 112,100

In 2003 only, an estate can claim an additional estate tax deduction if farm and qualifying business interests exceed 50 percent of the adjusted gross estate. The maximum business tax deduction is $675,000, but in no case can the total tax credit exceed $1,300,000. This allows for less tax to be paid and increases the value of property passed to family members. To qualify for this deduction, the business must remain in the family for 10 years after death. Otherwise, the IRS will recapture any additional taxes due.

Because most states also tax the estates of their residents, the IRS allows an estate tax credit for the amount of inheritance or estate taxes the estate paid to the decedent's state of residence. The maximum credit is equal to the taxable estate less $60,000 (a fixed amount) times the maximum credit rate. For 2003, the calculated credit amount is then reduced to 50 percent (25 percent in 2004, and a deduction in 2005) to arrive at the maximum credit allowed. The maximum credit rates are provided in Table 15.5.

Mrs. Hardman's taxable estate was $1,600,000 ($1,650,000 – $50,000 in deductions). As shown in the sidebar "Estate Tax Calculation Example," her maximum state death tax credit would be $35,400.

Mrs. Hardman's estate will benefit from total credits of $381,200.

STEP 6. CALCULATE THE NET ESTATE TAX LIABILITY
The estate tax credit determined in step 5 is subtracted from the gross estate tax to arrive at the net estate tax liability. After subtracting Mrs.

Table 15.5 Maximum State Death Tax Credit Rates

(1) Adjusted Taxable Estate Equal to or More Than	(2) Adjusted Taxable Estate Less Than	(3) Credit on Amount in Column (1)	(4) Rate of Credit on Excess over Amount in Column (1)
640,000	840,000	18,000	4.8%
840,000	1,040,000	27,600	5.6%
1,040,000	1,540,000	38,800	6.4%
1,540,000	2,040,000	70,800	7.2%
2,040,000	2,540,000	106,800	8.0%
2,540,000	3,040,000	146,800	8.8%
3,040,000	3,540,000	190,800	9.6%
3,540,000	4,040,000	238,800	10.4%
4,040,000	5,040,000	290,800	11.2%
5,040,000	6,040,000	402,800	12.0%
6,040,000	7,040,000	522,800	12.8%
7,040,000	8,040,000	650,800	13.6%
8,040,000	9,040,000	786,800	14.4%
9,040,000	10,040,000	930,800	15.2%
10,040,000	Unlimited	1,082,800	16.0%

Hardman's credit of $381,200 from her initial tax liability of $493,300, her tentative tax liability will be $112,100.

STEP 7. TOTAL GIFT TAXES PREVIOUSLY PAID

Few individuals make any payments toward their estate tax in advance. However, those who have transferred gifts of value exceeding the annual gift exclusion and exceeding the applicable exclusion amount may have paid a gift tax at the time of the gift. This will happen when the total value of excess gifts (those over $10,000 per person per year in the year 2001 and before or over $11,000 after 2001) exceeds $1,000,000. In such a case, the decedent would have been required to previously pay a gift tax. The amount of gift tax previously paid is now used to offset the estate tax.

Credit for these prior payments is given to the decedent's estate because the value of the gifts is included in the calculation of the gross estate to be taxed. Mrs. Hardman had not paid any gift taxes earlier.

STEP 8. CALCULATE THE TAX DUE

The amount of tax due equals the tentative estate tax liability calculated in step 6 less the total of any taxes previously paid as determined in step 7. Mrs. Hardman's estate is liable for estate taxes of $112,100.

Filing the Return   You will use Form 706 to calculate and file your parent's estate and gift tax return. The return is due 9 months after your parent's death. If an extension is needed, you may request one by using Form 4768. Filing an extension does not excuse one from paying any tax due within the 9-month time period. In fact, you must send a check for the amount of taxes you expect to be due with the extension request. The estate will pay interest and late payment penalties on any taxes paid after the 9-month period ends.

Getting a Release from the IRS   How do you know that the estate tax return you filed with the IRS was complete? Or, how do you know that you no longer have any liability? Once a Form 706 is filed, the IRS manually examines it. This process may take anywhere from 9 months to 3 years. Once the IRS accepts the Form 706 as correct and decides that all tax liabilities have been satisfied, you will receive an *acceptance of estate tax return* letter. Keep this letter. It is proof that neither the personal representative nor the estate has any more liability for estate taxes. The probate court will require you to have this letter before it closes the estate.

Filing the Decedent's Final Income Tax Return

Unfortunately, not even death can exempt a person from paying income taxes on income he or she received. The tax is assessed on all income received from January 1 through and including the day of death, and a return is required. You will use a regular Form 1040 to file your parent's final return, and the information provided in Chapter 6 of this book applies to the preparation of this return.

Generally speaking, the same types of income are taxed and the same deductions allowed as if your parent was still living. The personal representative will choose whether medical expenses paid by the estate within 1 year following death are deducted as an itemized deduction on the final Form 1040, Schedule A, or on the estate tax return, Form 706. The expenses are deducted on the tax return for the year in which the medical services were provided, not the year in which the cost was paid. Funeral, probate, and estate expenses may not be deducted on Form 1040, the decedent's personal, final return.

> If the estate is not required to file Form 706, then be sure to deduct medical expenses on the Form 1040 for the tax year in which the medical services were provided.

Filing a Return for a Single or Married Filing Separately Deceased Parent
Income earned from the first day of the year through the day of death must be reported on the final tax return. Likewise, itemized deductions for a deceased person are allowed only for expenses paid through the day of death. Deceased persons are credited with the full exemption and standard deduction amounts, even if they lived only 1 day during the tax year. The decedent cannot claim the personal deduction if someone else claims the decedent as a dependent. No standard deduction can be claimed if a surviving spouse is filing separately and itemizes deductions.

The personal representative should sign and file the tax return. When an estate is not probated, there is still a person who is in charge of the decedent's property. This person should sign the return followed by the words, "Personal Representative."

The personal representative must attach the letters testamentary or letters of administration to the tax return when claiming a refund. Form 1310 must be filed when a claim for a refund is made on an amended return or when the estate is not being probated and there is no court-appointed personal representative. It is not required if the refund request is made on the original tax return. Any refund that your parent is due will be paid to the estate and distributed according to the terms of the will.

Filing a Joint Return for a Deceased and a Surviving Parent   The personal representative and your surviving parent have the option of filing your parents' income taxes jointly, provided the surviving parent has not remarried by the end of the tax year. The personal representative will file your deceased parent's return using the "married, filing separately" status if the surviving spouse has remarried by the end of the year.

All income for the full year for the surviving parent and the income earned through the day of death for the deceased parent will be included if you decide to file a joint return with the surviving spouse. Income from assets that are held jointly with the spouse with rights of survivorship will be fully reported on the joint return. Allocate all deductions in the same manner. Of course, if you are filing a return jointly for your surviving parent and a deceased parent, the surviving parent is allowed itemized deductions for the full tax year.

The court-appointed personal representative must sign a joint return and include his or her title. This means that the personal representative signs for the decedent and the spouse signs for him- or herself. A spouse who is also acting as personal representative must sign the return twice. In addition, the personal representative must attach the letters testamentary or letters of administration to the return.

Estates that do not need to be probated have no court-appointed representative. In this case, the surviving spouse should write "Filing as Surviving Spouse" in the line for the decedent's signature and sign his or her name on the appropriate line.

The IRS will send a refund made payable to the surviving parent and the estate. In most cases, you will want the refund to be paid to the surviving parent only. Form 1310 can be used to request that the check be issued to only the surviving spouse. Attach a copy of the death certificate to the Form 1310.

The final return for a deceased parent is due by April 15 of the year following the year of death. You will be required to file this return before closing the estate. The IRS requires that the tax return be filed on the appropriate year's Form 1040. This means that you may have to keep the estate open in order to file the final income tax return on the correct forms.

You may also file a 4-month extension request on Form 4868. Penalties and interest will be charged on tax due amounts that are not paid by April 15. To avoid penalties and interest, you must pay any taxes due at the time you file an extension request.

Filing an Income Tax Return for the Estate

In addition to taxing income received during the year, but prior to the death of a taxpayer, the Internal Revenue Service also taxes income accruing to the estate after death and during the probate or settlement process. A trust also must pay income taxes on the income it receives during a tax year. You will report the estate or trust's income and deductions on Form 1041. This return must be filed if the estate has a gross income of $600 or more or if the estate has a non-U.S. resident beneficiary. Because tax rates on income to an estate or trust are more accelerated than those of most individual beneficiaries, you can choose to "pass through" the income and deductions. This means that each heir will pay income taxes on his or her share of the estate's taxable income, and the estate will not be taxed at the higher rates.

The gross income of an estate will include wages, interest, dividends, and the capital gain from the sale of any asset, including a home, when the proceeds were paid to the probate estate. The estate receives a $600 "personal" exemption and may employ standard deductions such as interest and property taxes paid. Funeral, probate, and legal expenses may be deductible on Form 1041 or Form 706. However, medical expenses paid from the estate for a decedent may not be deducted on Form 1041.

Life insurance proceeds paid to an estate are not taxable. However, withdrawals from retirement plans are taxable to an estate if no beneficiary was named.

> Because tax rates for an estate's income are more accelerated than the tax rates on personal income tax returns, you will want to have heirs, rather than the estate, withdraw funds from retirement plans.

The personal representative has a choice of whether to use many of the deductible items, such as legal fees, property taxes, and interest, on Form 1041, the estate income tax return, or Form 706, the estate tax return. You will want to consult a tax adviser to determine the most advantageous use of these deductions.

One Form K-1 (1041) is attached to the Form 1041 for each beneficiary. This form reports to the beneficiaries their share of the estate or trust income. The beneficiaries then report this information on their personal Form 1040s. It is normally better to pass through the income and deductions, and thus the tax, rather than have the estate pay the taxes because estate tax rates are normally much higher than the individual tax rates of the beneficiaries.

Form 1041, the estate's income tax return, is due on the fifteenth day of the fourth month after the close of the tax year. This may or may not be April 15. For a variety of reasons, including convenience, minimization of taxes, and the expected length of the probate process, many estates choose a tax year that ends on a day other than December 31. A 3-month extension may be requested on Form 2758, but as always, any taxes due must be paid with the extension request. A second 3-month extension may be granted upon filing of a second Form 2758. Form 8736 is used to request a 3-month extension for a trust tax return. The second extension request for a trust is filed on Form 8800.

Filing a State Estate Income Tax Return   Not all states tax estates and trusts. Consult with your state's tax office to determine if a return is required. If it is, you will need to file a return.

Final Thoughts

Settling an estate is time-consuming and requires attention to detail. The personal representative should be carefully chosen and not only be able to handle the details of the estate settlement but also be willing to serve. An attorney can be retained to advise, assist, or even serve as the personal representative. You will need to ensure that all of your parents' property is transferred according to their wishes as stated in their wills, or by owning property jointly with rights of survivorship or naming direct beneficiaries or payable on death designees. Finally, make sure that all tax returns are filed in a timely manner and that both tax liabilities and debts are fully satisfied prior to closing the estate. You can now sit back, relax, and know that you would have made your parents proud!

Part V

Epilogue

16

Using the Lessons
You've Learned

Pedro Hernandez, age 48, is married and has two grown children. In the past 3 years, both of his elderly parents have passed away. Pedro was very involved in assisting them physically, emotionally, and financially during their final months. During that time Pedro put his own financial affairs on the back burner, but now he recognizes that he and his wife must focus on their own financial future.

Pedro is the manager of a midsize conference hotel. He and his siblings each inherited $75,000 from their parents. Pedro wants to invest most of his inheritance for retirement because he has so little put away. Pedro makes a decent salary, and the hotel management company does provide health and life insurance benefits. It will also match some contributions to his retirement savings plan. But Pedro has no idea if the insurance the company offers is enough, and he has been saving only $75 out of his biweekly paycheck for retirement. He is trying to make a long-term financial plan.

PEDRO HAS COME THROUGH some trying times. He is probably tired of "taking care of things." Caring for his aging parents and their money was stressful. But it also gave him an opportunity to learn about some financial topics that were not yet part of his reality, such as Medicare, Medicaid, nursing home selection, and estate planning. His new knowledge should not be wasted. Now is the time for him to examine his own financial affairs and put them in order.

Now is the time for you to do this too. Perhaps you will inherit a few assets from your parents. Or perhaps you are nearing retirement and wish to devise a retirement plan for yourself. Maybe you've become an "empty nester" recently. It is important for you to make your own plan and take action to turn the plan into reality. Financial success is not a function of how much money you have but rather of how you manage it.

This chapter is designed to remind you of all the financial issues you will face as you age and to help you make and implement a plan for the future. Each section in this chapter parallels the earlier chapters in this book. A quick review of the major issues is provided, with a checklist for your use. In addition, several financial tips are emphasized.

Basic Money Management

Just as excellent golfers have a basic swing that they use over and over again, you should acquire good money management skills that can guide your economic decisions. All money management decisions should be based on economic reality. And you can't know your financial reality unless you prepare three basic financial statements: a cash flow statement, a balance sheet, and a budget.

Cash Flow Statement

A cash flow statement provides a history of your sources of income and how you have chosen to spend your money. It can confirm your priorities or expose bad spending habits. In either case, it is impossible for you to make a plan for the future without knowing what you did in the past.

Your checkbook register, credit card statements, pay stubs, and income tax returns will prove invaluable to you as you review your income and expenditure history. If these are not readily available for the past year, you will want to track your income and expenses for several months in order to establish your personal patterns. Use the sample cash flow statement in Chapter 2 as an example as you prepare your own. You may want to answer the questions in the sidebar, "Things to Consider about Your Cash Flow Statement."

Things to Consider about Your Cash Flow Statement

- How many sources of regular income do I have?
- How much income does each source provide?
- How much of my income is provided by my assets, not my labor?
- Where does my money go?

- What percentage of my income is used to provide for my housing expenses (mortgage, rent, utilities)?
- Am I surprised about how much I am spending in any category?
  - If so, which category?
    - Do I want to increase or decrease my spending in this category?
- Which expenses are difficult to change?
- Which expenses can I easily decrease?
- Which of my expenses are paid irregularly (not monthly, for example)?
- Is my income greater than my expenses?
- In which months does my income not cover my expenses?
- Do I save money to cover my expenses in those months in which my income is less than my expenses?

Balance Sheet

While the cash flow statement provides a history of your income and expenses over a period of time, the balance sheet will show your net worth or wealth at one point in time. Your assets are the positive side of the net worth coin—they show the value of what you own. Debts are the negative aspect of the balance sheet. They decrease net worth. Debts are listed at the current outstanding balance, or the amount of money it would take to pay off the debt today. Net worth equals assets minus debts. Use the sample balance sheet in Chapter 3 as you prepare your own.

The balance sheet is an informative tool in your planning kit. First, it tells you what you are worth (economically) and whether you are solvent or bankrupt. Second, upon closer examination, it tells you which assets are available to increase your income and which you are using in daily living. Each individual or family should have emergency funds that are held in liquid savings vehicles such as savings and money market accounts or certificates of deposit. Third, it tells you whether you have funds saved for retirement or for the long term. And, if you compare your balance sheet from year to year, you should see an increase in your net worth, which signifies either an increase in your assets or a decrease in your debt load. You may want to examine your balance sheet for the items outlined in the sidebar "Things to Consider about Your Balance Sheet."

Things to Consider about Your Balance Sheet

- What is your net worth?
  Is it increasing or decreasing from year to year?
- What is the total value of your liquid assets (checking, savings, and money market accounts and certificates of deposit)?
  How many months of expenses would your total liquid assets provide?
- What is the total value of your investment assets (checking, savings, money market, and brokerage accounts)?
  Is the value of your investment accounts increasing each year?
  Which investments are providing you with current income (interest, dividends, or rents)?
- What is the total value of your retirement or deferred assets [IRAs, 401(k)s, 403(b)s, annuities, and cash-value life insurance]?
  Is the value of your retirement accounts increasing each year?
- What percentage of your total debts does your first mortgage represent?
- What is the total value of all nonmortgage debt?
  Is your total debt decreasing from year to year?

Budget

A budget is the road map to successful financial planning. The purpose of a budget is to guide your spending so that you meet your income, spending, and savings goals. Without a budget, you may always be strapped for cash or may never satisfy your financial desires. Creating your budget is a personal process, and only you can do it.

Budgeting involves setting priorities, examining your income stream, and determining how you are going to spend your money. You can use paper ledgers or financial software to make the task easier. Regardless of how you budget, you will need to evaluate your budget and your progress toward your income and spending goals on a regular basis.

Many of us experience "too much month at the end of our money." You must decide how to respond when expenses exceed income. You can increase your income, reduce your expenses, withdraw money from savings and investments, or borrow money from others to make up for the shortfall. Examine your spending patterns first to see where you can reduce your expenses. Then decide if you can increase your income at your present place of employment or by assuming a second job. Because savings withdrawals and borrowing funds are only temporary fixes for budget shortfalls, consider them as a last resort. The information in the sidebar "Things to Consider about Your Budget" may help you in the budgeting process.

Things to Consider about Your Budget

- People who like to use cash may benefit from dividing their spending money into envelopes by category. When an envelope is empty, either stop spending on the particular item or move money from another envelope (category). This method may not work for impulse purchasers who constantly "borrow" from another category.
- Those who like to keep an ongoing record of expenses will prefer paying for most items by check. This can be costly if your financial institution charges a fee for each check you write.
- Disciplined spenders may successfully use a credit card for all purchases and then just have one large bill to pay at the end of the month. If you don't pay the bill in full, stop using this method.
- Save money each budget period for large, irregular expenses such as property taxes, auto or health insurance premiums, and home or auto repairs. This area is where most individuals fail at budgeting. When the large, irregular bills come due, there is no money to make the payment, and the individuals will borrow to do so.

Credit

Credit is the use of your future income for current consumption. When you borrow, you are buying something now and promising to work for it later. Overusing credit can hinder your long-term prospects for financial security. Most individuals who find themselves in debt trouble got there because they borrowed against future income and then for a variety of reasons the future income did not materialize. Research suggests that an unforeseen job loss, divorce, and unexpected medical expenses are the most likely causes of credit management problems. Individuals are able to manage quite well until one of these events take place. When income drops or expenses increase, a previously manageable debt load becomes unbearable.

In addition to reviewing your balance sheet for debt information, complete a debt inventory like the one you prepared for your parents in Chapter 5. Pay particular attention to the interest rates charged on each account. Close accounts that you no longer use. Consider using only one major credit card instead of having several store or special-purpose cards. And make a serious effort to reduce your credit card debt.

It is likely that you will need additional credit in the future, perhaps for a larger home or a new vehicle. Poor credit ratings will result in application denials and increased interest rates. Don't wait until you need to apply for a loan to check your credit rating. For a small fee you can request a copy of your credit report from your local credit bureau. If the report contains errors, report the errors to the credit bureau immediately. Repairing a bad credit report should be a financial priority. Consider the issues outlined in the sidebar "Things to Consider about Credit Cards" as you examine your credit situation.

Things to Consider about Credit Cards

- How many credit cards do you hold?
  How many of those credit cards do you use regularly?
  Which of the credit card accounts have an annual fee?
  What is the interest rate on each account?
- Do you use credit cards for convenience?
  If so, do you pay the balances in full each month?
- Do you only use credit to purchase durable goods that hold value or provide years of service?
- Do you have an employer-provided credit card?
  If so, when you are reimbursed for charges do you repay the credit card balance?
- Do you just make the minimum payments each month?
- Do you use one credit card to make payments on or pay off another?
- Do you take cash advances against your credit cards?

Income Taxes

They say the only two certainties in life are death and taxes. You cannot do much about the former, but you can manage the latter. Most people can't recall the total tax liability they incurred in the previous year. That's because they don't write a check for their taxes the way they do for groceries. But it is likely that income taxes are one of your largest expenses each year.

Review the last three income tax returns you filed. Pay attention to what types of income you had, the amount and type of itemized deductions you claimed, and your total tax liability. Take active steps to reduce your tax liability. The average person approaching retirement will save 27 cents in taxes for each dollar saved in an IRA or a qualified retirement plan through his or her employer. Do you have a student in the family? You can now take an income adjustment for the amount of interest you pay on student loans and for qualified tuition and related expenses. If you're self-employed, don't overlook the income adjustment for the health insurance premiums you pay each year.

Taxpayers who normally prepare their own return may benefit from a quick review by an accountant to ensure that they are claiming every deduction available to them. Or review your income tax returns and focus on the issues highlighted in the sidebar "Things to Consider about Income Taxes."

Things to Consider about Income Taxes

- Are you contributing to an individual retirement plan or to a 401(k) or 403(b) retirement plan at work?
  If so, consider using a bonus or salary increase to raise your contribution.
- Are you or is your spouse or a child a student?
  If so, are you deducting the cost of tuition?
  Are you deducting the cost of interest on your student loans?
- Are you or your spouse self-employed?
  If so, be sure to deduct 70 percent of your health insurance premium on the front of your Form 1040 (available only for non-employer-provided plans). Deduct the remaining 30 percent on Schedule A.
  Consider using a medical savings account to pay for your medical costs and deduct contributions to the plan.
  Deduct 50 percent of the self-employment tax you pay (Schedule SE) on the front of your Form 1040.
- Are your property taxes escrowed or paid as part of your monthly mortgage payment?
  If so, did you deduct the amount of property taxes you paid?

Things to Consider about Income Taxes *(continued)*

- Are you tracking your charitable contributions?
- Are you deducting the mileage you travel for charity or volunteer work?
- Are you deducting your out-of-pocket business expenses that are not reimbursed?
- Is your refund large?
- Have you reviewed your tax withholding information with your employer recently?

Protecting and Investing Your Assets

You work hard for your money. Both insurance and investments are based on theories of risk and return. Buying insurance protects you from losing financial assets that you have been accumulating over time and limits your exposure to future loss of income. And if you are a wise investor, you will have your money working for you instead of you working for your money.

Insurance

The concept of insurance is simply a trade: You pay a small, certain premium in return for the reimbursement of a large, uncertain economic or financial loss. Insurance is available to protect your home, auto, life, health, and income-producing ability.

What do you have to lose? That's the fundamental question related to insurance. You can lose the assets you own, such as your car, your boat, or your home. Assume that you own a home worth $150,000, and your mortgage balance is $100,000. Your home burns to the ground. Yes, you would need to repay the mortgage and buy another house. Without insurance, you would be out $300,000 (the $100,000 mortgage, $50,000 in home equity, and $150,000 for the new home)! Of course, lenders require mortgage holders to buy homeowner's insurance.

In addition to losing property, you can also lose financial assets. The liability part of auto and homeowner's policies pays benefits to others whom you have harmed. For example, if you are at fault in an auto accident you will be responsible not only for the victim's car but also for his medical expenses and possibly his lost income. Liability insurance covers these losses, but only up to the policy limits.

The greatest asset most people have is their income-earning ability. All of us are at risk of losing this asset because of an unexpected illness or accident or premature death. Disability insurance protects our income-earning ability should we cease to be able to work before normal retirement age. Life insurance does nothing for the insured, but it is designed to replace the income we are no longer able to provide in the event that we die prematurely. Life insurance protects our spouse, our children, and our other dependents if this should happen.

The cost of health care has historically increased much more rapidly than the cost of other consumer goods and services. On the one hand, health insurance premiums are expensive. On the other hand, few people can afford to be without health insurance. Hopefully, you're one of the lucky individuals whose employer provides health insurance as an employment benefit. If not, hold onto your wallet! Health insurance is expensive because the probability that you will use health-care services is high and the cost of these services is high. Shop around for health-care coverage. Investigate the availability of community health programs, health maintenance organizations, and preferred provider organizations. Reduce your risk of loss by maintaining good health and practicing preventive behaviors, such as regular exercise and good eating habits.

The underlying concepts of risk and financial loss should guide your insurance purchasing decisions. You will want to review the suggestions in the sidebar "Things to Consider about Insurance" as you analyze your insurance situation.

Things to Consider about Insurance

- Reduce your risk of loss by practicing preventive behaviors such as eating well, exercising, locking your car, and installing a security system.
- Reduce the severity of a loss by using products such as smoke alarms and seat belts.
- Insure the losses with the greatest possibility of occurring and the greatest severity of losses first.
- Increase deductibles and copays when appropriate.
- Make sure you have required insurances, such as homeowner's insurance if you hold a mortgage and auto insurance if your state of residence requires it.
- Evaluate the financial coverage you already have in place, such as savings and investments, social security benefits, and employer-provided insurance, before purchasing insurance.
- Do not overinsure in the hopes of receiving a windfall.

Investing

A good investment portfolio will be well diversified in terms of risks and estimated rates of return. The amount of risk you are willing to assume depends on your life stage, income, wealth level, and financial goals.

Generally speaking, younger investors and those with more secure incomes can take more risk with their investment funds. Funds that are needed to provide for short-term goals, such as the purchase of a new car in 2 years, should be kept in secure savings vehicles. Monies that are not needed for several years may be invested in low-risk bonds or securities. Growth-oriented stocks may be used for long-term retirement assets.

In addition to considering the purpose of investment funds and when the funds are needed when you allocate your funds among investment vehicles, you should always consider your personal risk tolerance. Never invest in any vehicle with which you are not familiar or in any investment that will keep you up at night worrying.

Things to Consider in Investment Planning

- List all of your investment goals.
- Prioritize your goals.
- Place a dollar value on each goal.
- Consider the time frame in which you hope to reach each goal.
- Match available investment vehicles with your goals, time horizons, and risk tolerance.
- Choose investments that offer current income or long-term growth, as appropriate.
- Consider your knowledge, your experience, and the amount of time you have to manage your investments.
- Put aside funds for investing on a regular basis—this reduces your risk and costs.
- Use mutual funds if you do not have the time or experience to research individual investments.
- Use no-load mutual funds to decrease the cost of investing.
- Invest for the long term; do not trade frequently.

Housing

Moving is probably the last thing on your mind. You're healthy and happy just where you are. Most people don't make a long-term housing plan. In fact, housing changes as people age and are most often precipitated by the death of a spouse or a sudden change in health status. But you can have a plan in mind, even though you don't implement the plan now.

Consider the type of housing you would like to have and the neighborhood you would like to live in if you decided to scale back. Condominiums, garden homes, and senior housing developments abound. For those who need some assistance, a myriad of choices are available, including life care facilities, assisted living apartments, and group homes. More care, including medical and skilled nursing care, is available in intermediate and skilled nursing facilities. Although Medicare coverage is limited, Medicaid often covers the cost of these types of care.

Discuss your housing preferences with your children because they are likely to be the ones making the decisions for you. Be open about what types of facilities you like and can afford. Consider their needs for convenience. And if it is likely you will live with them, make sure that appropriate legal and financial arrangements are made well in advance of the need for such documents.

Things to Consider about Housing

- Is your current home too large or too small?
- Are you able to maintain your home in good repair?
- Is the amount of yard and gardening work cumbersome?
- Is your home accessible to wheelchair-bound or physically disabled individuals?
- What adaptations would be required to make your home accessible if you became physically disabled?
- Does your home have a first floor bedroom?
- Does your home have a full bathroom on the first floor?
- Where are the laundry facilities located in your home?
- Can you afford your monthly payment, property taxes, and insurance costs?
- Can you afford utilities and repair and maintenance costs?
- What is the cost of renting similar housing?
- What type of housing would you like to have next?

Transferring Your Estate

Regardless of your age, developing and implementing an estate plan should be a priority item on your financial to-do list. The average age at which a person loses a spouse in the United States is 56. An adequate estate plan should meet three goals: appropriately provide for the distribution of your worldly (and financial) possessions, minimize the cost of settling your estate, and minimize your estate's tax liability.

Legal Documents

You should prepare a minimum of four legal documents immediately: a will, a power of attorney, a living will, and a health-care power of attorney. The first two documents provide for the management of your affairs should you become incapacitated or die. The latter two documents allow medical care providers and your chosen representative to make and implement health-care decisions should you become terminally ill or unable to approve medical care.

An ideal estate plan may also incorporate appropriate trusts. Trusts are legal entities that are often used to control the management and distribution of assets. In addition, couples often employ revocable living or testamentary trusts to minimize estate taxes. Single persons can minimize estate taxes by using irrevocable living trusts.

A letter of last instruction is not a legal document. However, it is an invaluable tool for providing relatives or close friends with information about your funeral and burial plans, the location of legal documents, and other pertinent details. Be sure to leave it in a convenient location that an appropriate party can easily access.

For a variety of reasons, many individuals do not want their estates probated. If you are among them, use the JTWROS ownership form, living trusts, named beneficiaries, and payable on death designees.

Things to Consider about Your Estate Plan

- What is the value of your estate?
- Is the value of your estate greater than the estate tax exclusion amount in effect this year?
- Are you willing to make gifts of money or property to reduce the size of your estate?
- Whom do you want to act as executor or personal representative of your estate?
- Do you have minor children who will need a guardian?
  Whom would you like to rear your children?

- Do you have minor children who will need a trustee to manage their monies if you die prematurely?

  Who would have the skills and be willing to act as trustee?
- How do you want your personal property distributed?
- How do you want your house, autos, and financial property distributed?

  Where possible, have you named beneficiaries on your financial accounts consistent with your distribution wishes?

Minimizing Estate Taxes

As we discussed in Chapter 14, you can avoid estate taxes only if the value of your estate is smaller than the exclusion amount that is in force during the year of your death. Reducing the size of your taxable estate requires that you either give everything except the exclusion amount to a spouse or charity or forgo control of your assets before your death. Employing a well-designed gifting plan can significantly reduce the size of your estate. Discuss any giving plan with an expert in estate planning. Be sure to consider the impact that gifts will have on the recipient's future income tax liability. Consider the issues discussed in the sidebar "Things to Consider about Settling Your Estate" as well.

Things to Consider about Settling Your Estate

- Have you shared your funeral and burial plans with a close relative or friend?
- Have you told a close relative or friend where your will is located?
- Have you told a close relative or friend where your letter of last instruction is located?
- What property in your estate will need to be probated (transferred by will or intestate succession)?
- What will be the cost of probating your estate?
- Do you want your personal representative to use an attorney?
- Do you want the distribution of your estate to remain a private matter?
- Will an estate tax return need to be filed if you die?

  If so, what do you estimate your estate taxes will cost?

Final Thoughts

We hope you have found this book to be both educational and insightful. It is full of things you can do to help your parents manage their finances in their remaining years. Knowing what to do and how to do it is only part of the equation, however. Behavior must follow. You will be challenged emotionally as you get more involved with your parents' finances. Your efforts will be much more successful if you can avoid being perceived as taking over. Instead, you want to assist. Make sure your parents understand that. As much as you can, keep them informed about what is going on with their money. Always present options objectively, with your perceptions of the pros and cons of each. When it does come time to take an action, make sure your parents know that you are going to do so and give you a clear okay to go ahead.

Like Pedro Hernandez, you probably recognize that adequately managing your own financial affairs will eventually reduce the stress your loved ones will experience should they need to assist you. Implementing an appropriate financial plan also allows you the peace of mind and freedom to live life to its fullest! We wish you the best.

Index

About the Authors

Sharon Burns, Ph.D., C.P.A., counsels families on the financial aspects of caregiving. She is executive director of the Association for Financial Counseling and Planning Education.

Raymond E. Forgue, Ph.D., is the director of graduate studies of the University of Kentucky Department of Family Studies.